D0945560

THE JURISPRUDENCE OF

JOHN MARSHALL

THE JURISPRUDENCE

OF

JOHN MARSHALL

BY ROBERT KENNETH FAULKNER

PRINCETON, NEW JERSEY

PRINCETON UNIVERSITY PRESS

1968

T O   M A R G A R E T

PREFACE

THIS is a study of the jurisprudence of the great Chief Justice of the United States, John Marshall. Jurisprudence in its customary sense comprises legal science, knowledge of, or practical skill in, the law. It is Marshall's blend of knowledge verging on the theoretical, with judgment eminently practical, that this volume seeks to portray. The blend might be called Marshall's "Constitutional understanding." His knowledge was attuned to the fundamental law of a particular nation; his judgment to the service of that law and nation. In this he was a typical statesman of the law. Only at the peak of legal knowledge, where jurisprudence loses its link with practice and shades into political philosophy, have thinkers like Plato in his *Laws* and Montesquieu in his *Spirit of Laws* endeavored to rise above the particular customs of diverse nations, picking and choosing among them according to reflections on the potentialities of human nature. Such philosophic inquiry was not Marshall's. He was a statesman engaged in building, and then governing, his nation. It is natural that his jurisprudence revolved about the Constitution of the United States as understood at its framing, varied somewhat with great events and changing conditions in America, and encompassed practical skills in application as well as knowledge of the broad principles and purposes of American law. An examination of Marshall's jurisprudence contributes chiefly to our understanding of American law, history, and political thought, and only incidentally to a more philosophic jurisprudence.

It is easy to see why Marshall's views have always been peculiarly illuminating to students of American institutions. His public service spanned the time from the Revolution to the later years of Jackson's presidency. As the last of the original Federalists he outlived his old enemy Jefferson and his friend Adams by nine years. He saw the war for independence from the British, America under the Articles, the founding of the government under which we yet live, its remarkable inauguration under Washington, and the subsequent developments of the country, its politics, and its economy during the next forty-five years.

The skeptical Justice Holmes once remarked that "If American law were to be represented by a single figure, skeptic and worshipper alike would agree that the figure could be one alone, and that one, John Marshall."[1] Marshall's opportunity was the greatest that ever fell to a judge, as Holmes has also said, and, one might add, the chance was grasped. In what was yet a new nation, with newer institutions, with deep divisions among the departments of government, Marshall and his Court were forced to contrive and even to record authoritative solutions to problems touching the very basis of the American order. Blessed with a fine intellect, the Chief Justice trained his judgment in life-long experience as lawyer, framer of constitutions, legislator, diplomat, general, and Secretary of State.[2] Moreover, choice combined with necessity to make him proceed without that helpful but obfuscating crutch of the law, precedent. His situation was essentially unprecedented. Besides, Marshall was disposed to reason out his findings in constitutional cases by proceeding from the most basic premises he believed the country, or at least its Constitution, presupposed. Thus his writings, especially those from the bench, supplement the greatest commentary on the Constitution, The *Federalist*, with the explanations and the revisions which experience with the new order inevitably demanded. Although his reflections cannot but represent a particular point

[1] Oliver Wendell Holmes, "John Marshall," *Collected Legal Papers* (New York: Peter Smith, 1952), p. 270. In Appendix I, *infra*, Holmes' estimate of Marshall is considered at length.

[2] A writer of some qualification has said, "The decisive claim to John Marshall's distinction as a great statesman is as a judge. And he is the only judge who has that distinction." Felix Frankfurter, "John Marshall and the Judicial Function," reprinted in *Government under Law*, ed. Arthur E. Sutherland (Cambridge: Harvard University Press, 1955), p. 7. Quoted by Samuel F. Konefsky, *John Marshall and Alexander Hamilton* (New York: Macmillan and Company, 1964), p. 15.

of view, they provide a perspective sufficiently discerning, comprehensive, and statesmanlike to shed light upon American law and thus upon the country's political thought and its history.

Indeed, one would suppose that Marshall's jurisprudence is of more than merely historical importance. Detailed prescriptions for the problems of our times cannot be expected from him; the United States has changed too much. To the extent that sound judgment about particulars, however, is guided by a broad understanding of the national interest, the national character, and the part which law should and can play, Marshall can help. Like others of the country's founders, he was compelled to consider more deeply than all succeeding statesmen, except Lincoln, the institutions which all but Lincoln could then take, in fundamentals, for granted. In these fundamentals we remain in more ways than is popularly believed the clay that Marshall and his generation molded, in the shape they gave us. The country is still democratic in a complicated manner involving representation, the rule of law for the sake of individual rights, and the discipline of an elaborately organized economic system moved by private enterprise. We are still troubled by the relation between the races, by the quality of our citizens and statesmen, by the proper functions of the several branches of our government, by the place of general and state governments, by an apparently undemocratic supreme court which presides over an ambiguously democratic order. It would be surprising if our reflections on these and other problems, which after 180 years still arise under the aegis of the Constitution, would not be deepened and stimulated by the thoughts of the "Expounder of the Constitution." Indeed, in view of the uncertainty and downright skepticism as to standards of judicial choice, now so worrying to lawyers and judges, a reconsideration of Marshall may be especially timely. Whatever our future course, in any event, we must understand his views if only to understand what we are. Justice Frankfurter did not much exaggerate when he remarked that, "It is shallow to deny that general ideas have influence or to minimize their importance. Marshall's ideas, diffused in all sorts of ways, especially through the influence of the legal profession, have become the presuppositions of our political institutions."[3]

These reasons for Marshall's importance to students of American law suggest also the relevance of his work to a more philosophic consideration of law, at least in this country. With rare exceptions, contemporary legal philosophers yet believe that Benthamite utilitarianism marked a great advance from the essentially Lockean liberalism, centering on natural rights, embodied in the jurisprudence of, say, Blackstone, as well as Marshall. They do not realize that Bentham's critique of Blackstone's jurisprudence in no important sense rebuts or deeply comprehends its subtle subject. And these thinkers remain entangled in the peculiarly abstract, sterile, and apolitical difficulties of Bentham's endeavor: his attempt to construct an essentially liberal science of the law while simultaneously cutting away the moral and political foundations of liberalism, or incorporating them *sub rosa* into an undefined "utility." Several writers, led by the British philosopher, H. L. A. Hart, have sought hesitantly to remedy these difficulties by restoring the foundations; they have returned to essentially Hobbesian reasoning. They overlook, however, the ingenious corrections made in the political philosophy of Hobbes by John Locke, corrections from which America especially has reaped the benefit. In these circumstances, perhaps, students of legal philosophy may find instructive a Lockean interpretation of liberty and law which is separated from neither moral considerations nor a certain kind of political wisdom, and takes into account, moreover, America's peculiar conditions.

An investigation of Marshall's legal and political principles

[3] Felix Frankfurter, *Mr. Justice Holmes and the Supreme Court* (Cambridge: Harvard University Press, 1961), pp. 4-5. Near the end of Appendix I, *infra*, I consider at greater length the peculiar pertinence, at the present time, of Marshall's jurisprudence.

can only complement the several works that tower over a considerable and still growing corpus of studies. Like all students of Marshall, I have benefited from Beveridge's deservedly famous *Life*.[4] It paints with vigor, good sense, and enormous detail the conditions, men, and problems which confronted Marshall's statesmanship. In his quest for the lively and dramatic, however, the Senator explicitly disavowed any deep or precise investigation of the Chief Justice's premises and reasoning. To remedy this deficiency, E. S. Corwin has provided scrupulous studies of "doctrines" basic to American constitutional law and Marshallian jurisprudence alike. His examinations of the principles underlying judicial review and of "The Basic Doctrine of American Constitutional Law" are especially valuable.[5] However, even in *John Marshall and the Constitution* Corwin did not provide an account of how all these doctrines are connected, or consistent, one with another, and how they serve the deeper purposes, economic as well as political, sought by the Chief Justice. Justice Oliver Wendell Holmes has written a very influential little essay, "John Marshall," many times reprinted, which does try to characterize the gist of Marshall's jurisprudence. I believe his argument is profoundly misleading, however. Not wishing to burden my introduction with an extensive consideration of Holmes' thought, I have chosen to treat his essay in Appendix I.

The older commentators[6] of the half-century after Mar-

---

[4] Albert J. Beveridge, *Life of John Marshall* (Boston: Houghton Mifflin Company, 1919).

[5] Corwin, *John Marshall and the Constitution* (New Haven: Yale University Press, 1919); Corwin, *The Doctrine of Judicial Review* (Princeton: Princeton University Press, 1914); Corwin, "The Basic Doctrine of American Constitutional Law," *Michigan Law Review*, XII (Feb. 1914).

[6] Joseph Story, *A discourse upon the life, character, and services of the Honorable John Marshall, LLD, Chief Justice of the United States of America . . .* , as published in *An Address by Mr. Justice Story on Chief Justice Marshall* (Rochester: Lawyers Cooperative Publishing Co., 1901); James B. Thayer, *John Marshall* (Boston: Houghton Mifflin, 1901); George van Santvoord, *Sketches of the lives*

shall's death in 1835 portrayed his legal principles devotedly, but their dedication to spreading his words was perhaps more politically salutary than illuminating. Story's remarkable celebration of his Chief's more fundamental intentions, while both discerning and a model of political eulogy, hardly was intended to provide or provoke a skeptical or even questioning attitude toward Marshall's views. Thayer did query judicial review and Marshall's interpretation of the contract clause, but he had no intention of confronting the basic premises of which these matters are but corollaries.

Of the more recent writers, Max Lerner[7] gives us a glimpse of a real and controversial economic ingredient of Marshall's thought, but his concern is not to bring out Marshall's own perspective in which the part found its place. Charles Grove Haines[8] shows how Marshall's opinions reflect certain policies for America which Haines is content to exhibit as "partisan." His historical interest, however, when coupled with a more or less debunking intent, does not encourage him to present Marshall's views as a whole, or to inquire deeply into the reasons, Marshall's deeper convictions, behind the policies he discovers. Another recent writer, Morton Frisch, has noted and deplored the absence of any "systematic exposition and analysis of [Marshall's] political ideas."[9] To correct that deficiency is an aim of this book.

---

and judicial services of the Chief-Justices of the Supreme Court of the United States (New York: Scribner, 1854); Henry Flanders, *Lives and Times of the Chief Justices of the Supreme Court* (Philadelphia: Lippincott, 1855-59).

[7] "John Marshall and the Campaign of History," *Columbia Law Review,* xxxix (March 1939), 396-431; see also V. L. Parrington, "John Marshall," *The Romantic Revolution in America* (New York: Harcourt, Brace and Company, 1927), pp. 20-27.

[8] *The Role of the Supreme Court in American Government and Politics, 1789-1855* (New York: Russell & Russell, 1944).

[9] "John Marshall's Philosophy of Constitutional Republicanism," *Review of Politics,* xx (January 1958), 34.

Taking my bearings from Marshall's views, then, and wondering chiefly about their soundness rather than their "cause" by "his times" or by some historical process, I follow in this study a topical rather than a chronological arrangement and seek even to imitate the order, so far as it exists, of his thoughts. Perhaps a summary of that order, and hence of the book's organization, will provide a useful guide for the reader.

The guiding star of Marshall's constitutional interpretation was his understanding of the purposes for which the fundamental law had been established: "The intention of the instrument must prevail." The gist of that intention, as he understood it, lay in the preservation of the nation's "great objects." Indeed, the Chief Justice always began his decisions with a consideration of the fundamental law itself, not with the country's goals as such. His reasonings were based upon careful examination of the particular words of the provision in question; he sought to distill, as he put it, their "natural and common import." The lucidity that distinguishes him from almost all American judges results, in good part, from his attention to the precise discriminations implicit in the "common-sense" meaning of these words in his time, in the common usage of those "for whom the instrument was intended." Often, however, the terms of a law must be finally interpreted according to the intention of the whole provision, for "the same words in different connexion have a different import."[10] Thus law points beyond itself to the purposes and policies which it serves. In the difficult and most interesting cases legal interpretation must turn upon an understanding of the law's ends. Marshall thought this peculiarly true of a Constitution whose character demands that "only its great outlines should be marked, its important

[10] For Marshall's remarks on the construction of legal language, see *Ogden* v. *Saunders*, 12 Wheaton (U.S.), 332 (1827); *Pennington* v. *Coxe*, 2 Cranch (U.S.), 52 (1804); *King* v. *Delaware Insurance Co.*, 6 Cranch (U.S.), 80 (1810); *Shore* v. *Jones*, I Brockenbrough 289 (1814).

objects designated, and the minor ingredients which compose those objects be deduced from the nature of the objects themselves."[11]

It seemed appropriate, therefore, to begin this book with Marshall's understanding of the Constitution's purposes, and of the kind of nation they implied. Most important to Marshall, as to all of the nation's founders, was the provision for human liberty as he understood it, the natural rights to life, liberty, and property. I show in the course of the first Chapter how these famous rights amount, in Marshall's words, to the "solid safety and real security" which the American "individual" and his "interests" should receive. This essentially humanitarian aim, often not fully appreciated because of our distrust of Marshall's concern for the property right, was expected to provide not only private safety and comfort, but also national wealth and power. In developing the Chief Justice's reflections on these subjects, I have not hesitated to turn for assistance to the modern philosophers, jurists, and economists, especially Locke, Blackstone, and Adam Smith, whose influence on Marshall, as on all of his generation, was marked.

For such a nation the very first necessity, as Marshall believed, was the powerful government which he understood the Constitution to erect. Chapter II considers the general character of "sovereign power," the special tasks of the judiciary branch, attuned to the citizen's rights, and of the "political" branches, which provide against foreign dangers, domestic unrest, and other evils. The chapter's last section explores Marshall's views on "union," which are not quite so simply "nationalistic" as is occasionally presumed. These matters possess a certain legalistic dryness, I am afraid. That quality, however, is itself a sign of the mechan-

[11] *McCulloch* v. *Maryland*, 4 Wheaton (U.S.), 407 (1819). See also John Marshall, *The Address of the Minority in the Virginia Legislature to the People of that State, containing A Vindication of the Constitutionality of the Alien and Sedition Laws* (Richmond, 1799), p. 7. For attribution to Marshall, see Beveridge, *Life of John Marshall*, II, 402 and references.

ical or politically neutral arrangement of powers which characterizes Marshall's style of government. And this style was intended to moderate, and hence to take precedence over, disputes about the naturally more appealing questions as to forms of government and the distribution of wealth, office, and privilege.

Still, Marshall surely possessed definite opinions about what we commonly call political matters, about the merits of democracy and republicanism, for example. Because of his very great caution as Chief Justice, however, which caused him to say little in writing and even to burn many of his papers, few of his reflections on these subjects remain. Obviously, he favored a republican arrangement of offices and authority. This meant, essentially, that form of popular government which could provide for the sovereign powers described in Chapter II. Chapter III considers the ingredients, popular sovereignty, representation, and balanced government, of popular government as Marshall conceived it. It dwells also on certain traces of an older and nobler aristocratic republicanism that has a distinct place in Marshall's thinking, a place made tenuous, however, by his Lockean jurisprudence oriented to men's low if solid "interests." These components of Marshallian republicanism determined his view of the epochal struggle between Federalists and Jeffersonian Republicans during the new regime's early years. The later parts of Chapter III discuss that struggle and the downfall of such political checks as representation and balanced government, designed, as Marshall thought, to filter out any serious departure by the popular will from its interests and from its representation by the more excellent citizens. At the chapter's end I contrast at some length the republicanism of Marshall with that of Jefferson.

Besides political checks upon the populace's excesses, there were also legal barriers. Chapter IV discusses at length judicial review and the political implications of a written constitution treated as law. It also considers the distinctive qualities of Marshall's judicial statesmanship, including, above all, his legal rhetoric and reasoning. In short, the book is less a treatise on American constitutional law than a study of one comprehensive political, economic, and legal persuasion by which the Constitution was to be interpreted. It discusses the chief principles of the American order as Marshall understood them, and closes by considering his efforts to fix a modern constitution embodying these principles upon a new and restively democratic nation.

I wish to clarify here a few peculiarities of the Marshallian writings on which this study relies. The materials are adequate, if by no means rich. A healthy share of Marshall's correspondence has not survived, by dint of his combination of careful burning and careless disdain. Those letters remaining are in scattered institutional and private collections, although a number of the most interesting have appeared in various books and magazines. The publication of a collected edition of Marshall's papers is still some years away. I have examined all of Marshall's unpublished correspondence now available, to the best of my knowledge, in institutional libraries, and have been generously permitted to benefit from the searches, largely but not fully completed, of Dr. Stephen G. Kurtz and his staff at The Papers of John Marshall.

Undoubtedly the most valuable materials are Marshall's many and elaborately reasoned judicial opinions. The Chief Justice's glory was his career on the bench and especially in the Supreme Court. If he was careless and secretive about his letters, he was scrupulous in preserving the manuscripts of his unpublished judicial dissertations.[12]

Yet there is a well-known problem in treating these opinions, especially those for the Supreme Court, as reliable indications of Marshall's own principles. They were in some sense a product of the Court. Marshall himself attested to the need for a judge's words to command the assent of the whole court, not merely of their author.[13] We have, more-

[12] See *Reports of Cases . . .* , ed. John W. Brockenbrough (Philadelphia: James Kay, Jr. & Brother, 1837), i, vii.

[13] "The course of every tribunal must necessarily be, that the

over, the testimony of Marshall's associate, Justice Johnson, that "in some instances" the Chief Justice delivered the opinions of the Court "even when contrary to his own Judgment and Vote."[14] Johnson once announced from the bench that the decision in *Sturges* v. *Crowninshield*, in which Marshall had delivered the Court's opinion, "partakes as much of a compromise, as of a legal adjudication."[15]

As a rule, however, I think it must be presumed that Marshall's judicial opinions represent his basic views, at least in the great cases bearing on constitutional and international law which are most relevant to this study. However much the evidence for the contrary notion has been repeated, I believe it not really convincing. Thus the Supreme Court's opinion in *Sturges* v. *Crowninshield* varies from Marshall's own principles only in a clearly incongruous concluding paragraph, evidently required by other justices, expressly restricting the argument of the opinion to the narrow facts of the case. With the opinion's argument Marshall later said that he had "never yet seen cause to be dissatisfied."[16] In support of the prevailing suspicion that Marshall's judicial opinions fail to represent his own views, W. W. Crosskey has given, it seems, the most ingenious arguments. Almost all, however, boil down to the attribution to Marshall of an unqualified nationalism which the Chief Justice never held. In

---

opinion which is to be delivered as the opinion of the court, is previously submitted to the consideration of all the judges; and, if any part of the reasoning be disapproved, it must be so modified as to receive the approbation of all, before it can be delivered as the opinion of all." John Marshall ("A Friend to the Union"), Philadelphia *Union*, April 28, 1819; reprinted in Alan Westin, ed., *An Autobiography of the Supreme Court* (New York: The Macmillan Company, 1963), p. 80.

[14] Quoted by William Winslow Crosskey, *Politics and the Constitution in the History of the United States* (Chicago: The University of Chicago Press, 1953), p. 1080.

[15] *Ogden* v. *Saunders*, 12 Wheaton (U.S.), 213 (1827). See *Sturges* v. *Crowninshield*, 4 Wheaton (U.S.), 272 (1819).

[16] *Ogden* v. *Saunders*, 12 Wheaton (U.S.), 333 (1827).

fact, the criticism with which Crosskey discredits Marshall's published opinions repeatedly leads him to discredit even Marshall's personal letters, which affirm only a qualified nationalism.[17] For this and other reasons it seems impossible to sustain Crosskey's suspicious skepticism. Marshall's prodigious influence over the Supreme Court in matters of constitutional law, the fact that he almost always formulated the Court's opinions on such matters, and the remarkable consistency of his judicial opinions both with one another and with his views elsewhere expressed, lead me to assume that the Court's constitutional expositions were shaped by Marshall to reflect at least his basic views. Controversy about particular cases will be treated when necessary, but in general I have tried to account for Justice Story's reference to Marshall's constitutional opinions as "those exquisite judgments, the fruits of his own unassisted meditations, from which the Court has derived so much honor. . . ."[18]

Apart from the judicial opinions, Marshall's *Life of George Washington* is surely the best source of his important views. It is stuffy, and its borrowings have aroused some rather querulous criticisms.[19] Still the book in its second edition, with its original Introduction, *A history of the*

[17] See *infra*, Chapter II, n. 39.

[18] Story, *Discourse*, p. 56. See also Story, reviewing Marshall's *A history of the colonies . . .* , North American Review, LVIII (January 1828), 36.

[19] William A. Foran, "John Marshall as a Historian," *American Historical Review*, XLIII (October 1937), 51-64. Compare Charles Beard's comments on Marshall as an "authority, whose knowledge of the period and whose powers of judgment and exposition will hardly be denied by the most critical," "a historian of great acumen," whose "masterly" *Life of George Washington* is a "great" work. Charles Beard, *Economic Origins of Jeffersonian Democracy* (New York: The Macmillan Company, 1915), pp. 1, 109, 159, 237ff., 242; Beard, *An Economic Interpretation of the Constitution* (New York: Macmillan, 1937), p. 296 and following.

Marshall was aware of a certain ponderous deliberateness in his style. In one of the rare letters that reveal the captivating nobility of manner the man evidently possessed, he affords a comparison with his audacious friend, John Randolph, by speaking of himself as "a man who, though he will not compare himself exactly to the animal who crawls with some one of his hundred feet always in contact with the

colonies . . . appearing as a distinct volume,[20] is invaluable for my purposes. It reveals Marshall's considered judgment on the Constitution's origin, the conditions it was to face, and its practical working during the first crucial decade. The neglect of Marshall's comprehensive reflections by Corwin and Beveridge may be seen in their rather slight reliance on the work. *The Life of George Washington* is in effect a commentary upon the colonies and America in independence, as well as the Constitution. Whatever its limitations, it is Marshall's most elaborate statement on American politics.

My profit from the studies of Beveridge and Corwin is already evident, as is my debt to Dr. Stephen G. Kurtz and The Papers of John Marshall, sponsored by The College of William and Mary and The Institute of Early American History and Culture. I might also acknowledge here three studies, too easily overlooked, from which I have benefited: Joseph Dorfman's "John Marshall, Political Economist,"[21] Morton Frisch's "John Marshall's Philosophy of Constitutional Republicanism,"[22] and Benjamin Munn Ziegler's thoughtful

---

subject on which he moves ever has and ever will feel a just pride in the friendship of the 'gallant horseman who at a flying leap clears both ditch and fence.' " Marshall to Randolph, March 6, 1828 (ALS, Association for the Preservation of Virginia Antiquities, John Marshall House). Marshall neglected to observe that Randolph's particular daring occasionally led to great spills as well as great triumphs. Randolph, or someone other than Marshall, annotated the letter: "that great master of the human heart."

[20] John Marshall, *The Life of George Washington* (Philadelphia: James Crissy and Thomas Cowperthwaite and Co., 1839); Marshall, *A history of the colonies planted by the English on the continent of North America, from their settlement, to the commencement of that war which terminated in their independence* (Philadelphia: Small, 1824). The text of the *history* to be cited is that reprinted as Volume i of John Marshall, *The Life of George Washington* (Fredericksburg: The Citizens' Guild of Washington's Boyhood Home, 1926). Hereafter cited as *A history of the colonies.* . . .

[21] The piece appears in W. Melville Jones, *Chief Justice John Marshall, A Reappraisal* (Ithaca: Cornell University Press, 1956).

[22] *Review of Politics,* xx (January 1958), 34-35.

examination of *The International Law of John Marshall.*[23] In addition, I have found my way smoothed by James A. Servies' judicious and reliable bibliography.[24] Mr. Servies has also generously provided me with a supplementary list of published material and an invaluable catalogue of Marshall's unpublished letters and their whereabouts, for both of which I am very grateful. Perhaps my acknowledgments to Mr. Servies, who is librarian at the University of West Florida, can serve as a token of my gratitude to the many librarians who have searched their collections for relevant materials and then forwarded copies or afforded hospitality.

This book began as a doctoral dissertation under the auspices of the Department of Political Science at the University of Chicago. It is a happy privilege to thank the distinguished faculty in constitutional law and political philosophy who guided my studies, Professors C. Herman Pritchett, Joseph Cropsey, Herbert Storing, and Leo Strauss. I have benefited from Professor Strauss's penetrating wisdom and relentless yet gentle and delightful spirit of inquiry in ways too many for adequate acknowledgment here. Herbert Storing's reflections on the nation's founding introduced me to the statesmen and problems connected with American institutions; he has assisted my study of Marshall from its inception.

Professors John Howe, Ralph Lerner, and Leo Weinstein helped me with comments on the manuscript. Professors Martin Diamond and Walter Murphy, William McClung of Princeton University Press, John Lamkin, and my wife, Margaret McConagha Faulkner, provided detailed criticism for which I am especially grateful. To the searching examination of my argument and prose by Professor Thomas Schrock I owe most of all. Mrs. Helen Wright of Princeton has been the model of a scholar's typist.

[23] Chapel Hill: The University of North Carolina Press, 1939.
[24] *A Bibliography of John Marshall* (Washington: United States Commission for the Celebration of the Two Hundredth Anniversary of the Birth of John Marshall, 1956).

CONTENTS

THE JURISPRUDENCE OF
JOHN MARSHALL

"Those who know human nature, black as it is,
must know that mankind are . . . attached to
their interest. . . ."

John Marshall,
in the Virginia Ratifying Convention, 1788.

"Then too, loftiness and greatness of spirit,
and courtesy, justice, and generosity are much
more according to nature than are selfish pleasure,
riches, and life itself."

Cicero, *De Officiis*.

CHAPTER I

LIBERTY, INTEREST,

AND EMPIRE

LIBERTY AND INTEREST

FOR JOHN MARSHALL, as for almost all eminent Americans, the encouragement of human liberty formed the great theme and purpose of political life. Around this object revolved Marshall's whole understanding of the United States, its Constitution, its government, its society, its nationhood. It was as "votary of liberty" that Marshall fought for independence from British rule, advocated the Constitution of 1788, welcomed the dawn of the French Revolution and damned its development, and damned both beginning and development of the Jeffersonian revolution at home. In the same faith, he served his nation as diplomat, legislator, minister of foreign affairs, and, most conspicuously, as Chief Justice.

Fundamentally, Marshall understood liberty as "private security," security of the individual's natural rights and, more basic yet, of his "interests." A qualification must be inserted here, however. Marshall's understanding of liberty was complicated and beset with a certain tension. He was a votary of a kind of political liberty as well, that republican freedom comprising political self-government of a nation by its citizens. In Chapter III Marshall's devotion to republican freedom will be considered. There it will be shown, however, that he favored self-government only so long as it provided good government, government capable of securing the citizens' rights and interests.

Marshall's understanding of human liberty revolved, then, about the natural rights to life, to liberty of movement and of opinion, and to the opportunity to acquire property. A good part of this chapter will be spent on the profound implications of this perspective, now so wearily hoary to many scholars that its true character is rarely penetrated. We must first agree, nevertheless, that in his fundamental orientation the Chief Justice did not differ from the other distinguished Americans of his time. Marshall's views are but one variant of the central concern with man's natural liberties and interest that guided Jefferson, Madison, Hamilton, Washington, and others of the generation that framed the Constitution of 1788. In each was the pervasive influence of the doctrines of liberalism or liberal individualism, in the form originally set forth by such thinkers as Locke, Montesquieu, and Hume. These philosophers had taught that political society existed to provide for certain interests of every man, traits understood as so basic as to be judged natural rights of all. The community was to preserve rights belonging to man before he entered communal life. One illustration of Marshall's acceptance of this view might be given here. In his dissent in *Ogden* v. *Saunders*, he was compelled to reveal the doctrinal foundation of those judicial opinions supporting vested contractual rights for which his career is well known:

> If, on tracing the right to contract, and the obligations created by contract, to their source, we find them to exist anterior to, and independent of society, we may reasonably conclude that those original and pre-existing principles are, like many other natural rights, brought with man into society; and, although they may be controlled, are not given by human legislation.
>
> [The obligation of contract is intrinsic and] results from the right which every man retains to acquire property, to dispose of that property according to his own

4

judgment, and to pledge himself for a future act. These rights are not given by society, but are brought into it. . . .

This reasoning is, undoubtedly, much strengthened by the authority of those writers on natural and national law whose opinions have been viewed with profound respect by the wisest men of the present, and of past ages.[1]

While there are occasional laudatory references to the individualistic philosophers scattered among Marshall's writings,[2] it is perfectly clear that his own basic orientation was absorbed from the climate of opinion about him. One might pinpoint especially the views prevailing in the area of his greatest deeds, his chosen profession of the law. As he sought in his mature years to apply the Constitution, the law of nations, and the common law, the works on which he relied are revealing. It is not open to question that *The Federalist* helped to fix Marshall's Constitutional constructions. Its influence is perhaps discernible even as he argued in the Virginia Ratifying Convention. He was later to describe the work from the bench as "a complete commentary on our constitution," always "considered as of great authority," whose "intrinsic merit entitles it to this high rank."[3] Madison's famous remark in Number 10—the "first object of government [is] the protection of different and unequal

[1] *Ogden* v. *Saunders*, 12 Wheaton (U.S.), 345-47 (1827). Relying essentially on this dissent, Nathan Isaacs has exhibited the influence of what he calls the "eighteenth-century" philosophers on Marshall's views on contract, "John Marshall on Contracts. A Study in Early American Juristic Theories," *Virginia Law Review*, Vol. vii, No. 6 (March 1921), 413-28.

[2] For Locke: see Marshall, *A history of the colonies* . . . , pp. 154-55; Hume: John E. Oster, *The Political and Economic Doctrines of John Marshall* (New York: Neale, 1914), p. 56; Burke: Marshall, *A history of the colonies* . . . , p. 418.

[3] *Cohens* v. *Virginia*, 6 Wheaton (U.S.), 418 (1821). For Marshall's other remarks on *The Federalist*, see *McCulloch* v. *Maryland*, 4 Wheaton (U.S.), 433 (1819); Marshall, *The Life of George Washington*, ii, 127.

faculties of acquiring property"—illustrates the influence of Lockean fundamentals.

In treating the law of nations, Marshall's favorite authority was Vattel. In *The Law of Nations, or, Principles of the Law of Nature; Applied to the Conduct and Affairs of Nations and Sovereigns*, the Swiss jurist expressly sought to derive an international law from the basis of free and independent individuals who unite to preserve their natural rights.[4]

More influential in shaping Marshall's views than commentators on the law of nations or perhaps even those on the Constitution were the great authorities on the common law. He understood the common law to contain the very "substratum" of the rules of law. It consists, he thought, chiefly of "unwritten" principles of justice which have been accepted by the United States' courts. It thus approaches more closely to the basic purposes of law than does the Constitution, while being more inclusive and authoritative than the law of nations. The common law, wrote Marshall in his most considered definition, is "really human reason applied by the courts, not capriciously, but in a regular train of decisions, to human affairs, for the promotion of the ends of justice."[5]

As counsellor in the "ends of justice" Marshall most ad-

---

[4] Emmerich De Vattel, *The Law of Nations, or, Principles of the Law of Nature; Applied to the Conduct and Affairs of Nations and Sovereigns* (New York: Samuel Campbell, 1796), esp. *Preface* and *Preliminaries*. See Book I, viii and xx, 254-55. See also Benjamin M. Ziegler, *The International Law of John Marshall* (Chapel Hill: University of North Carolina Press, 1939), p. 9.

[5] *Livingston v. Jefferson*, 1 Brockenbrough 203, 207 (1811). Compare, in the context of the law of nations, *The Venus*, 8 Cranch (U.S.), 297 (1814), and *Schooner Exchange v. McFadden*, 7 Cranch (U.S.), 117 (1812). See also John Marshall, *Address of the minority of the Virginia Legislature containing a vindication of the constitutionality of the Alien and Sedition Laws* (Richmond, 1799), p. 13; and David Robertson, *Reports of the Trials . . . for Treason & for a Misdemeanor . . . taken in short hand by David Robertson* (Philadelphia: Hopkins & Earle, 1808), II, 402, 482.

mired the shrewd and cautious Blackstone, whose *Commentaries on the Laws of England* had such a profound influence upon Americans generally. He cited Blackstone as often as Vattel, and the praise bestowed upon the English teacher of judicial statesmen was far higher. Marshall singled out Blackstone among the "best elementary writers" as the "authority" from whom "no man will lightly dissent."[6] He accepted his very definition of law, ascribing it to "a writer, whose definitions especially have been the theme of almost universal panegyric."[7] In various particular subjects, moreover, Marshall seemed to take the *Commentaries'* word as a true expression of common law doctrine.[8] And Blackstone, repeatedly citing Locke and Montesquieu in company with hosts of English jurists, followed the path of Montesquieu in weaving the corrosive individualism of Locke into a legal and political fabric comprising various national laws, customs, and institutions, all suitably reinterpreted.[9] In short, Marshall's references to authority permit one to describe him in words he himself applied to the Constitution's framers: "intimately acquainted with the writings of those wise and learned men, whose treatises on the laws of nature and nations have guided public opinion" with respect to basic concerns of the law.

[6] Marshall's reliance upon Blackstone is most explicitly indicated by his opinion in *Livingston v. Jefferson*, 1 Brockenbrough 209 (1811). See also Marshall, *An Autobiographical Sketch*, p. 5. Among the few studies of Blackstone existing, only that of Herbert J. Storing indicates the manner in which a fundamentally liberal or Montesquieuan political perspective guides subtly the English jurist's reshaping of English institutions and legal doctrines. "William Blackstone," in *History of Political Philosophy*, ed. by Leo Strauss and Joseph Cropsey (Chicago: Rand McNally & Company, 1963), pp. 536-48.

[7] Cf. *Ogden v. Saunders*, 12 Wheaton (U.S.), 347 (1827) with *Commentaries on the Laws of England in Four Books*, ed. by Thomas M. Cooley (Chicago: Callaghan and Company, 1884), I, 44.

[8] See, for examples of Blackstone's influence in particular cases, *Ex parte Bollman*, 4 Cranch (U.S.), 93-94, 96ff. (1807); *Marbury v. Madison*, 1 Cranch (U.S.), 168-69 (1803).

[9] Blackstone's most massive statements occur in I *Commentaries* 129ff.

The persuasion spread by those "treatises," we have observed, finds the purpose of political society to be the maintenance of man's prepolitical rights; "rights anterior to and independent of society," Marshall called them. Political society exists to promote purposes not intrinsic to political life itself. Man is not essentially a political animal and hence not naturally a citizen. He is naturally an "individual," a word characteristic of Marshall's prose. His rights belong to him as a man.[10]

Marshall's view of natural rights turns on what might be called his psychology, more exactly, his particular understanding of that desire he understood to dominate most men, "interest." Man's natural rights are precisely the legitimate forms of the basic desires to live, to act according to one's will, and to increase one's possessions. Together these form a unity called by Marshall "interest," roughly identifiable as the legitimate desire for safety and profit. Man's rights are natural in the sense that they are linked to a strong and even predominant force in the human animal. "Those who know human nature, black as it is, must know that mankind are . . . attached to their interest. . . ."[11] Even if "interest" is not always the most potent motive, it is supposed to be at least the most safe and reliable basis for planning a polity. Being low and solid, its existence in most men may be depended upon with few risks. It is then a "legitimate" basis for political calculation. From it man's rights and hence the form and bounds of his political society may be most prudently deduced. From this root assumed as necessary by classical liberalism follows the whole tone of sober inevitability and the severe and necessary deductions that distinguish Mar-

---

[10] Marshall frequently refers to "the original right to transfer property," or "the original capacity [of the individual] to contract." See *Sicard's Lessee* v. *Davis*, 6 Peters (U.S.), 136 (1832); *Head* v. *Providence Insurance Co.*, 2 Cranch (U.S.), 168 (1804).

[11] Jonathan Elliot, *The Debates in the Several State Conventions on the Adoption of the Federal Constitution* (Philadelphia: J. B. Lippincott Company, 1836), III, 562.

shall's judicial opinions. Let us then consider Marshall's understanding of this peculiar passion in greater detail. Marshall was perfectly aware of exceptions to the sovereignty of "interest." Some of the people most of the time, and most of the people some of the time, may rise to higher aspirations than continual pursuit of profit and safety. Like all of the framing statesmen, Marshall distinguished quite sharply between the few best and the many. He tended to make that distinction one of character, rather than merely of talents, as will be indicated more fully in Chapter III when his genuine admiration for human excellence will be discussed. Those of exceptionally fine character are not moved by "the motives which usually guide the human mind," but "act upon principles of disinterestedness." Such men are special, perhaps by dispensation of nature itself, and therefore rare. Wolfe, Montcalm, and the few at Breed's Hill defending Boston from the British, "were endowed with more than a common portion of bravery."[12] Washington was "endowed by nature with a sound judgment, and an accurate discriminating mind." His "superiority," like that of other great statesmen, was in part "that ascendancy which is the prerogative of a superior mind."[13]

Even common men may not be ruled always by common desires. Marshall the historian could hardly help observing that New England was indebted for its first settlement to religion, "a stronger motive than even interest."[14] Similarly, the "spirit of enthusiastic patriotism . . . for a time, elevates the mind above all considerations of individual acquisition."[15]

Nevertheless, Marshall considered such behavior by the generality of men to be exceptional actions depending on a basically unreliable "enthusiasm." Ardor elevates most men only temporarily. "Enthusiastic patriotism," for example, op-

[12] Marshall, *A history of the colonies* . . . , p. 475.
[13] Marshall, *The Life of George Washington*, II, 129, 448; I, 41, 105.
[14] Marshall, *A history of the colonies* . . . , p. 74.
[15] *Ibid.*, p. 419.

erates but "for a time."[16] Religion's sway may be more lasting, but is still untrustworthy. For the zealous faith required to raise men's aspirations above profit and safety necessarily provokes its own evils. By aiming so high, it risks falling very low. The colonial New Englanders, especially in Massachusetts, were often engaged in godly persecution of dissenters who were not godly after their own manner. Occasionally, ordinary persecution was overshadowed by a veritable "frenzy" of pseudo-religious fervor. Marshall dwelled on the witch trials in a long and horrified note. They gradually culminated in a "prevailing infatuation . . . infecting every class of society," a "destructive rage," evoking a "reign of popular frenzy." "Never was there given a more melancholy proof," Marshall quoted from the historian Hutchinson, "of the degree of depravity of which man is capable when the public passions countenance crime."[17]

Political rather than religious enthusiasm, however, was more characteristic of Marshall's own time. Although favorably disposed to the French Revolution at its onset, Marshall grew disillusioned as the struggle's "visionary" character became evident. The Revolution was "visionary" in supposing that men generally might be raised to a kind of flawless character. Once caste and convention were stripped off, it was thought, an essentially good or "perfectible" human nature would be revealed. In Marshall's analysis, the great uprising's eventual breakdown into a twofold tyranny was inevitable. Those seeking to realize their vision had to become increasingly autocratic in their attempt to perfect the imperfectible human passions. Government thus became a "furious despotism, trampling on every right, and sporting

[16] Marshall quoted from a letter of Washington: "When men are irritated, and their passions inflamed, they fly hastily and cheerfully to arms; but after the first emotions are over, to expect among such people as compose the bulk of an army, that they are influenced by any other motives than those of interest, is to look for what never did, and I fear never will happen." Marshall, *The Life of George Washington*, I, 104-05.

[17] Marshall, *A history of the colonies* . . . , pp. 477-81, note 1.

with life." And the populace generally, freed from any order, eventually became a kind of mob tyranny. "Indiscriminate massacre" followed. In a private letter to Charles Cotesworth Pinckney, Marshall wrote of the Revolution's essential premise: "This new doctrine of the perfectibility of man, added to the practice of its votaries begins to exhibit him I think as an animal much less respectable than he has heretofore been thought."[18]

The excesses provoked by a trust in "enthusiasm," political and religious, only confirmed in Marshall's mind the need to turn to "interest" as the solid touchstone of political planning. Every country, it may be said, must provide for its citizens' interests: for the security of their lives and possessions. What distinguishes Marshall's account of liberty, however, is the peculiar importance given to what might be thought only the minimal conditions of community life. Far from being a necessity kept in its place by other and choicer goods, safety of person and property expands to be the principal purpose of political society. The reason has been in-

[18] Marshall to Pinckney, November 21, 1802, *William & Mary Quarterly* (Ser. 3), xii, No. 4 (October 1955), 646; *The Life of George Washington*, ii, 155, 239, 250, 252, 267ff., 323, 353. See also Marshall's brief evaluation of Gouverneur Morris' diplomatic despatches from France (Appendix, Note xvi, 17ff.). Jefferson, while deprecating "enthusiasm," distinguished it nevertheless from "bigotry" or "Jesuitism," and seemed to see in it at least some saving virtue. Enthusiasm is the disease of "the free and buoyant," while bigotry, on the other hand, is but the "disease" of "morbid minds." "Education and free discussion," he went on to say, "are the antidotes of both." Letter from Jefferson to John Adams, August 1, 1816, printed in Lester J. Cappon, ed., *The Adams-Jefferson Letters* (Chapel Hill: The University of North Carolina Press, 1959), Vol. ii, 484. Jefferson's more sanguine and sympathetic view of the liberal and republican movement sweeping the Western world allowed him a far more charitable view of the French Revolution's development. Still, he opined occasionally that the Jacobins had ignored the harsh possibilities of which human nature unchecked is susceptible. Letter to Jedidiah Morse, March 6, 1822. Albert Ellery Bergh, ed., *The Writings of Thomas Jefferson* (Washington: Thomas Jefferson Memorial Association, 1907), Vol. xv, 360.

dicated: on the foundation of low but solid interests can be constructed a solid and workable politics. This basis may not be noble, honorable and magnanimous. Adam Smith himself was not unaware that his commercial order might depreciate a certain "liberal or generous spirit."[19] Such an order was nevertheless appropriate or at least "legitimate" because "realistic" in its accord with the bent of most men. It is this exclusive attention to low but solid calculation that especially distinguishes Marshall's kind of jurisprudence not only from the "visionary" French influenced by Rousseau, but also from such writers as Cicero or Aristotle or Plato. The classics generally agreed with Marshall, vis-à-vis the "visionary" descendants of Rousseau, that "most men pursue wealth and petty ambition." They agreed as well that certain safeguards, as, for example, a regime affording some checks and balances, were thus as a rule expedient. Although the ancient authors understood that a statesman has to compromise with baseness, they nevertheless believed that he should also leaven it. As for anything worthwhile, some risks are involved. Politics, they argued, should take its fundamental bearings from excellence of character, shoring up the finer men and the finer parts of most men by some religious orthodoxy, by moral and patriotic rhetoric, and by the effectual but not absolute rule of that aristocratic or oligarchic class likely to nurture the better men or at least to discipline most men. The tradition that informed Marshall, however, was content not to distill the gold from the dross but to build on the passions characteristic of the mass. In summing up the fundamental teaching of Machiavelli, Spinoza, Locke, and Montesquieu, Hume is unusually plain: "But as these [ancient] principles are too disinterested, and too difficult to support, it is requisite to govern men by other passions, and animate them with a spirit of avarice and industry, art and luxury."[20]

[19] *The Wealth of Nations* (New York: Modern Library, 1937), p. 332. See also pp. 556, 718.
[20] David Hume, "Of Commerce," in *Essays Moral, Political, and*

Thus, an assumed necessity gives birth to liberty. With man's prevailing passions for life, liberty, and property are to go the natural rights whose protection yields "solid safety and real security" for the individual. Upon his return from some exasperating negotiations with the French of the Directory, Marshall sought to distinguish for his fellow citizens their "actual" freedom from its spurious French counterpart:

> To a citizen of the *United States,* so familiarly habituated to the actual possession of liberty, that he almost considers it as the inseparable companion of man, a view of the despotism, which borrowing the garb and usurping the name of freedom, tyrannizes over so large and so fair a proportion of the earth, must teach the value which he ought to place on the solid safety and real security he enjoys at home. In support of these, all temporary difficulties, however great, ought to be encountered. . . .[21]

In discussing the sphere to be secured, one must dwell on Marshall's devotion to the rights of life and liberty as well as that of property. It is necessary to confront that exaggeration of Marshall's economic concerns which is one cloudy legacy of the watered Marxism in commentators such as Lerner and Parrington. These writers, while never really clarifying just what Marshall understood the rights of property to be, so emphasized them as to imply that he cared hardly at all about the other liberties. Thus they failed utterly to show how all three of these rights are connected in Marshall's scheme, that of property being an indispensable means to the rest. In general, they followed fashion in making economic forces or interests the center of their interpretation, instead of remaining true to

---

Literary (Oxford: Oxford University Press, 1966), p. 269; cf. pp. 264-66. On the contrast between ancients and moderns, see Leo Strauss, *Natural Right and History* (Chicago: University of Chicago Press, 1953), Chaps. iv, v.

[21] "General Marshall's Address to the Citizens of Richmond, Virginia." Reprinted in Beveridge, *Life of John Marshall,* ii, 572.

Marshall's own political economy with its political justification and circumscription of the property right.

Marshall's devotion to the safety and freedom of the citizen is easily shown. He was thoroughly modern in his concern that "penal laws" affecting life and liberty be "construed strictly," a principle "founded on the tenderness of the law for the rights of individuals." He argued powerfully for the Supreme Court's authority to issue writs of *habeas corpus*, the key legal check upon a government's ability to oppress its citizens.[22] (The English *habeas corpus* act had been called by Blackstone a "second *magna carta*, and stable bulwark of our liberties."[23]) Still, these are hardly the most forceful illustrations of Marshall's views.

Presiding over the famous treason trial of Aaron Burr in 1807, the Chief Justice gave an opinion that influences legal doctrine and controversy to this day. He interpreted so strictly the Constitution's requirements for a treason conviction that, in effect if not in his explicit statements, only persons engaged bodily in warring against the nation—by means of visible and unambiguous acts to which two witnesses might testify—could receive the dire penalties prescribed for this worst of political crimes. Common sense, and even the English common law at that time, regarded the planning and procuring of treason as at least as criminal as its perpetration. Marshall, however, was disposed throughout the trial to understand the constitutional definition of treason, "levying war," as "perpetrating war," and to limit accordingly those who might be accused. He granted for the sake of argument that the definition might encompass "procuring" of a war perpetrated by others. But he required such stringent proof of an act of "procuring" as to make it difficult in the extreme to convict Burr for anything but per-

[22] *United States* v. *Wiltberger*, 5 Wheaton (U.S.), 94 (1820); *Ex parte Bollman* and *Ex parte Swartwout*, 4 Cranch (U.S.), 93-100 (1807); cf. *Meade* v. *Deputy Marshall*, 1 Brockenbrough, 328 (1815), *The Mary*, 9 Cranch (U.S.), 144 (1815).

[23] Blackstone, *Commentaries on the Laws of England*, Book i, Chapter 1, 137.

petration. These strict limits were to be followed, even though those originators who were "in truth the chief traitors," as Marshall himself called them, would go free.[24] It seems that the Chief Justice applied on a grand scale his injunction, invoked in the Burr trial specifically with respect to procedures for admitting evidence, to treat the defense in criminal prosecutions "with as much liberality and tenderness as the case will admit."[25]

Marshall respected liberty of speech and opinion as well as freedom from bodily arrest. Writing about France in 1797, he condemned the Directory's "banishment of the printers to the slavery of the press."[26] As a Federalist candidate for Congress a year later, he declared against his party's Alien and Sedition Acts and, after his election, he voted, despite intense pressure from his party, to repeal that section of the Sedition Act defining and punishing seditious speech.[27] This vote of the most prominent southern Federalist, and the only leading Federalist to declare publicly against the party's controversial measures, ruined Marshall's chances for political advancement in the ordinary American sense.[28]

Marshall's respect for free speech was by no means confined to political statements. He celebrated Roger Bacon's religious tolerance. His criticism of Puritan bigotry has al-

[24] Robertson, *Reports*, II, 440, 436-37. Edward S. Corwin, *John Marshall and the Constitution*, pp. 109-10. See also Appendix II.

[25] Robertson, *Reports*, II, 534; cf. I, 178, 186. Marshall displayed such a "tenderness" for the accused that Corwin and others consider his opinion the product of political bias, not of judicial principle. This view cannot be sustained. See Appendix II.

[26] Marshall to Washington, September 15, 1797; *American Historical Review*, II (1896-97), 300.

[27] *Marshall's Answers to Freeholder's Questions*; reprinted in Beveridge, *Life of John Marshall*, Appendix II, 577. Marshall also voted against an amendment by Bayard which would have affirmed ". . . the offences therein specified [to] remain punishable at common law" with the qualification that truth was a ground of exoneration. U.S. Congress, *Annals*, 6th Congress, 1st Session, pp. 419, 423.

[28] Beveridge, *Life of John Marshall*, II, 451.

ready been mentioned. The New Englanders' punishment and persecution of deviant opinions constituted a violation of "rights of conscience" and "religious liberty." He wrote in 1797 a characteristically compassionate description of the "consternation and fright" of Antwerp's inhabitants, in the face of the suspension of their customary religious worship by the conquering French.[29]

Still, security of person and property had greater importance for Marshall than freedom of speech. Marshall feared general arbitrariness endangering men's "real" interests more than suppression of opinion as such. His spirit is perhaps less close to the contemporary respect for unlimited exchange of ideas as the principal means for "development" of individual and society alike, than to Locke's *Letter on Toleration*. He believed government should keep its hands off speech not because of any great progress of the mind which will develop from free public discussion, but because its primary business is the protection of body and property, not the saving or even cultivating of souls.

> . . . The political society is instituted for no other end [wrote Locke]; but only to secure every man's possession of the things of this life. This the safeguard of men's lives, of the things that belong unto this life, is the business of the commonwealth . . . the business of the laws is not to provide for the truth of opinions, but for the safety and security of the commonwealth, and of every particular man's goods and person.[30]

Marshall deplored the Directory's unqualified suppression of a free press as much, perhaps, as an occasion for the "banishment" of the printers as for its effect on freedom of speech. He viewed Antwerp's situation not as an example

[29] Letter from Marshall to Charles Lee, September 22, 1797. MS. Emmett Collection, 2137, New York Public Library. Marshall, *A history of the colonies . . .* , pp. 96, 97, 86, 87.

[30] John Locke, *Letter on Toleration*, ed. John Gough (Oxford: Oxford University Press, 1946), p. 151.

16

of religious suppression *per se*, but as a kind of tyranny, ". . . as great as if the town was to be given up to pillage." He did not deny but rather affirmed the constitutionality of the Sedition Act.[31] He attacked it, however, as foolish and inflammatory. Instead of encouraging national unity, the act undermined it. Shortly after his return from France, Marshall told his potential constituents that, had he been in Congress, "I should have opposed [the Alien and Sedition Acts] because I think them useless; and because they are calculated to create unnecessary discontents and jealousies at a time when our very existence, as a nation, may depend on our union."[32] Similarly, Marshall's criticism of Puritan intolerance dwelled on the deprivation of the dissenters' "choicest" political rights rather than liberty of conscience as such. He disparaged as well the "perpetual discontents," and the endless discord over "metaphysical points," that attended the colonists' efforts to enforce religious uniformity.[33]

It is not strange that Marshall's devotion to the property right has been emphasized and lately exaggerated. He believed it not much inferior, at least in political importance, to the fundamental right to life itself. In the leading contract clause case of *Fletcher* v. *Peck* Marshall equated the "rules of property" with "certain great principles of justice" and asked, "If any [limits to the legislative power] be prescribed, where are they to be found, if the property of an individual, fairly and honestly acquired, may be seized without compensation?" In this opinion and in others he called the property right "sacred." Marshall considered it to be unequivocally a natural right, thus following such liberal republicans as Locke and Adam Smith, if differing slightly from Blackstone and radically from such a classical republican as Cicero.[34]

[31] Marshall, *Address of the Minority* . . . , pp. 10-14.
[32] *Marshall's Answers to Freeholder's Questions*; reprinted in Beveridge, *Life of John Marshall*, II, 577.
[33] Marshall, *A history of the colonies* . . . , pp. 86-87, 101-02, 116. Cf. pp. 96, 212.
[34] John Locke, *Two Treatises of Civil Government*, ed. Thomas L.

Why is private property so important, even natural? The question will occupy us until the chapter's end, as we observe the manner in which Marshall believed both private advantage and public interest to be served by its protection. The answer must begin with Marshall's understanding of property itself. He used the term to stand for tangible possessions, yet that common meaning does not penetrate to the core of his usage and that of the philosophy which informed his thought. Property was fundamentally the product of human labor; conventional and legal titles to things should embody as much as possible man's "natural right to the fruits of his own labor." The right of property was not so much the right to possess as the right to possess what one has worked for. This was the premise, developed in Chapter V of Locke's *Second Treatise*, which Marshall took to be "generally admitted," and from which his arguments on property in general, and on vested contractual rights in particular, took their beginning.[35]

Cook (New York: Hafner Publishing Company, 1956), II, 27, 28; Adam Smith, *The Wealth of Nations*, ed. Edwin Cannan (New York: The Modern Library, 1937), Book I, Chapter X, Part II, pp. 121-22; Blackstone, *Commentaries on the Laws of England*, Book I, Chapter I, 127, Book II, Chapter I, especially p. 11. Cicero, *De Officiis*, I, vii, 21, "there is no private ownership by nature. . . ." See, however, II, xxi, 73. *Fletcher* v. *Peck*, 6 Cranch (U.S.), 133, 134-35 (1810). This case in particular, and the Constitution's contract clause in general, is illuminated by C. Peter Magrath's recent and comprehensive investigation, *Yazoo, Law and Politics in the New Republic, The Case of Fletcher v. Peck* (Providence: Brown University Press, 1966).

[35] In the case of the *Antelope*, Marshall described the "unnatural slave-trade," and implicitly slavery itself, as in violation of nature's laws because it deprives men of those fruits of labor which are their "natural right." "That [the slave-trade] is contrary to the law of nature will scarcely be denied. That every man has a natural right to the fruits of his own labor, is generally admitted; and that no other person can rightfully deprive him of those fruits, and appropriate them against his will, seems to be the necessary result of this admission." *The Antelope*, 10 Wheaton (U.S.), 120 (1825). Marshall's view of slavery is discussed in the first section of Chapter II. Compare Blackstone: ". . . Bodily labour, bestowed upon any subject

The implications are immense. What is fundamentally protected is a dynamic force for production, not existing products; the industrious acquisition of more possessions, not possessions as such. Security of property in the ordinary sense of tangible goods is then only a secondary object. Protection of labor, in the sense of industry devoted to production, is basic. In no way would Marshall have differed from Madison in *Federalist* X: the first object of government is the protection of the "different and unequal faculties of acquiring property." Thus ways of obtaining property other than "self-reliance," or "making one's fortune," or "getting ahead," are depreciated. Nothing like an aristocratic concern to provide for the continuance of stable and fixed family estates characterizes Marshall's judicial opinions on contract; they protect commercial agreements, contracts for mutual gain. Nowhere do his writings express remorse at the expulsion of entail and primogeniture from the laws of his native Virginia. Throughout, as we will see, is the celebration of commerce and industry (in both senses). In place of an aristocratic view of property is the acquisitive individualism underlying modern economics. This view is closely connected with the decision to rely, politically speaking, upon "interest." The Lockean understanding of property takes account of the powerful passion for gain, which cannot easily be suppressed but can be "channeled": "Everything in the world is purchased by labour; and our passions are the only causes of labour," wrote Hume, who elsewhere spoke of "avarice, the spur of industry." To conclude, Marshall's view amounts to protection of that peculiarly grasping passion which, properly guided, proves the fundamental means of production. In its most primitive or natural form this force is the passion for gain linked with habits of industry; in its developed form, making use of a thorough division of labor, and labor-saving technology, it is

---

which before lay in common to all men, is universally allowed to give the fairest and most reasonable title to an exclusive property therein." *Commentaries on the Laws of England*, II, 5; consider 1-15.

"private enterprise" moving modern "industries." The right to pile up for oneself material goods without moral limit, is the premise at the heart of that system of free enterprise unequivocally devoted to the accumulation of ever more wealth, capitalism.[36] What, after all, is capital but wealth devoted to the production of more wealth, and what is capitalism but a system of private inducements to produce ever more wealth? At this point we may appropriately consider the question the contemporary reader will have asked already: in what manner do the individual rights of which Marshall is so fond, take account of the needs of society?

PRIVATE INTEREST AND PUBLIC INTEREST

Perhaps the calculated ingenuity of Lockean liberalism, and thus of Marshall's jurisprudence, is best seen in the public uses to which the private passions are put. The peculiar interests and rights that Marshall defended go hand in hand with a complementary social expediency. We are still familiar with the formula of this solution: "private interest, public gain." That statement sums up not only the economic arrangements from which it is generally known, but the tenor of all of liberal society. When Tocqueville remarked that the Americans combat a merely selfish individualism by constantly preaching the "principle of self-interest rightly understood," he was only confirming the dissemination of the basis of their liberal institutions. "In this country," Marshall remarked at the Virginia Convention called to consider ratification of the Constitution, "there is no exclusive personal stock of interest. The interest of the community is blended and inseparably connected with that of the individual. When he promotes his own, he promotes that of

---

[36] On capitalism's origin in liberal political philosophy, see Leo Strauss, *Natural Right and History*, pp. 60, n. 22, 234ff.; C. B. MacPherson, *The Political Theory of Possessive Individualism* (Oxford: Clarendon Press, 1962), pp. 194-221; Joseph Cropsey, *Polity and Economy, An Interpretation of the Principles of Adam Smith* (The Hague: Martinus Nijhoff, 1957).

the community. When we consult the common good, we consult our own."[37]

This easy reconciliation of private conduct and public need, we may observe, marks the elemental force attending liberalism's orientation by humanity's more ordinary desires. The stake of most men in the security of their "interests" hardly requires subtle demonstration, at least when men are "liberated" from constraining moral customs and religious devotion. The connection of these obvious concerns with the minimal duties and institutions of civil society can be shown without much greater difficulty, at least to that potential majority of sober men possessed of some property. In short, the informed devotion to the public good that is produced by general enlightenment, is possible only when the message is pitched to the aspirations which most men share.[38]

The mating of private preference and public welfare implies that the community's goals are as mundane as those of the individual. The nation is but an artificial construction, concerned with "regulating" the pursuits upon which its members are determined by their inherent and ordinary promptings. "That grand corporation which the American people have formed," is, like any corporation, only "an artificial being, invisible, intangible, and existing only in contemplation of law."[39] It follows that the form of government is not of essential importance to the character of the community. Any government of whatever form should provide the requisite channels for private endeavors. In the event of a change of governments, Marshall remarked in connection with the transfer of Florida from monarchic Spain to the republican United States, "the people change their allegiance, their

[37] Elliot, *Debates*, III, 232.

[38] Marshall's desire for widespread propagation of such subjects as Blackstonean jurisprudence and Smithian political economy is treated in the third section of Chapter III, *infra*.

[39] *Dartmouth College* v. *Woodward*, 4 Wheaton (U.S.), 636 (1819); *William Dixon et al.* v. *United States*, 1 Brockenbrough, 181 (1811). Cf. *American Insurance Co.* v. *Canter*, 1 Peters (U.S.), 542 (1828).

relation to their ancient sovereign is dissolved; but their relations to each other, and their rights of property, remain undisturbed."[40] Corresponding to the rule of private interest, then, is the "public interest":[41] peace within, defense from without, and what we now call a "rising standard of living." Public interest corresponds to private interest, public "policy" to private prudence.

According to Marshall, the rights of the individual are not only harmonious but even serviceable to the public interest thus understood. Security of life and liberty tends to eliminate the most bitter kinds of political and religious strife. At the very basis of Marshall's restrictive limitations on prosecutions for treason, for example, was the premise that treason is "the charge which is most capable of being employed as the instrument of those malignant and vindictive passions which may rage in the bosoms of contending parties struggling for power."[42] Similarly, the right of free speech reduces the danger of one kind of political oppression, and toleration of varying religious views avoids "perpetual discontents" and discords over "metaphysical points." Someone might add that toleration of many religions renders the claims of any one less compelling, and the weakening of religion allows greater sway to the reliable passion of interest.

We must spend more time considering Marshall's view of the utility of the property right, a right, after all, less obvi-

[40] *United States* v. *Percheman*, 7 Peters (U.S.), 87 (1833). Cf. *United States* v. *Clarke*, 8 Peters (U.S.), 444-45, 448 (1834). Cf. especially *Soulard and others* v. *The United States*, 4 Peters (U.S.), 511 (1830).

[41] See Herbert Storing, "The Crucial Link: Public Administration, Responsibility, and the Public Interest," *Public Administration Review*, Vol. xxiv, No. 1 (March 1964), 39.

[42] Robertson, *Reports*, ii, 13-14. See also *infra*, Appendix ii. Aristotle observes the dangers attending "political trials, which when not well conducted cause party divisions and revolutionary disturbances." *Politics*, 1300b, 37-38. For Marshall's own description of the misery accompanying indiscriminate executions during domestic strife, see *The Life of George Washington*, i, 395; ii, 16ff., 24n.

ously or intrinsically defensible than those to life and liberty. Its peculiar importance issues from its peculiar usefulness; its protection is in the highest degree politic, Marshall supposed, as well as right. Indeed, it seems that Locke thought that private property's rightness originated with its policy. The natural right of acquiring property results from the contribution of acquisitions to satisfying the fundamental natural claim to self-preservation. Marshall surely recognized property's utility, and interpreted the right so that it would be useful, although he seemed to presume its independent rightness as well.[43]

To some extent the property right was seen as a legal "fence," to use Locke's term, protecting the individual from both his fellows and his government. "Sacred" property would serve to protect whatever parts of a man's activities are involved in his property. Moreover, concern with property and its acquisition would heighten in liberal society. The emphasis upon accumulation and production would lead to what R. H. Tawney has called the "acquisitive society." Thus, a considerable sphere of life and power becomes circumscribed by the legal wall of "property rights" or "freedom of contract," during the movement "from status to contract" which the individualistic philosophers provoked. Marshall's old-fashioned liberal suspicion of public meddling in private "affairs" is illustrated by a remark made in a private letter, when he was by no means in a crotchety dotage:

> I consider the interference of the legislature in the management of our private affairs, whether those affairs are

[43] This is one illustration of the way Marshall's views depart from the merely calculating character of Locke's essentially selfish moral outlook. The Chief Justice speaks of "those principles of abstract justice, which the Creator of all things has impressed on the mind of his creature man." His opinions are in harmony, however, with what might be called the "public face" of Locke's complicated moral philosophy. *Johnson and Graham's Lessee* v. *M'Intosh,* 8 Wheaton (U.S.), 572 (1823). As to Locke's views, see *Two Treatises of Government,* I, 86-90; II, 26-28.

committed to a company or remain under individual direction, as equally dangerous and unwise. I have always thought so and I still think so. I may be compelled to subject my property to these interferences, and when compelled I shall submit; but I will not voluntarily expose myself to the exercise of a power which I think so improperly usurped.[44]

The property right not only provides a "fence" about the individual but also creates a certain peaceableness within society generally. It tends to preclude that perennial cause of civil strife, the struggle between "haves" and "have-nots." The haves are protected in what they possess, but the road to having is opened to all by a fundamental protection of acquisition, not possession. Again and again Marshall recalled that the post-Revolutionary state legislatures, during what he, like the historian John Fiske, would have called the "critical period," had used the "power of interfering with contracts" to vary "the relative situation of debtor and creditor." Rather delicately he alluded to the possibility of class strife between rich and poor.[45] This danger was chiefly the

[44] Letter from Marshall to Greenhow, October 17, 1809. MSS "Judges and Eminent Lawyers," Massachusetts Historical Society. Cited in Beveridge, *Life of John Marshall*, iv, 479-80. Marshall was not unaware that the first thing necessary to preserve liberty was government; protection from government was only the second. See *infra*, ii, at the end of the second section.

[45] "The power of changing the relative situation of debtor and creditor, of interfering with contracts, a power which comes home to every man, touches the interest of all, and controls the conduct of every individual in those things which he supposes to be proper for his own exclusive management, had been used to such an excess by the State legislatures, as to break in upon the ordinary intercourse of society, and destroy all confidence between man and man. This mischief had become so great, so alarming, as not only to impair commercial intercourse, and threaten the existence of credit, but to sap the morals of the people, and destroy the sanctity of private faith. To guard against the continuance of the evil . . . was one of the important benefits expected from a reform of the government." *Ogden* v. *Saunders*, 12 Wheaton (U.S.), 213, 354-55 (1827). See also Marshall, *The Life of George Washington*, ii, 103-05.

fruit of an "instability" in principles securing rights of property, principles "which ought, if possible, to be rendered immutable. . . ."[46] Such a guarantee would not only preclude strife, but even engender a kind of harmony. For substantial acquisition requires commerce, and commerce promotes mutual dependence and hence mutual helpfulness. With respect to the advantages of a projected trade route in Virginia, Marshall remarked:

> The intimate connection which generally attends free commercial intercourse, the strong ties . . . formed by mutual interest, and the interchange of good offices, are well calculated to cherish those friendly sentiments, those amicable dispositions, which at present unite Virginia to a considerable portion of the western people.[47]

Secure property, however, is useful principally because it encourages productive labor. Marshall was familiar with the community ownership characteristic of early Jamestown and Plymouth—the former due to "the unwise injunction contained in the royal instructions," the latter tinged with a certain Christian communism. In both places there occurred an identical and "constant" difficulty: "The public supplies were generally inadequate to the public necessities." The citizens "were often in danger of starving; and severe whipping, administered to promote labor, only increased discontent." The cause lay in "their adherence to the pernicious policy of a community of goods and of labor." The solution lay in providing "industry its due reward," "exclusive property in the product of its toil." When this was in part provided among the colonists at Jamestown, "a sudden change was made in their appearance and habits. Industry, impelled by the certainty of recompense, advanced with rapid

[46] Marshall, *The Life of George Washington*, II, 104. Cf. *Ogden v. Saunders*, 12 Wheaton (U.S.), 354-55 (1827).

[47] Increased commerce would "cement more closely the union" of states as well. John Marshall, *Report of the Commissioners . . . appointed to view certain rivers* (Richmond, 1816), p. 38. See Marshall, *The Life of George Washington*, II, 68.

strides; and the inhabitants were no longer in fear of wanting bread either for themselves, or for the emigrants from England." Unlike Jamestown, Plymouth failed to change its ways with dispatch. The eventual result of the New Englanders' "pernicious policy," combined with their thin soil, was not indeed continued starvation. Marshall wrote only that "they increased [in numbers] more slowly than the other colonies."[48] Increasing population, however, was intimately connected in Marshall's mind with the provision of resources and men for national defense, as we will indicate in the sequel. Besides, wealth serves national strength more directly. "In modern war," Marshall quoted Washington, "the longest purse must chiefly determine the event." Thus, the liberation of individual interest provides the wherewithal for both subsistence and defense, and avoids at the very same time harsh measures such as "whipping, administered to promote labor," which endanger the safety and comfort of the laborer.

It is only in light of the political purposes of peace and an ever-growing "national product," that Marshall's judicial interpretation of property rights can be made intelligible. His great legal opinions did not fundamentally involve "property" as such. Marshall's thematic concern was "vested rights." These were legal claims to ownership which come to exist, or "vest," in one party, simply by virtue of a legitimate contract with another party. It is the doctrine of security for "vested rights," and thus for private contracts, that E. S. Corwin described as the "basic doctrine of American constitutional law." That doctrine served to protect private exchange, that is, commerce. It affirmed the warrant of nature itself not only for the acquisitions of individual labor, but also and especially for the commerce required for substantial gain. Nature dictated not only gain but unlimited gain, and hence the right to contract no less

---

[48] The discussion on which this paragraph rests occurs in Marshall, A history of the colonies . . . , pp. 42-43, 45-46, 77-79. Compare pp. 253-55.

than to acquire. Thus originated the "intrinsic" obligation of contract, familiar to students of the Constitution, which Marshall struggled so hard to prove in his *Ogden* v. *Saunders* dissent. The obligation of contract is intrinsic and "results from the right which every man retains to acquire property, to dispose of that property according to his own judgment, and to pledge himself for a future act. These rights are not given by society, but are brought into it."[49] The point for our present discussion is that the very basis of the Marshallian doctrine of property rights supposes the necessity of a kind of society: the minimal society required for productive exchange. Nature dictates not only rights of man but "relations between man and man," to use Marshall's habitual phrase. Built into the individualistic doctrine he shares with Lockean liberalism, then, is the presupposition that personal property may be regulated in accord with the requirements of commercial society and of a government capable of protecting that society.

It is Marshall's understanding of the circumscribed place of contractual freedom, even within a political society constructed upon the principle of free contract, that ultimately guides his judicial protection of vested rights. On the one hand, the Chief Justice maintained that an inviolable obligation was created by private agreements themselves. He defended this view by pointing to the words of the contract clause, to the framers' avowed intentions, and finally to the great national purposes served by making private contracts absolutely secure. Like Webster's argument for Saunders, Marshall's dissenting opinion in *Ogden* v. *Saunders* began and ended with an invocation of the great national purposes —Webster had even called them *political* purposes—at stake. On the other hand, the Chief Justice willingly admitted that the obligation of certain contracts freely undertaken by individuals may be denied or not enforced by civil laws. "Statutes of frauds, of usury, and of limitations," can legitimately deny the obligation of eligible contracts or at

[49] 12 Wheaton (U.S.), 346 (1827).

least deny enforcement to them.[50] How are the limitations which state laws impose on private contract reconcilable with the natural liberty of contract which the Constitution forbids state laws to impair? Marshall's explicit answer is beset with difficulties. That answer, when pruned of its problems, seems to amount finally to a limitation of free commerce according to the needs of commerce itself and of a commercial society.

Marshall insisted that the state laws in question do not affect the obligation of an existing contract. Either they act only upon the legal remedy for a contract already broken, or they precede the making of a genuine contractual obligation by merely "prescribing the circumstances on which the original validity of a contract shall be made to depend." This is hardly satisfactory, as Warren B. Hunting has shown in his study of Marshall's opinions on contract.[51] Some refusals of remedy may in effect impair the contractual obligation the Constitution protects. Similarly, to allow a state to prescribe the original circumstances in which a contract shall be judged broken or valid, is to allow the existence of a contract to depend on state edict, not on individual undertaking.

In fact, what guides Marshall's use of these distinctions is a willingness to hold valid those restrictions on contract which he judged necessary to liberal commercial society. It is significant that at a crucial stage in the *Saunders* argument he relied on universal agreement in the community to justify a state law of this kind. "All have acquiesced in [statutes of limitations], but have never considered them as being of that class of laws which impair the obligation of contracts."[52] He resorted to his own judgment as well as to common judgment. "It would be a mischief not to be tole-

---

[50] *Ibid.*, 344ff.

[51] *The Obligation of Contracts Clause of the United States Constitution*, in *Johns Hopkins University Studies in Historical and Political Science* (Baltimore: The Johns Hopkins Press, 1919), p. 44.

[52] 12 Wheaton (U.S.), 349.

rated [if] stale obligations" might at any time be invoked. His procedure amounts to a presumption that contracts are to be interpreted to avoid those "mischiefs" which preclude good contractual relations. This suggestion is confirmed by a subsequent and much more striking passage from the *Saunders* dissent. In implied contracts, the Chief Justice wrote, "the parties are supposed to have made those stipulations, which, as honest, fair, and just men, they ought to have made. When the law assumes that they have made these stipulations, it does not vary their contract, or introduce new terms into it, but declares that certain acts, unexplained by compact, impose certain duties, and that the parties had stipulated for their performance."[53]

In a similar fashion Marshall provided for the indirect as well as the direct conditions of good "relations between man and man." He refused to interpret what he at least called a contract (in this case a state grant of a bank charter) to imply an exception to the state's taxing power. "That the taxing power is of vital importance; that it is essential to the existence of government; are truths which it cannot be necessary to reaffirm. They are acknowledged and asserted by all. It would seem that the relinquishment of such a power is never to be assumed."[54] In short, if legal ob-

---

[53] *Ibid.*, 341-42. Consider Blackstone's analogous argument.

"From these *express* contracts the transition is easy to those that are only *implied* by law. Which are such as reason and justice dictate, and which therefore the law presumes that every man has contracted to perform; and upon this presumption makes him answerable to such persons as suffer by his non-performance.

"Of this nature, are, first, such as are necessarily implied by the fundamental constitution of government, to which every man is a contracting party. And thus it is that every person is bound and hath virtually agreed to pay such particular sums of money as are charged on him by the sentence, or assessed by the interpretation of the law. For it is a part of the original contract, entered into by all mankind who partake the benefits of society, to submit in all points to the municipal constitutions and local ordinances of that state, of which each individual is a member." *Commentaries on the Laws of England*, III, 158.

[54] *Providence Bank* v. *Billings*, 4 Peters (U.S.), 514 (1830).

stacles to contractual freedom had to bear a presumption of wrong, the presumption could be rebutted by showing a real connection between the law in question and the whole social fabric of which contractual freedom was but a part.

Although Marshall interpreted the personal right to property so as to fit within the requirements of the public interest, he was convinced that the public interest is served by fundamental *laissez faire*, by essentially free exchange. Marshall recognized full well that the "claims of the creditors stand on high ground" in the United States—higher ground, perhaps, than "in every [other] commercial country known to us."[55] He could not but be aware that such "tenderness" towards the rights of creditors would occasionally result in an untender pressing of debtors. Yet he rejected the more "humane" alternative because, it has been argued, of the political purposes served by liberty of contract. The natural liberty at the basis of Marshall's law went hand in hand with the "system of natural liberty" characteristic of his economics; the liberal jurisprudence of Blackstone provided for the almost unconstrained opportunity for acquisition required by the liberal economics of Adam Smith.[56]

[55] *Brashear* v. *West and others*, 7 Peters (U.S.), 615 (1833); see *Bayley* v. *Greenleaf*, 7 Wheaton (U.S.), 55 (1822).

[56] A remark of Sir Henry Maine illuminates the point: "It is certain that the science of Political Economy, the only department of moral inquiry which has made any considerable progress in our day, would fail to correspond with the facts of life if it were not true that Imperative Law had abandoned the largest part of the field which it once occupied, and had left men to settle rules of conduct for themselves with a liberty never allowed to them till recently. The bias indeed of most persons trained in political economy is to consider the general truth on which their science reposes as entitled to become universal, and, when they apply it as an art, their efforts are ordinarily directed to enlarging the province of Contract and to curtailing that of Imperative Law, except so far as law is necessary to enforce the performance of contracts. The impulse given by thinkers who are under the influence of these ideas is beginning to be very strongly felt in the Western world. Legislation has nearly confessed its inability to keep pace with the activity of man in discovery, in invention, and the manipulation of accumulated wealth. . . ." Sir Henry Sumner Maine, *Ancient Law*

Thus, the basic doctrine of American constitutional law provides for the chief endeavor to which the country's energies have been devoted: the increase of production. Marshall regarded manufacturing and agriculture alike as means to "national prosperity," welcomed without reserve the country's astounding economic growth, and admired the rise of the technology that ministers to economic development.[57] His legal doctrines catered to all of these. Security of exchange and property quickens commerce and industry, and they in turn stimulate one another. Marshall shared the common opinion that paper money and a lax enforcement of contracts under the Articles of Confederation had in

---

(London: Oxford University Press, 1931), pp. 253-54. See Joseph Cropsey, "On the Relation of Political Science and Economics," *The American Political Science Review*, Vol. LIV, No. 1 (March 1960), 3-14.

I have seen no explicit reference by Marshall to Smith, but it is perfectly clear that he was at least influenced by his political economy. He often used Smith's language, as the economic historian Joseph Dorfman has pointed out. "John Marshall: Political Economist," in W. Melville Jones, ed., *Chief Justice Marshall*, pp. 126, 128. "Let us buy and sell as dear as possible. Let commerce go wherever individual, and consequently national interest will carry it." *Ibid.* He praised "free competition" (*A history of the colonies* . . . , p. 50) and damned the "avaricious spirit of commercial monopoly" (*The Life of George Washington*, II, 284). Marshall wished an adequate knowledge of economics to be spread in America. He complimented a budding political economist by saying that he thought it fine that an American study the subject, "as important as it is abstruse," although he had some disagreement with the author's conclusions. Marshall to Daniel Raymond, September 25, 1821. Printed in D. Raymond, *Elements of Constitutional Law and Political Economy* (4th ed., Baltimore: Cushing & Brother, 1840), pp. ix-x.

[57] See Marshall, *The Life of George Washington*, II, 63; *Grant v. Raymond*, 6 Peters (U.S.), 218 (1832). See also Marshall's encouragement, tempered with judicious admonitions, of "scientific researches" into agriculture, itself "a science in which society is deeply interested." Marshall to Henry Bidleman Bascom, November 19, 1827. Printed in Rev. M. M. Henkle, *Life of Henry Bidleman Bascom, Late Bishop of the Methodist Episcopal Church, South* (Louisville: Morton & Griswold), p. 194.

effect diminished "the mass of national labor, and of national wealth." The more stringent provisions of the new Constitution were to arrest this decline: the "great and visible economic improvement occurring around 1790" was in part due to

> . . . the influence of the constitution on habits of thinking and acting, [which] though silent, was considerable. In depriving the states of the power to impair the obligations of contracts, or to make anything but gold and silver a tender in payment of debts, the conviction was impressed on that portion of society which had looked to the government for relief from embarrassment, that personal exertion alone could free them from difficulties; and an increased degree of industry and economy was the natural consequence of this opinion.[58]

[58] Marshall, *The Life of George Washington*, II, 192, 104. Cf. Elliot, *Debates*, III, 231. Harold J. Laski made a discriminating appraisal of the influence upon the United States of the doctrine of vested rights. "In no other country has economic development been so largely shaped by judicial decision. Anyone who examines the first fifty years of the court's history will find the clue to its attitude in that line of decisions of which *Fletcher* v. *Peck* and the *Dartmouth College Case* are the most notable, where the purpose of the Judges was to protect the vested interests of property from invasion by state legislatures which were being driven by the economic difficulties of their constituents to inflation, the reduction of debts, and the cancellation of property rights. This epoch of judicial nationalism, so remarkably inaugurated by Marshall, was obviously an expression of Federalist effort to secure the conditions under which commerce could flourish without interference from those who had suffered through the poverty resulting from the Revolutionary War. This explains the court's view both of the Commerce Clause, as in *Gibbons* v. *Ogden*, and the "obligation of contract" clause in the Constitution.

"These first fifty years summarize a period in the history of the United States in which the pattern of a modern industrial society is only beginning to emerge. The work necessary for that stage was well accomplished by Marshall and his immediate successors." Laski, *The State in Theory and Practice* (New York, 1935), pp. 156-59. Quoted by Charles Grove Haines, *The Role of the Supreme Court in American Government and Politics*, p. 651.

It is illuminating here to stand back a bit from Marshall's own understanding of his economic principles. With the benefit of hindsight it is commonly acknowledged, to say the least, that disadvantages as well as benefits have followed the liberation of private acquisitiveness. In the face of a rigid protection of commercial exchange, ethics and politics alike tend to be subordinated to the provision of open and secure channels of gain. Thus, the doctrine of vested rights is the vehicle of a thoroughgoing commercialization of manners and institutions. It encourages an ever-growing specialization of labor as well as an ever-increasing concentration of the means of production. It is then the legal bulwark of that proliferation of enormous productive corporations characteristic of capitalism, and of the individual's increasingly minute place as "organization man" in ever more organized arrangements, as cog in an ever more efficiently productive social machine. The individual fulfils increasingly the role which the framers of the liberal order assigned to him as by nature's order: a tool of production. No stronger confirmation could be provided of the peculiar conformity of individual rights, especially property rights, to what classical liberalism understood by the public interest.

PUBLIC INTEREST AND THE ETHICS OF MASS SOCIETY

There thus emerges a more or less homogeneous mass of individuals whose life is in their property and their work, who readily conform to their role in the protective social mechanism. Marshall's jurisprudence, as we have observed, fails to encourage high and unusual aspirations, while providing unequivocally for useful channels in which the more ordinary desires of men might flow. It is not surprising that Marshall's country comes to be characterized by men who fit easily into the common and ordinary pursuits of everyday affairs, who make a life of earning a living. These men are pettily selfish yet nevertheless benevolent and useful—with respect to the tastes and wants of most men. The whole of liberal individualism, not merely the pervasive leveling of society on which Alexis de Toqueville fixes, is the deepest root of the common mores and mass conformity he so masterfully discerned in America's liberal democracy. Marshall's jurisprudence encourages the "morals" of the humane, peace-loving, restless and acquisitive modern middle class: "a flock," Tocqueville looked soberly at what was emerging, "of timid and industrious animals of which the government is the shepherd."[59]

Since all individuals possess the same rights, all individuals should equally respect the rights of others. Besides, and perhaps more to the point, how could any man expect to obtain what he wants unless he allows others an opportunity to obtain what they want? These implications of Marshall's jurisprudence point to the moral dispositions of peaceableness and humanity as complements to the right to life, and of tolerance as adjunct to the liberty of opinion. Marshall always considered himself a "philanthropist." He spoke feelingly of "the various improvements which struggling humanity has gradually engrafted on the belligerent code." And he himself favored such projects as the "humane designs for civilizing the neighboring Indians."[60]

[59] *Democracy in America*, 2 volumes (New York: Vintage Books, 1954), II, 337. The classic discussion-cum-propagation of the mores of mass society is Locke's pervasively influential *Thoughts on Education*, many times translated and reprinted. Consider also Hobbes' *Leviathan*, Part I, especially Chapters 6 and 11; David Hume, *Enquiry Concerning the Principles of Morals*, Sect. VI, "Of Qualities useful to Ourselves."

[60] *Worcester* v. *Georgia*, 6 Peters (U.S.), 557, 562 (1832); Marshall, *The Life of George Washington*, I, 237. Cf. Samuel Pufendorf (whose works were frequently cited by Marshall), *De Jure Naturae et Gentium* (Oxford: The Clarendon Press; London: M. Milford, 1934), Preface, III, p. iii. Marshall's frequent and extensive praise of the natural feeling of humanity, an excellence especially strong in the female sex, marks the closeness of his views to the later liberalism of Hume and Adam Smith, rather than to the original source in Hobbes and Locke. See Joseph Cropsey, "Adam Smith," in Leo Strauss and Joseph Cropsey, eds., *History of Political Philosophy* (Chicago: Rand

Tolerance inclines one to be broadminded where matters of "mere" opinion and character, unconnected with more solid interests in life, liberty and property, are concerned. Our previous discussion of Marshall's devotion to liberty of opinion requires little amplification. Beveridge notes that Marshall displayed but trifling care for religious disputes as such. He was concerned principally, it might be said, to conciliate them. Similarly, the savage character of the Indians did not deter him from favoring the politic intermarriage of white settlers with them. When a bill to that effect failed of passage in the Virginia legislature, he wrote to Monroe, "Our prejudices . . . oppose themselves to our interests, and operate too powerfully for them."[61]

The dispositions to peaceableness, humanity and toleration were secondary to man's fundamental drives, however. They were not expected to prevail in instances of conflict. As Marshall commented while deriving certain rules of international law, "humanity dictates and its wants require" the rules. Where "wants" conflict with "humanity," however, the "wants" ought to prevail. His remarks on Indian policy deserve quotation at some length:

McNally & Company, 1963), pp. 549-72. Cf. David Hume, *Treatise of Human Nature*, Book III, Part III, Sections i, ii; *Enquiry Concerning Morals*, Sections I, v, Part II; App. II.

[61] Letter from Marshall to James Monroe, December 2, 1784, quoted by Beveridge, *Life*, I, 241; cf. I, 240; J. Herman Schauinger, *William Gaston, Carolinian* (Milwaukee: The Bruce Publishing Company, 1949), pp. 160-61. To the letter of the Reverend Frederick Beasley, who had enclosed his "Vindication of the Orthodox Faith," Marshall made, in part, the following reply: "It is not for me sir to discern 'any point not sufficiently made out' if indeed there is any. My reading on controversial questions of Theology has been very limited, while yours has obviously been very extensive. I have been content with the faith received from my fore Fathers, and with the revelation contained in the holy scripture as generally understood, and have not entered into those metaphysical enquiries which perplex and I fear cannot enlighten the human understanding." November 9th, 1831. (ALS, The American Philosophical Society.)

any censure which philanthropy may bestow upon [our forefathers' expulsion of the Indians] ought to be qualified. [T]he Indians were a fierce and dangerous enemy whose love of war made them sometimes the aggressors, whose numbers and habits made them formidable, and whose cruel system of warfare seemed to justify every endeavour to remove them to a distance from civilized settlements.

It was not until after the adoption of our present government that respect for our own safety permitted us to give full indulgence to those principles of humanity and justice which ought always to govern our conduct towards the aborigines when this course can be pursued without exposing ourselves to the most afflicting calamities.[62]

As benevolence and toleration contributed to others' life and liberty as well as to one's own, so industry, frugality, and honesty contribute to production which benefits all while it profits oneself. Marshall would follow Adam Smith in condemning "idle people who produce nothing." His admiration for those who acquire was restricted to those who acquire by increasing the common product. He gave no praise to men who sought wealth without labor, whether guided by "the avaricious spirit of commercial monopoly" or by the Spanish "disease" of "an insatiate passion for gold."[63]

[62] Letter from Marshall to Story, printed in Massachusetts Historical Society, *Proceedings*, 2nd series, xiv (November 1900), 337. *The Schooner Exchange v. McFadden*, 7 Cranch (U.S.), 136 (1812). "However retaliation may wound the feelings of humanity," Marshall wrote as Secretary of State, "a just regard for the lives of our citizens and sound policy [may] compel us to resort to it." Marshall to David M. Clarkson, Department of State, August 1, 1800. U.S. Office of Naval Records and Library, *Naval Documents related to the quasi-war between the United States and France* (Washington: G.P.O., 1935-38), vi, 215.

[63] Marshall, *A history of the colonies* . . . , pp. 10, 126; compare p. 30; *The Life of George Washington*, ii, 284, 102-03. Smith, *Wealth of Nations*, pp. 278-79. "God gave the world to men in common; but since he gave it them for their benefit and the greatest conveniences of life they were capable to draw from it, it cannot be

Instead, Marshall admired "industry." Industry was simply the disposition to labor intensely, a habit or attitude that is the real source of prosperity. He praised also frugality or "economy," the willingness to forego the present fruits of labor for the sake of the capital required for further production. He admired honesty, especially that "private faith" which contributes to commercial exchange. The whole spirit of Marshall's ethics is shown in his commendations of the "sober industrious" people of New England, who "improved the advantages which the times afforded them by industry and attention to their interests," and by his praise of John Smith's strong rule at Jamestown, where "a spirit of industry and subordination" had been created "which was the parent of plenty and of peace." What Marshall the historian admired is the increase in wealth and power; the religious zeal of the colonists he implicitly condemned. There is no evidence that Marshall's capitalism owes anything to Calvinism. He distinguished the New Englanders' quarrels about "abstruse theological points" from "those solid acquisitions which permanently improve the condition of man." "Sober, industrious, and economical, they labored indefatigably in opening and improving the country, . . . [and furnishing] themselves with those supplies which are to be drawn from the bosom of the earth," thereby tending to "surplus" and "profitable market." It is the modern politico-economic project, "the relief of man's estate," that moved him. Marshall did not admire the true Puritan character, but what he called "the sound mercantile character."[64] With

---

supposed he meant it should always remain common and uncultivated. He gave it to the use of the industrious and rational—and labour was to be his title to it—not to the fancy or covetousness of the quarrelsome and contentious"; Locke, *Two Treatises of Government*, II, 34. Blackstone suggested "punishing the dissolute and idle," and "protecting the peaceable and industrious." *Commentaries on the Laws of England*, Introduction, I, 8.

[64] "Report of the Commissioners . . . appointed to view certain rivers." In Virginia, House of Delegates, *Journal* (1812/13), pp. 83-89. Marshall, *A history of the colonies* . . . , pp. 104, 33; cf. p. 126.

benevolence and toleration it provides the conditions of peace, comfort and strength that "solid safety and real security" require.

THE APPREHENSIVE EMPIRE

We have sketched the wary calculations, underlying Marshall's better-known deeds and doctrines, by which politics and law are reliably grounded on man's solid interest. This must be so because these interests will prevail, and it should be so because even if they might be subordinated, the effort required makes for risky politics. From this safe starting point issue the rights of man to life and liberty, and, most controversially, to property. Secure property accords with the desires to possess and to gain, and by its encouragement of acquisition provides comfort and the means of defense. To these ends that ethic which seems hardly more than social expediency makes men co-operative and industrious. The result is not merely economic and social but also political: a modern, massive, growing nation-state.

Private interest properly channeled breeds wealth, and wealth breeds power, power in the nation as well as in the wealthy. Marshall saw the United States destined to a "legitimate greatness" which would be centered upon its wealth, population, extent, and military equipment—or, more precisely, on its "progress" in the increase of these. When Marshall justified his *History of the colonies* by reference to the "present state of greatness" which occasioned a "history of their progress," it was to their growth that he pointed. "In arts, in arms, and in power, they have advanced, and are advancing, with unexampled rapidity."[65] The peaceful United States wanted no involvement in European wars of conquest, Marshall told Talleyrand in the course of the XYZ mission in 1797-98, for they would obtain eminence by a different kind of conquest. They would exploit their territories, "on which bountiful nature has bestowed, with a lavish hand, all

[65] Marshall, *A history of the colonies* . . . , pp. 1-4; *Address of the Minority* . . . , p. 15.

the capacities for future legitimate greatness."[66] And thus a great and expanding republican empire would be America's future. "This vast republic" was to be "a great powerful, and independent nation," extending "from the St. Croix to the Gulph of Mexico, from the Atlantic to the Pacific." Phrases like "this our wide-spreading empire," "this newly created empire," our "rising empire," came easily from Marshall. He could admire "the magnificent purchase of Louisiana"[67] with neither the constitutional doubts of Jefferson nor the sectional jealousies of the Northern Federalists.

If the United States was to be an empire, however, it would be of a peculiar kind. One might call Marshall's nation an empire in means, but not in ends, a society always preparing tremendous power, yet not devoted to conquest and rule. Its greatness was a "legitimate greatness," which would not violate the American principle of legitimacy: the only title to rule is the consent of those ruled. Not men but the land was to be conquered. Whether this aim of infinite expansion of power might not indirectly lead to imperial rule is not a question upon which Marshall can be seen to have speculated. There is a difficulty here. It is symbolized, of course, by the plight of the American Indians, the men on the land to be conquered. We will consider in Chapter II Marshall's sober and humane views on the Indian problem. Here we can at least say that rule was not the aim of the American nation as Marshall understood it. The American republic, for which commerce was action and money was blood, was to resemble the model set down by the greatest advocate of commercial republicanism, Montesquieu: ". . .

<hr>

[66] Marshall, "American Envoys to the Minister of Foreign Affairs of the French Republic," Paris, January 27, 1798. *American State Papers, Foreign Relations*, II, 170.

[67] *Johnson and Graham's Lessee* v. *McIntosh*, 8 Wheaton (U.S.), 587 (1823); Marshall, *Address of the Minority* . . . , p. 15; *McCulloch* v. *Maryland*, 4 Wheaton (U.S.), 408 (1819); Marshall, *The Life of George Washington*, II, 440; II, 64; cf. 143; *Loughborough* v. *Blake*, 5 Wheaton (U.S.), 319 (1820); Marshall, "General Marshall's Answer . . . ," in Beveridge, *Life of John Marshall*, II, 572.

a nation under a kind of necessity to be faithful, pacific from principle, and that seeks to gain and not to conquer."[68]

According to Marshall, the United States was to take merely its legitimate place as a nation among the other nations of the world, all to abide by the law of nations. Marshall understood that law as more or less analogous to common law within the United States. It provided for the relations between nation and nation as the common law did between man and man. As the Blackstonean common law embodied in civil society the natural legal principles, so the law of nations embraced among "civilized" nations "the great and immutable principles of equity and natural justice, the simple and natural principles."[69] Common law and international law were each understood as but specific applications of those natural principles that should govern relations among men everywhere. Marshall could write in the famous domestic case of *Gibbons* v. *Ogden* that the right to conduct commerce "derives its source from those laws whose authority is acknowledged by civilized men throughout the world."[70] There is a tendency toward cosmopolitanism, and even toward an increasing homogeneity of peoples, inherent in these Lockean political principles supposed to derive from universal human nature.

In the process a definite sort of international law emerges by which the United States is to abide. Marshall argued that the law of nations was part of the law of the land.[71] Since natural rights belong to man as man, the American nation ought accord a due deference to all other nations, recognizing their legitimate needs and engaging in mutual exchange.[72] In his grand opinions on the law of nations, the

[68] *The Spirit of Laws*, transl. Nugent and Prichard (London: G. Bell and Sons, 1914), xx, 8.
[69] The Venus, 8 Cranch (U.S.), 297 (1814).
[70] *Gibbons* v. *Ogden*, 9 Wheaton (U.S.), 211 (1824).
[71] *The Nereide*, 9 Cranch (U.S.), 423 (1815).
[72] *The Antelope*, 10 Wheaton (U.S.), 122 (1825). See Ziegler, *International Law of Marshall*, p. 31. In discussing Marshall's law

Chief Justice steadily endeavored to promote the "modern" and "humane, civilized" trend encouraging commerce[73] and lessening the rigors of war on person and property. In obeying such a law the United States, while indeed giving to man's common humanity its due, was also serving the nation's own peace and prosperity.[74] While gain might result, however, conquest for empire was ruled out. "Contemplating man, even in a different society, as the natural friend of man," Marshall wrote in one of a series of diplomatic papers addressed to the perhaps bemused Talleyrand, "a state of peace, though unstipulated by treaty, was considered [by the United States] as imposing obligations not to be wantonly violated." "Only necessity, not . . . choice" would compel the United States "to contemplate and prepare for war as a probable event."[75]

---

of nations, I have relied extensively upon Ziegler's collection of sources as well as his sound discussion. See also *Schooner Exchange* v. *McFadden*, 7 Cranch (U.S.), 137 (1812).

[73] *The United States* v. *Percheman*, 7 Peters (U.S.), 86-87 (1833); cf. Vattel, *Law of Nations*, III, Chapter XIII, Section 200. Cf. Locke, *Two Treatises on Civil Government*, II, 179ff.

[74] *Schooner Exchange*, 7 Cranch (U.S.), 136 (1812). "The prosperity of the United States is, in a peculiar degree, promoted by external commerce. A people almost exclusively agricultural have not within themselves a market for the surplus produce of their labor, or a sufficient number and variety of articles of exchange to supply the wants of the cultivator: they cannot have an internal, which will compensate for the loss of an external commerce: they must search abroad for manufactures, and for many other articles which contribute to the comfort and convenience of life, and they must search abroad also for a market for that large portion of the productions of their soil which cannot be consumed at home. The policy of a nation thus circumstanced must ever be to encourage external commerce, and to open to itself every possible market for the disposition of its superfluities, and the supply of its wants." Marshall as Envoy, Memorial to the Minister of Foreign Affairs. United States, *American State Papers*, Foreign Relations, II, 176-77. Compare *A history of the colonies . . .* , p. 34.

[75] Marshall as Envoy, United States, *American State Papers*, Foreign Relations, II, 169; *The Nereide*, 9 Cranch (U.S.), 419 (1815); *Brown* v. *United States*, 8 Cranch (U.S.), 122 (1814).

Still, such a necessity might well arise. Marshall never believed that his country could rest content with reliance on international law and its own good will. National power was the necessary instrument of defense, if not of conquest. Whatever the soothing aspirations for "man . . . as the natural friend of man," which he put in his message to Talleyrand, Marshall was aware of those "black" ingredients in men and nations which make arms necessary. "A defenceless country cannot be secure," he argued at the Virginia Ratifying Convention. "The nature of man forbids us to conclude that we are in no danger from war. . . . Until mankind shall cease to have ambition and avarice, wars will arise. . . . The passions of men stimulate them to avail themselves of the weakness of others."[76]

A question arises, however. Every thoughtful statesman, even every statesman, could agree with Marshall's insistence upon preparations for defence. But why the need for a constantly expanding amount of power, for "progress" in riches, population, arms? The answer is clear, if dour. "The exigen-

---

[76] Elliot, *Debates*, III, 227; *Ogden v. Saunders*, 12 Wheaton (U.S.), 346 (1827). The character of Marshall's opinions on international affairs, as well as the man's considerate and sober judiciousness, are revealed in the following letter. It may be quoted in full as a very small, but illustrative, gem.

To the publisher of the Essay on "A Congress of Nations for the amicable adjustment of national differences."

Sir,—I have received your pamphlet proposing A Congress of Nations for the amicable adjustment of national differences, for which I thank you, together with your note requesting my opinion on it. I have read it with deep interest, and a sincere wish that the attainment of its object were practicable. The argument is well arranged and well supported. The quotations from the New Testament are directly applicable, and the whole spirit of the Sacred Volume inculcates peace. The human race would be eminently benefitted by the principle you advance. The religious man and the philanthropist must equally pray for its establishment. Yet I must avow my belief that it is impracticable.

With great respect, I am your ob't servant
J. Marshall.
The Calumet, November-December, 1832, p. 290.

cies of nations," Marshall argued at the Virginia Ratifying Convention, "have been generally commensurate to their resources."[77] Evils are to be anticipated, to the extent of whatever resources one can pile up. All a nation can do in providing for the necessities of life is not too much. To concern the nation with the good life, with a life of excellence or even pleasure, is "unrealistic," whatever may be the appearance of safety and comfort. Interest rather than honor, businessmen rather than gentlemen, work rather than leisure, must rule the citizens' lives. The nation requires not merely strong means of defense, but an ever-growing pile of such means, accumulated through industry and commerce rightly stimulated and regulated. At the basis of the acquisitive society is apprehension,[78] fear of future dangers. To a considerable extent Marshall's politics is a great preparation in the name of peace for the needs of war. Its sober forethought is nicely and typically expressed in his praise of the mid-seventeenth-century New Englanders:

> They maintained external pcacc . . . and improved the advantages which the times afforded them by industry and attention to their interests. In this period of prosperity, they acquired a degree of strength and consistency

[77] Elliot, *Debates*, III, 235.

[78] "Fear was given us as a Monitor to quicken our Industry, and keep us upon our Guard against the Approaches of Evil. . . ." John Locke, *Thoughts on Education* (*The Works of John Locke Esq.*) (London: John Churchill, 1714), III, Section 115, p. 50. "It is objected; it is so improbable that men should grow into civil societies out of fear, that if they had been afraid, they would not have endured each other's looks. They presume, I believe, that to fear is nothing else than to be affrighted. I comprehend in this word fear, a certain foresight of future evil; neither do I conceive flight the sole property of fear, but to distrust, suspect, take heed, provide so that they may not fear, is also incident to the fearful." Hobbes, *De Cive*, Book I, Chapter I, note 2. "But yet of fear there may be made some use; for it prepareth patience and awaketh industry. . . ." Francis Bacon, "Of Earthly Hope," in *Meditationes Sacrae*, in *The Works of Francis Bacon, Lord Chancellor of England, with a Life of the Author by Basil Montagu, Esq.* (Philadelphia: M. Murphy, 1876), I, 168.

which enabled them to struggle through the difficulties that afterwards assailed them.[79]

The United States was thus intended by Marshall to become what in good part it has become, an enormous nation peaceful and tolerant but apprehensive as to future dangers, benevolent but continually attending to war-like provision for its interests. Under the influence of such a persuasion the country was thus moved to what appears as the American paradox—the petty, anxious, profoundly ascetic, and restlessly unhappy exploitation of the most generous abundance ever lavished upon a people. The consequences for the quality of life, of this preoccupation with the necessities of life, were not lost upon the French observer Tocqueville. "It would seem," he wrote as he concluded his study of the first new nation, "as if the rulers of our time sought only to use men in order to make things great; I wish that they would try a little more to make great men; that they would set less value on the work and more upon the workman. . . ."[80] This too must be put in the balance as we weigh the remarkable freedom and toleration for each, and peace and prosperity for almost all, that has been obtained from the liberation of private interest.

[79] Marshall, *A history of the colonies* . . . , p. 126. See also *McCulloch* v. *Maryland,* 4 Wheaton (U.S.), 408, 409, 415, 423 (1819).
[80] *Democracy in America,* ɪɪ, 347.

CHAPTER II

SOVEREIGN GOVERNMENT

THE NEED FOR GOVERNMENT

ALTHOUGH the American nation's success depended above all upon the restless application of private energies, their calculated coordination could be secured only by a public force, government. Marshall was in the long modern tradition of Machiavelli, Hobbes, Locke, and their followers in the way he believed one supreme government, state above church, with a superior or sovereign power to command all within its jurisdiction, the primary condition for a proper nation. He saw the channeling of men's desires as impossible without the enlightenment, and where education is insufficient, the compulsion, provided by government. Men may well be ignorant of their rights and interests, or at least of their duties to be peaceable, tolerant, industrious; aware of their duties, men may nevertheless ignore them. In most men, Marshall remarked, "judgment is completely controuled by the passions." The laudable disposition to improve one's condition may be crowded out by "the avaricious spirit of commercial monopoly." The counciliating helpfulness content to profit by mutual exchange may give way to war-like "ambition and avarice . . . , which stimulate [men] to avail themselves of the weakness of others."[1] "Regulation" by an artificial sovereign is needed to overcome all the "irregularities" which tend to upset the system of natural liberty.

[1] Elliot, *Debates*, III, 226-27. Marshall to Story, July 13, 1821, printed in Massachusetts Historical Society, *Proceedings*, 2nd series, XIV (November 1900), 329. Marshall, *The Life of George Washington*, I, 76; cf. II, 146, 189, 205, 209, 229, 238, 284. As to "regulation,"

Marshall's appraisal of society without civil authority is illustrated by his assessment of America under the Articles of Confederation. True, he did not see the thirteen societies as completely reduced to a "state of nature"—a condition without government and more or less tending to a state of war. Yet political rule under the Articles was at best weak and becoming weaker. The consequences were inevitable. A spread of debtor politics, together with such outbreaks as Shays' rebellion, indicated that most of America was gradually breaking away from the sound and politic principles "of all reflecting men." The financial liabilities of the Revolution went largely unpaid and in some states without interest. Treaty obligations to Britain were ignored while Britain insulted the newly independent states with impunity. Trade languished, partly because of British restrictions, but essentially because exchange was insecure. And resentment against debts bubbled over into violent efforts to overthrow the power of creditors, and of the courts which protected them and their claims. One of Washington's correspondents went so far as to call the situation "a beginning of anarchy with all its calamities." Marshall himself, in his sober way, wrote that it was this unenlightened and impassioned turbulence which demonstrated the need of a strong government to protect "the rights of the peaceable and quiet."[2]

Government, in that dry and abstract Lockean sense which in its essentials remains with Americans to this day, is an artificial construction. It is a public representative with enough force to provide against the dangers confronting the weak individual (as all are assumed to be). Its object is less the provision of goods desired, than protection against evils to be feared. Its distinctive feature is power in the hands of public officials, sharply distinguished from private individuals. Government, Marshall wrote as Chief Justice, "is

see Joseph Cropsey's remarkable essay, "Adam Smith," in Strauss and Cropsey, *History of Political Philosophy*, pp. 549-72.

[2] Marshall, *The Life of George Washington*, ii, 94-129, esp. 104, 105; i, 429.

an investment of power for the general advantage, in the hands of agents selected for that purpose; which power can never be exercised by the people themselves, but must be placed in the hands of agents, or lie dormant."[3] While men surely do not surrender to the sovereign their natural claims to life, liberty, and property, they surrender the right of enforcement. "When men come into society they can no longer exercise this original and natural right of coercion. It would be incompatible with general peace, and is, therefore, surrendered. Society prohibits the use of private, individual coercion, and gives in its place a more safe and certain remedy."[4]

The true harbor of liberty is, then, the civil society built by human artifice. Only by the power of the great sovereign can security be assured. "The very essence of civil liberty," Marshall remarked in *Marbury* v. *Madison* with characteristic force, "certainly consists in the right of every individual to claim the protection of the laws, whenever he receives an injury."[5]

Thus, Marshall followed his great teachers in insisting that civil society is ruled by the laws of government, not by the maxims of nature as such. Students of utilitarian jurisprudence may note that Marshall repeated approvingly the Blackstonean definition of law: "a rule of Civil conduct prescribed by the supreme power in a State."[6] The Chief Justice readily admitted that "the whole subject of contracts is under the control of society." "The right of society to prescribe those rules by which property may be acquired and preserved is not, and cannot, be drawn into question."[7] Sovereign government might even deprive men of their very inherent freedom or of property indubitably

[3] *Gibbons* v. *Ogden*, 9 Wheaton (U.S.), 189 (1824). See also Elliot, *Debates*, III, 233; *Fletcher* v. *Peck*, 6 Cranch (U.S.), 132-33 (1807).

[4] *Ogden* v. *Saunders*, 12 Wheaton (U.S.), 350 (1827).

[5] *Marbury* v. *Madison*, 1 Cranch (U.S.), 163 (1803).

[6] See *supra*, Chapter I, n. 7.

[7] *Ogden* v. *Saunders*, 12 Wheaton (U.S.), 319, 348 (1827).

theirs by nature. Despite its obvious denial of the Negro's natural right to the fruit of his labor, slavery had to be judged legal by virtue of the laws of states, Union, and even of nations generally.[8] Similarly, the Indians were surely the naturally rightful owners of their American lands. They enjoyed "pre-existing rights," "original natural rights, as the undisputed possessors of the soil from time immemorial." When their land claims conflicted, however, with those given priority by the United States, wrote the Chief Justice in *Johnson and Graham's Lessee* v. *McIntosh*, the settled law of the country now dominant must prevail. "However this restriction may be opposed to natural right, and to the usages of civilized nations, yet, if it be indispensable to that system under which the country has been settled, and be adapted to the actual condition of the two peoples, it may, perhaps, be supported by reason, and certainly cannot be rejected by Courts of justice."[9]

Still, these examples should not mislead us. Marshall exhibited no Austinian or Holmesian exultation at this demonstration of positive law's practical and theoretical supremacy. Government's authority to suppress the natural rights of men, members of its civil society or not, appeared to the Chief Justice as but a regrettable necessity incidental to government's fundamental purpose: preserving the natural rights of its own society's members so far as possible. In Marshall's view slavery was no better than an evil and ultimately dangerous necessity. Similarly, the vacating of Indian claims to land otherwise appropriated by American law could be painfully justified only as "indispensable" to the American system, especially where "the property of the great mass of the community originates" in those appropriations. We will illustrate these remarks on the relation of natural liberty and civil authority by considering at some

[8] For Marshall's views on slavery see the following paragraphs.

[9] *Johnson and Graham's Lessee* v. *McIntosh*, 8 Wheaton (U.S.), 591-92, cf. 572 (1823); *Worcester* v. *Georgia*, 6 Peters (U.S.), 543, 559ff. (1832).

length Marshall's views on slavery and the Indian problem. In each case he qualified human liberty for the sake of short-run expediency, while believing in the long-run expediency, as well as justice, of liberty.

Marshall thought the "peculiar institution" wrong by nature on sound liberal grounds. It was a clear deprivation, he said in words similar to those of Lincoln, of every man's "natural right to the fruits of his own labor." Whatever the violation of true justice, however, positive right in America had declared slavery legal. Property rights might vest in men. Slavery was built into the country's mass of property, then, into rights whose preservation was not only legally right but even expedient in the short run, for the sake notably of safety and peace, as well as property. The legal security which slavery thus received from Marshall is most clearly exhibited in *Mima Queen v. Hepburn.*[10]

Mima Queen was a Negro slave petitioning for freedom on the legal ground that her grandfather had been free. She hoped to establish her ancestor's status by hearsay evidence and especially by hearsay of hearsay. It appears from argument before the Supreme Court and from the very inadequately reported argument before the Circuit Court, District of Columbia, that the Circuit Court admitted hearsay evidence but denied admission of hearsay of hearsay. Exception to this latter ruling was the plaintiff's chief plea in appealing to the Supreme Court.[11] Marshall for the Court, Duval alone dissenting, affirmed the Circuit Court's decision. He opined, moreover, not merely that hearsay of hearsay would not be allowed to prove the specific fact of an ancestor's freedom, but that no hearsay evidence might prove the fact. He admitted several exceptions to the general rule forbidding hearsay evidence as proof of specific cir-

[10] *Mima Queen v. Hepburn*, 7 Cranch (U.S.), 290 (1813); *The Antelope*, 10 Wheaton (U.S.), 114 (1825).

[11] *Mima Queen et al. v. Hepburn*, 20 Federal Cases, 11, 503 (1810). See also the Circuit Court's opinion in the succeeding case of *Queen v. Neale* and Supreme Court Justice Duval's dissenting opinion in *Mima Queen v. Hepburn*.

cumstances. He said, however, that this kind of case did not fall easily within those. Fundamentally, Marshall seemed indisposed to enlarge the instances where hearsay evidence might be allowed, for "no man could feel safe in his property, a claim to which might be supported by proof so easily obtained." In the opinion's key sentence Marshall said that the case involves no preferred right which might rebut the general policy of laws securing property:

> However the feelings of the individual may be interested on the part of a person claiming freedom, the Court cannot perceive any legal distinction between the assertion of this and of any other right, which will justify the application of a rule of evidence to cases of this description which would be inapplicable to general cases in which a right to property may be asserted.[12]

If property in men was socially expedient in the short run as well as legally right, it was socially inexpedient in the long run as well as naturally wrong. Slavery was a "danger, whose extent can scarcely be estimated." Apart from the incendiary threat of slave revolts, it discouraged progress in wealth and power. Marshall's Lockeanism is marvelously illustrated in a remark that emancipation would render work once again respectable in Virginia and halt the emigration of the able and industrious—those who are "the power of the state."[13]

The Chief Justice surely rejected the principled radicalism of the Abolitionists. In their attempts to improve civil society they would destroy not only property rights, but perhaps civil society itself. The "malignant effects" of "insane fanaticism" would "defeat all practicable good by the

[12] *Mima Queen* v. *Hepburn,* 7 Cranch (U.S.), 295, 296, cf. 290 (1810).

[13] Quoted in Sallie E. Marshall Hardy, "John Marshall," *The Green Bag,* VIII, No. 12 (December 1896), 479, 488; Marshall to Pickering, March 20, 1826, Massachusetts Historical Society, *Proceedings,* 2nd Series, XIV, 321. See also Marshall, *A history of the colonies . . . ,* p. 50.

pursuit of an unattainable object." But he also believed foolish the fanatic antipathy of the Southern slave-holders to measures of gradual alleviation. He concurred with Pickering in thinking

> that nothing portends more calamity & mischief to the Southern States than their slave population. Yet they seem to cherish the evil & to view with immovable prejudice & dislike every thing which may tend to diminish it. I do not wonder that they should resist any attempt, should one be made, to interfere with the rights of property, but they have a feverish jealousy of measures which may do good without the hazard of harm that is, I think, very unwise.[14]

With respect to particular measures, Marshall seems to have favored colonization, using federal, state, and private funds, the wealth of Western lands, and discriminatory legislation against freedmen, to at once emancipate slaves and promote their emigration to Africa. On the other hand, he is supposed to have seen colonization as a mere "palliative," and "slavery incurable but by convulsion." He was surprised at the success of the British act of 1833 eliminating slavery in the colonies, and rejoiced in it as a possible example to the South.[15]

[14] Marshall to Pickering, March 20, 1826, *loc. cit.*; Marshall to Alliott Cresson, February 22, 1835, *Niles' Weekly Register*, xlviii (May 9, 1835), 162.

[15] Marshall's discussions of ways to mitigate slavery can be found in the following sources: Sallie E. Marshall Hardy, "John Marshall," *loc. cit.*, pp. 479, 488; Marshall to Edward C. Marshall, February 15, 1832, printed in Oster, *Doctrines*, p. 60; Marshall to R. R. Gurley, December 1831, American Colonization Society, *Annual Report*, xv (1832), vi-viii; Marshall to (unknown), *African Repository and Colonial Journal*, xii (May 1836), 165. Beveridge has a valuable discussion (*Life of John Marshall*, iv, 472-79).

The Chief Justice's grave apprehensions, and his encouragement of those seeking to colonize freedmen, is best reflected in a letter heretofore unpublished: "Will you pardon me," he writes, "if I deem this a fit occasion to express my profound sense of your strenuous and con-

If slavery seemed necessary to secure America's continuance, the restriction of the Indians' land claims was required for the country's very existence. While the Indians possessed the "original natural rights" to the land, the Americans possessed the land—if only by claims originating in conquest. This harsh situation, where justice was confronted by forces too strong for her, called forth a fine illustration of Marshall's stern but humane judicial statesmanship. His course accorded perfectly with the peculiar blend of subdued "realism" and conspicuous humanity guiding Locke's discussion of conquest in Chapter XVI of the *Second Treatise*. While the Chief Justice affirmed unequivocally that the laws and hence the titles of the conqueror must control the conqueror's courts, he presumed that the conquered will be left, where possible, with the use and possession of their property and even of their independence, both theirs until voluntarily ceded to the conqueror. These principles govern the three great Marshallian cases dealing with the Indian problem.

In *Johnson and Graham's Lessee* v. *McIntosh*, the very precedence of conflicting claims to the same land in Illinois was at issue. The plaintiffs showed a title from the Illinois Indians, who at the time of the grant in 1775 had been in full possession of the lands. Yet the lands were also at that time within the limits of Virginia, which after independ-

---

tinued exertions in that great cause of humanity—the restoration of the descendants of Africans in these United States to the land of their ancestors. No object unites more entirely in its favor those motives which actuate the Christian, the Philanthropist, and the Patriot; and you have promoted it not only by large pecuniary contributions, but by those laudable researches which may furnish inducements to the intelligent statesman to embark in an enterprize which promises great future advantages to his country. Go on sir,—assured of the approbation of your own heart, and of a great portion of the wise and the good.

J. Marshall"

Addressee unknown, no place, no date (ALS, Princeton University Library, Manuscript Division; copy at the Papers of John Marshall, Williamsburg).

ence ceded its Western lands to the United States. In turn, the United States had granted this particular tract to the defendants. Marshall began his opinion by presuming that the title to lands must depend on "the law of the nation in which they lie," not merely on "abstract justice." He then showed that the law of the European discoverers, and of their American successors, held that discovery gave title to the lands discovered. Thus the Indians' rights, although not entirely "disregarded," were "necessarily, to a considerable extent, impaired." Marshall characterized the impairment thus: the Indians remained "the rightful occupants of the soil, with a legal as well as just claim to retain possession of it, and to use it according to their own discretion," but they lost the right to dispose of it as they pleased. The Europeans claimed a power "to grant the soil," even "while yet in possession of the natives. These grants have been understood by all to convey a title to the grantees, subject only to the Indian right of occupancy." That title, on which much of the lands now possessed by the United States depend, must be affirmed, whatever the original stature of the claims:

> We will not enter into the controversy, whether agriculturists, merchants, and manufacturers, have a right, on abstract principles, to expel hunters from the territory they possess, or to contract their limits. Conquest gives a title which the Courts of the conqueror cannot deny, whatever the private and speculative opinions of individuals may be, respecting the original justice of the claim which has been successfully asserted. The British government, which was then our government, and whose rights have passed to the United States, asserted a title to all the lands occupied by Indians, within the chartered limits of the British colonies. It asserted also a limited sovereignty over them, and the exclusive right of extinguishing the title which occupancy gave to them. These claims have been maintained and established as far west as the

river Mississippi, by the sword. The title to a vast portion of the lands we now hold, originates in them. It is not for the Courts of this country to question the validity of this title, or to sustain one which is incompatible with it.[16]

Marshall did not rest, however, with affirming the basic authority of American land titles. His additional argument is most revealing, and was foreshadowed by argument of neither counsel so far as the *Reports* indicate. He passed by any attempt to defend the Europeans' own contention, that of title by discovery. Instead, he presented, if in a temperate and even tentative manner, what he clearly believed to be a truer and more just account of the merits of the controversy. "Although we do not mean to engage in the defense of those principles which Europeans have applied to Indian title, they may, we think, find some excuse, if not justification, in the character and habits of the people whose rights have been wrested from them." While making "character and habits" central, he was clearly not moved by the Europeans' "pompous claims" that they deserved to rule what they discovered because they brought "civilization" and "Christianity" to the heathen, or even by the argument of defendant's counsel, somewhat Lockean itself, that the more productive, cultivators, can justly push out the less so, in this case hunters.[17] Each of these arguments would permit in the name of civilization or progress a kind of slavery, or at least a continuing displacement from the land of savage tribes like the Indians. Marshall's contempt for such unnatural presumption, as he viewed it, is manifest. Instead he excused the displacement which had occurred by the most narrow argument possible: the Indians' war-like savagery made their physical proximity a mortal danger to the conquering settlers, and only to the

[16] *Johnson and Graham's Lessee* v. *McIntosh*, 8 Wheaton (U.S.), 588-89, 572-74 (1823).

[17] *Ibid.*, 569, 589, 590, 573. See also *Worcester* v. *Georgia*, 6 Peters (U.S.), 543 (1832).

extent of that danger might their lands be appropriated. The argument that follows will show how Marshall reduced the justification for depriving the Indians of their property to the most minimal of which liberal jurisprudence is capable— the right of providing for the colonists' self-preservation.

The Chief Justice was content to begin merely by acknowledging the need, the inevitable need, to recognize the claims of the Europeans. Superior power, where it undeniably exists, must be accommodated; this is undeniably an ingredient of the Chief Justice's, and of Locke's, "realistic" views. Conquest alone, he briefly remarked, gives a title or at least an actual sovereignty which is "conceded by the world" and must be admitted by those on whom it descends. This in two sentences. The great question, however, for Marshall no less than Locke, is how sovereignty is to be rendered tolerable, that is, careful of the lives and properties of the conquered. At once the Chief Justice went on to urge that the conqueror, moved by "humanity" as well as "wise policy," forego oppression so far "as is compatible with the objects of the conquest." Thus he will encourage the "mingling" of "old and new members of the society" to make "one people" or at least will allow the Indians to be "safely governed as a distinct people." Thus "the rights of the conquered to property should remain unimpaired" so that "confidence in their security" will encourage assimilation. This is "that law which regulates, and ought to regulate in general, the relations between the conqueror and conquered."

Yet, Marshall went on, the Indians were in 1775 and thereafter of a war-like savagery which did not permit assimilation or voluntary subordination. The settlers' superior arms and agriculture drove the Indians and their game far "into thicker and unbroken forests," leaving the nearer lands vacant. "The soil, being no longer occupied by its ancient inhabitants," was parcelled out by the British; claims under the grants were made. Thus the "character and habits" of the Indians made the usual rule governing the relation of conqueror and conquered inapplicable. A new rule was needed and every rule "which can be suggested will be found to be attended with great difficulty." Marshall then concluded his remarks in *Johnson and Graham's Lessee* v. *McIntosh*: "However extravagant the pretension of converting the discovery of a nation into conquest may appear; if the principle has been asserted in the first instance, and afterwards sustained; if a country has been acquired and held under it; if the property of the great mass of the community originates in it, it becomes the law of the land, and cannot be questioned. So, too, with respect to the concomitant principle, that the Indian inhabitants are to be considered merely as occupants, to be protected, indeed, while in peace, in possession of their lands, but to be deemed incapable of transferring the absolute title to others. However this restriction may be opposed to natural right. . . ."[18]

In this first judicial opinion on Indian affairs, the Chief Justice seemed to be showing his fellow-citizens that the exceptional and harsh treatment of the savages involved in America's settlement could be interpreted in the light of liberal and humane principles—and thus could be understood as exceptional. To discourage such brutal treatment where possible, as in his own time, was the great endeavor of Marshall's other judicial utterances on the subject, *Cherokee Nation* v. *Georgia* and *Worcester* v. *Georgia*. These decisions involved the state of Georgia's assertion of sovereignty over the Cherokees and their lands. Since both cases have been well discussed by Beveridge,[19] only the gist of Marshall's reasoning will be considered here.

In *Cherokee Nation* v. *Georgia*, Marshall determined that the Cherokees were not a "foreign nation" as they claimed, and hence could not on that ground receive benefit of the Supreme Court's original jurisdiction. Yet he began his opinion with expressions of deep sympathy at the plight of the tribe, roughly subordinated to Georgia law, their land overrun by Georgia's citizens. He concluded with a reference,

[18] *Ibid.*, 589-91.
[19] *The Life of John Marshall*, IV, 539-52.

hardly to be missed, to President Jackson's responsibility to protect these Indians from state wrongs both "inflicted" and "to be apprehended." The Cherokees, although not strictly a foreign nation, were nevertheless "distinct political societies," if "domestic dependent nations" in a state of "pupilage." "Their relation to the United States resembles that of a ward to his guardian." Following indeed the generally accepted interpretation of the relevant laws and treaties, Marshall emphasized that the Cherokees "have an unquestionable, and heretofore unquestioned right to the lands they occupy, until that right shall be extinguished by a voluntary cession to our government. . . ."[20]

With a defensible jurisdiction over *Worcester* v. *Georgia*, and in the face of Jackson's positive encouragement of the extinction of the Cherokee nation and its titles, Marshall declared the relevant laws of the state void. They violated United States treaties assuring the Indians' security. The Constitution granted the national government sole power to extinguish the Indian claims. From its inception the government had treated the Indians as independent nations, extinguishing only with their consent, and, moreover, "civilizing and converting them from hunters into agriculturists." Marshall indicated that the act endeavoring to accomplish this "laudable" amelioration, itself showed the country's "settled purpose to fix the Indians in their country by giving them security at home." True, on Georgia's side there were parties, like McIntosh in the first Indian case, claiming land by virtue of titles descending from an original discovery. These claims, however, reflected no settled national policy on which a mass of property depended. Georgia's citizens were in fact violating a humane national policy by only now rushing greedily upon the land. Here, moreover, was no ferocious and disappearing tribe of savages. The Cherokees were in the disputed land and had "made considerable progress" in "improvement," taking up agriculture, adopting a constitution with three separated powers, becoming "civi-

[20] *Cherokee Nation* v. *Georgia*, 5 Peters (U.S.), 15-20 (1831).

lized Christians and agriculturists" willing, as the bill in *Cherokee Nation* v. *Georgia* put it nicely, "to submit to a comparison with their white brethren around them."[21] In the face of almost certain rejection by the only officer capable of enforcing upon Georgia the Court's decision, Marshall and his Court had the courage to acknowledge to the Indians, and to state for other times and conditions, the generous, as well as just, wise, and humane, reconciliation of Indian rights with the sovereign American law. It might well be that the greater generosity displayed to the Indians, compared to the slaves, was owing to Marshall's belief that danger from the Indians was no longer to be expected, while the awful possibilities connected with Negro enslavement yet remained.

Slaves and Indians were those unfortunate men essentially outside of America's civil society, but ruled by it. The tension between natural liberty and civil government is not restricted to them, however. It appears within the American nation itself as the tension between "liberty and order," the famous problem intrinsic to Lockean government. Consider the definition of civil liberty given by Blackstone, Marshall's great judicial collaborator in embodying Lockean liberalism in enduring institutions. "Political . . . or civil liberty," he wrote, "which is that of a member of society, is no other than natural liberty so far restrained by human laws (and no further) as is necessary and expedient for the general advantage of the public."[22]

What follows will consider first the way the principles of human liberty manage to guide the American order, and then the fundamental character of a governmental system that in a sense limits man's natural liberty and in a more profound sense preserves it. These are the two parts of that distinctively modern constitutionalism which finds its origin, if not the full refinement given by Montesquieu, in the political philosophy of Locke: a provision for natural rights or the rights

[21] *Ibid.*, 6; *Worcester* v. *Georgia*, 6 Peters (U.S.), 556-62 (1832).
[22] 1 *Commentaries on the Laws of England*, 125.

of man on the one hand, a rigid system of necessary public powers, on the other.

As Marshall understood the American Constitution, it provided for man's natural rights by explicit provisions and, perhaps more important, by assuming the continuance of the old English common law. This law, he thought, had ruled in the thirteen states until they entered the Union. The original colonists "had brought with them the laws of England both statute and common law as existing at the settlement of each colony, so far as they were applicable to our situation." Marshall admitted that these rules might have been sloughed off at the Revolution, "either expressly or necessarily by the nature of the governments which we adopted." He maintained, however, that neither explicit enactments nor political novelties had in fact diminished the rule of the common law.

> [The Revolution did not change in any degree] the relations of man to man, or the law which regulated those relations. In breaking off our political connexion with the parent state, we did not break off our connexion with each other. It remained subject to the ancient rules, until those rules should be altered by the competent authority.[23]

What the common law embodied, the Constitution was to preserve. It is true that the common law varied from state to state. The laws of these "distinct societies," "though originating in the same great principles, had been variously modified." Still, in all the states the "great principles" of the common law were the same; they formed the "substratum of the laws of every state." And when the people of these societies became one society for the most important

[23] *Livingston* v. *Jefferson*, 1 Brockenbrough, 211 (1811). See also *Dartmouth College* v. *Woodward*, 4 Wheaton (U.S.), 651 (1819); Marshall to unknown correspondent, November 27, 1800, quoted in Crosskey, *Politics and the Constitution*, p. 1356, n. 45. See Robertson, *Reports*, II, 401ff.; *Murdock & Co.* v. *Hunter's Representatives*, 1 Brockenbrough 141 (1808).

purposes by adopting the Constitution of 1788, the principles of the common law became the "substratum of our laws" generally, "the law of the land," "the common or unwritten law which pervades all America."[24]

Marshall did not consider the Constitution to have "adopted" the common law. Adoption means a new promulgation, which would imply that American society was being originated or remade. Far from being newly established, even from being reestablished, however, the society was merely being preserved in its essentials. These essential principles were then simply assumed by the Constitution, and, to begin with, they formed the canons for interpretation of the document's words in most cases. To illustrate: "For the meaning of the term *habeas corpus*, resort may unquestionably be had to the common law."[25] The common law might even confer jurisdiction. Before Marshall became subject to the constraints of judicial office, he publicly affirmed a common law jurisdiction for the national courts. Such an authority is implied, he wrote in 1799, in section 2 of Article III, in which the judicial power of the United States is extended to all cases in law and equity arising under the Constitution, as well as under the laws of the United States.

What are cases arising under the constitution, as contradistinguished from those which arise under the laws made pursuant thereof? They must be cases triable by a

[24] Marshall, *Address of the Minority* . . . , pp. 12, 14. *Wayman* v. *Southard*, 10 Wheaton (U.S.), 46 (1825); Robertson, *Reports*, II, 481-82, 402.

[25] *Ex parte Bollman*, 4 Cranch (U.S.), 93-94 (1807). With respect to the constitutional term "treason," Marshall remarked that "it is used in a very old statute of that country whose language is our language, and whose laws form the substratum of our laws. It is scarcely conceivable that the term was not employed by the framers of our Constitution in the sense which had been affixed to it by those from whom we borrowed it." Robertson, *Reports*, II, 402ff. For a useful collection of materials and discussion, see Julius Goebel, Jr., "The Common Law and the Constitution," in Jones, *Chief Justice Marshall*, pp. 115ff.

rule which exists independent of any act of the legislature of the union. That rule is the common or unwritten law which pervades all America. . . .[26]

Apart from its assumption of the common law's essentials, the Constitution put express and, be it noted, separate limits on the state and general governments, providing what Marshall went so far as to call "a bill of rights for the people of each state,"[27] as well as the better known Bill of Rights for the nation. The harmony of constitutional provision and common law was not perfect. Where the "supreme law of the land" conflicted with the "law of the land," the Constitution must prevail. One example of such a conflict, that involving differing definitions of treason and of necessary safeguards surrounding trials for treason, is discussed in Appendix II. As a rule, however, the Constitution did not vary the common law and was content to make explicit some of its leading maxims, forbidding, for example, to the

[26] Marshall, *Address of the Minority* . . . , p. 12; see pp. 13-14. Crosskey very helpfully points out the remarks of Justice Story indicating that Marshall probably dissented when a Supreme Court majority in *United States* v. *Hudson & Goodwin*, 7 Cranch (U.S.), 32 (1812), held that the Court lacked a common law jurisdiction, *Politics and the Constitution*, pp. 767-84; p. 782, n. 73 and references.

[27] *Fletcher* v. *Peck*, 6 Cranch (U.S.), 138 (1810). *Barron* v. *Baltimore*, 7 Peters (U.S.), 243 (1833). Marshall's serene assertion here that the Bill of Rights applied only to the general government was but a reiteration of an opinion expressed on circuit during the Burr trial some 26 years earlier. Robertson, *Reports*, I, 99-100. This by itself destroys Crosskey's thesis raised on the merest hypothesis that Marshall's opinion in *Barron* v. *Baltimore* was compelled by Jeffersonian judges: the Chief Justice *really* believed the Bill of Rights to apply to the states. Crosskey, *Politics and the Constitution*, pp. 1076-82. Also, Crosskey's argument fails to account for the tone of certainty which he himself acknowledges, and for Marshall's and Story's failure to dissent, as they did with the property right alone at stake in *Ogden* v. *Saunders*. Crosskey's argument amounts to the assertion that Marshall must have differed because he obviously held that the national government was directly to govern the state governments. But that is untrue. See the discussion of "union" in the final section of this chapter.

states laws impairing the obligation of contracts and to both states and nation *ex post facto* laws and bills of attainder.[28] Thus there was a constitutional mandate to regulate the essential daily and ordinary affairs of men according to rules suggested by nature itself. Warren B. Hunting's remarks on the judicial interpretation of contracts during this period might be applied more generally: "As to private contracts, civil law supersedes natural law, but it impliedly adopts the principles of natural law unless it expressly enacts otherwise."[29] A perfect illustration of the natural core uniting in the Constitution common law and express provision occurs in *Fletcher* v. *Peck*. If Georgia's legislature was to decide a question of title, Marshall wrote, then it ought to have obeyed "those rules of property which are common to all the citizens of the United States." Marshall's interpretation of these "rules" turned finally on the premise that property rights vest "absolutely" in persons by virtue of a legitimate private agreement. This is but a corollary of the doctrine, made explicit in Marshall's *Ogden* v. *Saunders* dissent, that private agreements in civil society are intrinsically binding because they are expressions of the natural right to acquire and exchange property. Even if Georgia were an independent state, her act rescinding a grant of land might be challenged. She was not simply sovereign, however. She was a "member of the American Union" and thus subject to the Constitution's prohibition to the states of laws impairing the obligation of contracts. This is precisely the clause interpreted according to the natural right to contract in *Ogden* v. *Saunders*. Nature's liberties underlie both "these rules of property which are common to all the citizens of the United States" and the Constitution's contract clause. Georgia's revocation was then void, wrote the Chief

[28] *Ogden* v. *Saunders*, 12 Wheaton (U.S.), 344-45 (1827). See with respect to bills of credit, *Craig* v. *Missouri*, 4 Peters (U.S.), 431-32 (1830); *Byrne* v. *Missouri*, 8 Peters (U.S.), 40 (1834). Cf. Charles Grove Haines, *The Role of the Supreme Court in American Government and Politics, 1789-1835*, p. 285.

[29] Hunting, *Obligation of Contract*, p. 47.

Justice in concluding his basic argument, "either by general principles which are common to our free institutions, or by the particular provisions of the constitution of the United States."[30]

Whatever the Constitution's provision for the principles of natural justice, its chief concern was to erect suitable institutions. In its first and critical articles it established the three branches—legislative, judicial, executive. The Lockean philosophy as refined by Montesquieu dictated not merely a sovereign power, but a rigid system of distinct powers duly separated and balanced. The three departments correspond in their tasks to the three deficiencies or evils that Locke had observed outside of civil society. There existed neither "an established, settled known law . . . ," "a known and indifferent judge," nor "power to back and support the sentence when right."[31] The "power" of each department was then complicated in its meaning, at once implying all the means necessary for its task and a definite task to which the department was to be limited. The three departments together comprised the kinds of powers which the people were to be understood to have given up. Thus Marshall understood the Americans' ratification of the Constitution of 1788, as Chapter IV will suggest. The people had agreed to bestow their individual powers upon that great public power which, by its "machinery of government," and by an ingenious mechanical system setting ambition against ambition, would protect against danger while not being itself dangerous. From a consideration of men's low but solid interests, and the deficiencies of their natural condition, there can be deduced the second part of modern constitutionalism. Corresponding to the natural private law governing the relations between individuals, is what has been well called a "natural public law"

[30] *Fletcher* v. *Peck*, 6 Cranch (U.S.), 132-36, 139 (1810).

[31] Locke, *Two Treatises of Civil Government*, II, 124, 125, 126. See Marshall's opinion for the Supreme Court in *Wayman* v. *Southard*, 10 Wheaton (U.S.), 46 (1825).

controlling the government's activities. It is a sort of natural constitution behind the written constitution.[32]

This kind of rigidly defined and ingeniously arranged institutional system is often called "limited government." If the provision for the individual's security is sometimes praised, the constraining effect upon leadership is also deplored. With respect to its narrow tasks Lockean government has even been compared to a night-watchman. The analogy with a security-officer of the store has merit. It is essential, however, to observe Lockean government's virtually unqualified authority within its sphere. It is narrow in its pursuits, but not weak. On the contrary. In principle aloof from controversy about such "unrealistic" subjects as how wealth, honor and power should be distributed, or true religion followed, the "energy" of sovereign government can thus be unqualified and unhindered in providing for the individual's "real" interests and wants. Corresponding to the liberation of the acquisitive passions, and thus of great productive forces needing to be channeled, is a government meant above all to be "efficient" and "effective" in "administration," in performing regularly and reliably its necessary tasks. It assures the social machine's "working." It is the whole society's defender, the economy's supervising engineer. Marshall's jurisprudence encourages the sovereign protector of mass men, that new leviathan preoccupied with providing efficiently for the conditions of life for as many people as possible. It goes without saying that the full character of the bureaucratic state would become fully visible only generations later. The possibility was already seen, however, by

---

[32] There are many repetitions in Marshall's judicial prose of a thought similar to the following: "[The United States'] powers are unquestionably limited; but while within those limits, it is a perfect government as any other, having all the faculties and properties belonging to a government, with a perfect right to use them freely, in order to accomplish the objects of its institutions." *United States* v. *Maurice et al.*, 2 Brockenbrough 109 (1823). On the origin of "natural public law" in Hobbes' political philosophy, see Strauss, *Natural Right and History*, pp. 190-196.

the prescient Tocqueville, visiting the United States in 1831-32. Almost at the end of his great work he considered "What sort of despotism democratic nations have to fear." Above a sheep-like race of men, Tocqueville speculated, may stand "an immense and tutelary power, which takes upon itself alone to secure their gratifications and to watch over their fate. That power is absolute, minute, regular, provident, and mild. It would be like the authority of a parent if, like that authority, its object were to prepare men for manhood; but it seeks, on the contrary, to keep them in perpetual childhood: it is well content that the people should rejoice, provided they think of nothing but rejoicing. For their happiness such a government willingly labors, but it chooses to be the sole agent and the only arbiter of that happiness; it provides for their security, foresees and supplies their necessities, facilitates their pleasures, manages their principal concerns, directs their industry, regulates the descent of property, and subdivides their inheritances: what remains, but to spare them all the care of thinking and all the trouble of living?"

"JUDICIAL POWER": PRIVATE RIGHTS SECURED

In treating Marshall's views with respect to the judiciary department, I postpone until Chapter IV discussion of its most distinctive and controversial feature, judicial review. Judicial review being an American variation on the judiciary's place in liberal government, that place must be first understood. The ordinary, "civil" task of the legal or judicial power (Marshall used these names interchangeably) must be explained before considering the additional complication of judicial review. The helpfulness of modern commentators eager to exhibit the Court's "political" role is reduced when they fail to make this distinction. True, even the "judicial power," the distinctive authority assigned to the courts by their very character according to Marshallian doctrine, is "political" in some sense. But that assertion is not particularly enlightening unless the precise sense is portrayed, a task which requires first an articulation of the judiciary's function even in the spirit in which Marshall saw it. Thus one must follow the Chief Justice's understanding through premises which, until the explanation is complete, will no doubt seem of a child-like naïveté to many readers very conscious of present-day notions on these matters.

According to Marshall, legal or judicial power is the authority to construe laws as they apply to individuals. Since in civil society laws are fundamentally what the government says they are, and since the law-making department is the legislature, the judges might seem to be essentially secondary officials only carrying out the will of their superiors. It is well known that this was Marshall's view. Ordinarily the courts' duty "is to decide upon individual rights, according to those principles which the political departments of the nation have established," as he wrote while construing a treaty. Marshall was not unaware of what astute commentators are wont to point out, that this alone gives to the judiciary a wide jurisdiction. Going so far in adherence to the new canons of Montesquieuan political science as to hold that "the judicial department of every government is the rightful expositor of its law," the Chief Justice insisted that its province stretched as far as the laws it served. Perhaps remembering Jefferson's campaign to reduce the high-flying judiciary, he extolled not infrequently the "great political principle . . . that the legislative, executive, and judicial powers of every well constructed government are co-extensive with each other." The function he attributed to the courts is clearly part of a comprehensive *political* understanding, then. Yet that function itself, *according to that understanding*, is not political. The judiciary's power over "the rights of individuals" concerns, the Chief Justice wrote, "objects unconnected with government." As to the governmental policies which bear in civil society on individual rights, these are given by the laws which the

66

courts obey. Marshall is famous, today ridiculed, for his solemn repetition of the maxim for republican countries, taken up by Blackstone from Montesquieu, that courts are but tools of the law. "Judicial power, as contradistinguished from the power of the laws, has no existence." "Courts are the mere instruments of the law, and can will nothing. When they are said to exercise a discretion it is a mere legal discretion, a discretion to be exercised in discerning the course prescribed by law. . . ." So baldly stated, of course, the contention may look impossible. Even granting that the policies which bear on individual rights are not originated by the courts, the reconciliation of policies and rights—and hence the policies permitted—is made by judges, the result of judicial choice. Yet Marshall of course knew this and granted it. His most precise formulation, the clue to his understanding of judicial choice without judicial willfulness, occurred during the trials of Aaron Burr. "This is said to be a motion to the *discretion* of the court," he remarked at one important point. "But a motion to its *discretion* is a motion, not to its *inclination*, but to its *judgment*; and its judgment is to be guided by sound legal principles."[33]

The key to his views on the subject is the notion of "sound legal principles" which are to guide judicial choice. Marshall here referred to the "general principles" of the common law that we have already discussed. The judges' subordination to these was not opposed to a fundamental ministry to the national laws. For the laws themselves, as we have noted of the fundamental law, are meant to protect, and are certainly to be presumed to respect, the general principles governing private rights. The point is happily evident in a passage,

[33] Robertson, *Reports*, ɪ, 182. *Forster & Elam* v. *Neilson*, 2 Peters (U.S.), 307 (1829); *Bank of Hamilton* v. *Dudley's Lessee*, 2 Peters (U.S.), 524 (1829); *Osborne* v. *Bank of United States*, 9 Wheaton (U.S.), 818-19, 866 (1824); *Dartmouth College* v. *Woodward*, 4 Wheaton (U.S.), 518 (1819). See also U. S. Congress, *Annals*, 6th Congress, 1799-1801, p. 606; *Marbury* v. *Madison*, 1 Cranch (U.S.), 87 (1803).

quoted by Marshall, from *The Federalist*'s characterization of the Supreme Court: ". . . that tribunal which is destined to unite and assimilate the principles of natural justice and the rules of national decision."[34]

In the deepest sense, then, it is nature as well as the legislature which controls the judiciary's function; the judicial power is one special form of that authority defined by "natural public law." "The question whether a right has vested or not," Marshall remarked at a key turn of his argument in *Marbury* v. *Madison*, "is in its nature, judicial, and must be tried by the judicial authority." He elaborated the point in the leading contract clause case of *Fletcher* v. *Peck.* Courts are by definition "those tribunals which are established for the security of property and to decide on human rights." Thus, it would seem equitable that the Georgia legislature's decision to revoke its grant of land "should be regulated by those rules which would have regulated the decision of a judicial tribunal. The question was, in its nature, a question of title, and the tribunal which decided it was either acting in the character of a court of justice, and performing a duty usually assigned to a court, or it was exerting a mere act of power in which it was controlled only by its own will." As natural private rights vest under private contract, so a kind of natural judicial power vests by virtue of the social contract.[35]

[34] *Cohens* v. *Virginia*, 6 Wheaton (U.S.), 420 (1821). So appropriate is the remark to my argument that I must regret telling the reader that its authenticity may be suspected. For *The Federalist*, #82, has "principles of national justice" where the *Reports* have "principles of natural justice." Martin Diamond has pointed out to me, however, that, if no mere typographical or reportorial error is to blame, the argument of the text is perhaps strengthened. If Marshall changed *Federalist* #82, deliberately or not, it is probably because the change better expresses his own understanding of the issue.

[35] "The original power of judicature, by the fundamental principles of society, is lodged in the society at large," wrote Blackstone following Locke, "but as it would be impracticable to render complete justice to every individual, by the people in their collective capacity, therefore every nation has committed that power to certain select

Therefore, to fulfill their tasks properly the courts had to be at once independent of all pressures that would sway them from duty and dependent upon the counsel of liberal jurisprudence as to where their duty lay. This was roughly Marshall's prescription for the American judiciary. As one of the most distinguished members of the Virginia Consti-

---

magistrates, who with more ease and expedition can hear and determine complaints." I *Commentaries on the Laws of England* 267. *Marbury* v. *Madison*, 1 Cranch (U.S.), 167 (1803). *Fletcher* v. *Peck*, 6 Cranch (U.S.), 133 (1810). An argument analogous to that of *Fletcher* v. *Peck* is given by Marshall more elegantly in *Ogden* v. *Witherspoon*, II Haywood's *Reports*, 228-29 (1800). "The separation of these powers [legislative, executive, and the "supreme" judiciary] has been deemed by the people of almost all the states as essential to liberty. And the question here is, does it belong to the judiciary to decide upon laws when made, and the extent and operation of them; or to the legislature? If it belongs to the judiciary, then the matter decided by this act, namely, that the act of 1789 be a repeal of the 9th section of 1715, is a judicial matter, and not a legislative one. The determination is made by a branch of government, not authorized by the constitution to make it; and is therefore in my judgement void. It seems also to be void for another reason; the 10th section of the first article of the federal constitution, prohibits the states to pass any law impairing the obligation of contracts. Now will it not impair the obligation, if a contract, which, at the time of passing the act of 1789, might be recovered as by the creditor, shall by the operation of the act of 1789, be entirely deprived of his remedy?"

It would seem that Crosskey is correct in inferring from Marshall's praise of Story's opinion in *Martin* v. *Hunter's Lessee*, a similar opinion that "The language of Article III is . . . mandatory upon the legislature." Story went on: "Its obligatory force is so imperative, that Congress could not, without a violation of its duty, have refused to carry it into operation. . . . The object of the constitution was to establish three great departments of government; the legislative, the executive and the judicial departments. . . . The judicial power must, therefore, be vested in some court, by congress. . . . If it is a duty to vest the judicial power of the United States, it is a duty to invest the whole judicial power." *Martin* v. *Hunter's Lessee*, 1 Wheaton (U.S.), 328-30 (1816). Compare *Cohens* v. *Virginia*, 6 Wheaton (U.S.), 423 (1821). Story himself said that Marshall had concurred "in every word" of his opinion. On the whole matter see Crosskey, *Politics and the Constitution*, II, 817, 1245.

tutional Convention of 1829-30, the Chief Justice fought vehemently for "the independence of all those who try causes between man and man, and between a man and his Government. . . ." "This Convention can do nothing that would entail a more serious evil . . . ," he declared, "than to destroy the tenure by which her judges hold their offices." ". . . The Judicial Department, comes home in its effects to every man's fireside: it passes on his property, his reputation, his life, his all. Is it not, to the last degree important, that he should be rendered perfectly and completely independent, with nothing to influence or controul him but God and his conscience."[36]

While judges were to be independent in dispensing justice, they were to be familiar with the "sound legal principles" at the core of liberal justice. Marshall was not, like Jefferson, an evangelistic propagandist for liberal doctrine. He took for granted, however, the truths and even the general circulation of his more sober yet essentially liberal jurisprudence. When he called for "judges of capacity, and of legal knowledge," he no doubt presumed that their learning would encompass "those . . . treatises on the laws of nature and nations [which] have guided public opinion on the subjects of obligation and contract." The warm welcome he extended to Story's *Commentaries on the Constitution*, especially to that edition directed to the law schools, was probably occasioned more by Story's nationalism than by his largely Blackstonean liberalism. It is perfectly certain, however, that Marshall's whole portrait of the judicial role was colored by the function he understood it to serve. The judges' peculiar sanctity in his eyes issued from their supervision of "every man's . . . property, his reputation, his life, his all";[37] the judiciary is the only branch of government directly attuned to the innate rights which are the very object of government itself.

[36] Hugh B. Grigsby, ed., *Proceedings and Debates of the Virginia State Convention of 1829-30* (Richmond: Ritchie and Cook, 1830), pp. 615-17, 619.
[37] *Ibid.*, p. 616.

It is in the spirit of American law, then, that the judiciary's constructions should amount essentially to an enforcement of "the system of natural liberty" upon all concerned. Wherever a court might be found interpreting the country's law, be it common law, the Constitution itself, statutes, or the customs and treaties of nations, its peculiar function was to construe positive law in light of that which the law itself was presumed to wish. This was of immense importance, especially within the states whose officials occasionally failed to recognize the direction in which their laws were intrinsically pointed.

With respect to the common law, Marshall's method can be seen most appropriately in his endeavor to restore the law of creditors' rights to its natural stringency, a task which inevitably rendered the Court a kind of supervisor of the state governments. Primary authority over the ordinary life of Americans, and hence over civil and criminal procedures, had always rested with the states. It remained with them under the Constitution. Their governments afford the common remedies for enforcing contracts, Marshall observed, "and administer the remedy in tribunals constituted by themselves." To a considerable degree, however, these "independent societies" had deviated during the "critical period" from a strict justice to creditors. They had departed from what Marshall in characteristic fashion and prose called "that course of administering justice between debtor and creditor, which consisted, not only with the spirit of the constitution, and, consequently, with the view of the government, but also with what might safely be considered as the permanent policy, as well as interest, of the States themselves."[38] To eliminate these aberrations was one of

[38] *Wayman* v. *Southard*, 10 Wheaton [U.S.], 46-47. The passage, dealing with the federal judiciary's revision of the states' procedure with executions, deserves full quotation. Congress had prescribed a judicial system encompassing "distinct societies," a system further complicated by the deviation of many of the states from a proper administration of "justice between debtor and creditor. In adopting the temporary mode of proceeding with executions then prevailing

the chief tasks of the federal courts. Marshall encouraged a "return to the ancient usage, and just, as well as wise, principles," by exploiting various opportunities in the courts' common-law jurisdiction. Because this jurisdiction was merely concurrent, the federal courts' authority was somewhat qualified. Yet their influence could be pervasive and perhaps decisive. By affording an alternative forum, by influencing with their opinions the judges and lawyers of the states "on great commercial questions especially," the national judiciary could go far toward restoring a proper strictness. Indeed, the federal courts should not ignore the modifications of the common law in the various states. These variations should be respected to the point where the "great principles" in which all originated were threatened—but the courts need then feel no compunction about revising, according to the "ancient established rules," the judicial judgment of any government, state or general.

The best example of a Marshallian seizure of jurisdiction on the ground of "general principles" alone occurred in 1805 in the case of *Huidekoper's Lessee* v. *Douglas*. Marshall interpreted a Pennsylvania grant of land very strictly so as to favor the original grantees. It did not trouble him that the grant in question was a Pennsylvania statute, which had been construed in precisely the opposite manner by a Pennsylvania court. The Pennsylvania grant was not an ordinary posi-

---

in the several States, it was proper to provide for that return to ancient usage, and just, as well as wise principles, which might be expected from those who had yielded to a supposed necessity in departing from them. Congress, probably, conceived, that this object would be best effected by placing in the Courts of the Union the power of altering the 'modes of proceeding in suits at common law,' which includes the modes of proceeding in the execution of their judgments, in the confidence, that in the exercise of this power, the ancient, permanent, and approved system, would be adopted by the Courts, at least as soon as it should be restored in the several States by their respective legislatures." Consider also the letter from Marshall to the Hon. Dudley Chase, February 7, 1817. Reprinted in Crosskey, *Politics and the Constitution,* II, 1246.

tive law, of the kind to be finally construed by the courts of Pennsylvania. It was in its nature "a contract; and although a state is a party, it ought be construed according to those well-established principles, which regulate contracts generally." "All those principles of equity, and of fair dealing, which constitute the basis of judicial proceedings,"[39] permitted construction and dictated a strict interpretation securing rights of the original grantee.

We need not dwell at length here upon the manner in which the federal courts were to interpret according to

[39] 3 Cranch (U.S.), 70-71 (1805). I find myself continually in debt to William Winslow Crosskey's assiduous and ingenious scholarship, but almost as frequently in disagreement with his interpretations. He supposes that Marshall's willingness to construe the Pennsylvania law in this case, and in a manner opposite to that of a Pennsylvania court, demonstrates the Chief Justice's belief in the general judiciary's power to revise state constructions of state law. Leaving aside the complication that the state court decision was not that of Pennsylvania's highest court, the law in question was in its nature a contract, Marshall said. His construction is obviously intelligible as the construction of a contract and on this ground alone. To hold otherwise occasions a scramble like Crosskey's to explain away Marshall's many unqualified assertions of the finality of state construction of state laws—assertions presented not only in judicial opinions, but also in private letters. See Crosskey, *Politics and the Constitution*, II, 843-44, 847-49, 1076-82, 1245-46, and especially, Marshall to his brother, July 9, 1822 (ALS, Library of Congress): "Thus the exposition of any state law by the courts of that state, are considered in the courts of all the other states, and in those of the United States, as a correct exposition, not to be reexamined. The only exception to this rule is where the statute of a state is supposed to violate the constitution of the United States, in which case the courts of the Union claim a controuling & supervising power. Thus any construction made by the courts of Virginia on the statute of descents or of distribution or any other subject, is admitted as conclusive in the federal courts, although those courts might have decided differently on the statute itself. The principle is that the courts of every government are the proper tribunals for construing the legislative acts of the government." See also Crosskey's deprecatory treatment of Story's remarks, in *Swift* v. *Tyson*, pointing to the final authority of state courts in construing state legislation and settled customs, remarks which confirm the interpretation given here. II, 858-60.

Lockean "general principles" the Constitution's own civil provisions. Our previous discussions of the treason clause and of the prohibition to the states of laws impairing contracts are sufficient. Indeed, the judicial power could not *directly* intervene when the executive or legislature of some state confiscated debts or land, or paid the state's liabilities in paper money. Nevertheless, as Marshall quietly remarked after counsel had referred to the federal courts' incapacity in such a happenstance,

> suppose a State to institute proceedings against an individual, which depended on the validity of an act emitting bills of credit, suppose a State to prosecute one of its citizens for refusing paper money, who should plead the constitution in bar of such prosecution . . . that would be a case arising under the constitution, to which the judicial power of the United States would extend.[40]

Marshall's mode of interpreting statutes, as distinguished from common law and Constitution, is perhaps best illustrated by a criminal case decided on circuit in 1833, *Ex parte Randolph*. The Chief Justice managed to free Randolph from the excessively eager clutches of federal officials by a very strict construction of the law under which they had acted. The statute authorized certain administrators to determine debts owed by delinquent collectors of revenue, and then to issue warrants to recover the money by seizing and selling the collector's goods, and even by committing him to prison. It thus came very close, Marshall obviously believed, to vesting "judicial power" unconstitutionally in the executive department. But a court will consider the "constitutionality of a legislative act," he went on to say, only when "indispensably necessary." Instead Marshall interpreted the statute so as not to apply to an "acting" collector of revenue, as Randolph chanced to be, and justified his narrow construction thus:

[40] *Cohens* v. *Virginia*, 6 Wheaton (U.S.), 403, 405, 391-92 (1821).

If we take into consideration . . . the extreme severity of its provisions, that it departs entirely from the ordinary course of judicial proceeding, and prescribes an extreme remedy, which is placed under the absolute control of a mere ministerial officer, that in such a case the ancient established rule is in favour of a strict construction; my own judgment is satisfied that this is the true construction.[41]

Ex parte Randolph illustrates not only the Marshallian manner of statutory construction, but also the sway over the other or political departments yielded to the courts by this power—without even the additional authority to declare statutes void as unconstitutional. The classic illustration of this sway, at least as it applies to the executive branch, occurs in *Marbury* v. *Madison.* Marshall's opinion may be divided into three parts, the third of which makes the famous argument for judicial review that we will consider in Chapter IV. The first discusses the question as to whether Marbury, the office-seeker disappointed by President Jefferson, had a right to his commission signed by President Adams but not delivered by Jefferson's Secretary of State, Madison. The second considers whether Marbury could obtain a legal remedy, a remedy from the courts. Marshall's discussion turns upon a distinction between the President's "political" power and any "specific duty assigned by law" where "individual rights depend on the performance of that duty." Political authority is exercised according to the President's discretion; he is accountable only to those he represents and "to his own conscience." Where duties are assigned by law, however, he must obey the laws under which rights have vested, and the courts, with their duty to protect individual rights, can hold him therein accountable. In the case in point, the law allowed the President discretion as to whom to nominate and even as to the appointment of the person nominated, but with the appointment of a person not re-

[41] *Ex parte Randolph,* 2 Brockenbrough 447, 483 (1833).

movable at his behest, the President's freedom of choice ceased. In respect of Marbury's right to his commission, violated by the President's failure to obey the law, the President is accountable to the judiciary. "The question whether a right has vested or not," Marshall intoned, "is in its nature, judicial, and must be tried by the judicial authority."[42]

In construing laws among nations the Chief Justice followed similar principles providing for the safety of men and their property. Chapter I has rehearsed sufficiently the manner in which his decisions endeavored to restrict the belligerent's privileges and to correspondingly enlarge the prerogatives of neutrals.[43] A similar inclination might be observed in his construction of treaties, part of the "law of the land" like the law of nations and the Constitution itself. Yet the case of treaties is more complicated, in a manner which again points up the complicated relation in Marshall's jurisprudence between private rights and political powers. Because treaties are engagements between sovereign nations, they differ from ordinary contracts. They deal with political considerations as well as "general principles" of law.

[42] *Marbury* v. *Madison*, 1 Cranch (U.S.), 167, 171, 166, 170 (1803). See also *Foster and Elam* v. *Neilson*, 2 Peters (U.S.), 307, 309 (1829).

[43] Compare, on Congress's power to violate the law of nations, Marshall's remark in *Murray* v. *The Charming Betsy*, 2 Cranch (U.S.), 118 (1804). "An act of Congress ought never to be construed to violate the law of nations if any other possible construction remains, and consequently, can never be construed to violate neutral rights, or to affect neutral commerce, further than is warranted by the law of nations as understood in this country." See also *The Brig. Wilson* v. *the United States*, 1 Brockenbrough, 437 (1820): ". . . There is a portion of [Congress's sovereign power over commerce] as far as respects foreign vessels, which it is unusual for any nation to exercise, and the exercise of which would be deemed an unfriendly interference with the just rights of foreign powers. . . . I will not say, that this is beyond the power of a government, but I will say, that no act ought to have this effect given to it, unless the words be such as to admit of no other rational construction." See also *The Nereide*, 9 Cranch (U.S.), 423 (1815).

In construing such ticklish arrangements involving "great national concerns," the letter is to be followed as closely as possible, even to the extent of ignoring the rights so solicitously cared for in "mere private cases between individuals."[44] If the letter of a treaty should be unclear, however, Marshall would have no hesitation in presuming it to embody "that security to private property which the laws and usages of nations would, without stipulation, have conferred. No construction which would impair that security further than the positive words require would be admissible."[45]

In short, for state, nation, and foreign countries, over subsidiary courts and sovereign political powers alike, the federal judiciary was to perform the liberal tasks for which it had been erected, as Marshall thought, by the people. Judicial review ensured that its judgments could not be authoritatively challenged. The individual's rights were secured, his protector dominant. As the sphere of private interest was extended by Lockean liberalism to edge out the dignity intrinsic to community life, and thus to depreciate the importance of political stature, office, and action, one might note that the place of that judiciary which protects

---

[44] "In mere private cases between individuals, a court will and ought to struggle hard against a construction which will, by a retrospective operation, affect the rights of parties, but in great national concerns, where individual rights, acquired by war, are sacrificed for national purposes, the contract making the sacrifice ought always to receive a construction conforming to its manifest import; and if the nation has given up the vested rights of its citizens, it is not for the court, but for the government, to consider whether it be a case proper for compensation." *United States* v. *Schooner Peggy*, 1 Cranch (U.S.), 110 (1803). "If at any time, policy may temper the strict execution of the contract, where may that political discretion be placed so safely as in the department whose duty it is to understand precisely the state of the political intercourse and connexion between the United States and foreign nations . . . ?" Marshall, in his speech on the Robbins case, U.S. Congress, *Annals*, 6th Congress, 1799-1801, pp. 614-15.

[45] *The American Insurance Co.* v. *Canter*, 1 Peters (U.S.), 542 (1828).

private rights increased correspondingly. The polity was broken into state and society, the first ministerial to the second. The judiciary was the branch of the state that directly secured to men the place earned by industrious talent exercised in the economy, as well as a chance to engage as they wish in the other, less fundamental activities of society. As liberal society elevated the ordinary and everyday interests of most men to unqualified primacy, the courts as guardians of such concerns became pervasive in extent as well as first in dignity among the departments. Man, wrote David Hume almost at the beginning of his essay *Of the Origin of Government,* "is engaged to establish political society, in order to administer justice, without which there can be no peace among them, nor safety, nor mutual intercourse. We are, therefore, to look upon all the vast apparatus of government, as having ultimately no other object or purpose but the distribution of justice, or, in other words, the support of the twelve judges. Kings and parliaments, fleets and armies, officers of the court and revenue, ambassadors, ministers, and privy counsellors, are all subordinate in their end to this part of administration." Liberalism as well as judicial review accounts for the place of courts in America, and, as we will see, judicial review itself was, in good part, a means of preserving liberalism.

Still, private liberty and its guardian were to be confined by the political departments as well as protected from them. For the political authorities are indispensable to the protection of liberty, and even natural rights must bow to the means of their own preservation. Order as well as liberty is needed. "However absolute the right of an individual may be," Marshall remarked, "it is still in the nature of that right, that it must bear a portion of the public burdens; and that portion must be determined by the legislature."[46] Thus the judiciary's task boils down to the protection of individual rights—so far as is not incompatible with the needs of the political branches. Even a conclusive account of the

[46] *Providence Bank* v. *Billings,* 4 Peters (U.S.), 563 (1830).

judiciary's own authority, then, requires a description of the extent of the other departments. A "bill of rights," Marshall insisted in the Virginia Ratifying Convention of 1788, "is merely recommendatory. Were it otherwise, the consequence would be that many laws which are found convenient would be unconstitutional." Best illustrating that obeisance to political convenience to which necessity commits the individual, according to Marshall, is a remark concerning the constitutional prescription that the trial of all crimes shall be by jury. This provision, Marshall noted in 1799, "has never been construed to extend to the trial of crimes committed in the armed forces."

> Had such a construction prevailed, it would most probably have prostrated the constitution itself, with the liberties and the independence of the nation, before the first disciplined invader who should approach our shores. Necessity would have imperiously demanded the review and amendment of so unwise a provision.[47]

POLITICAL POWER

According to Marshall, the Constitution's political departments were also to serve the individual's security, but without the direct solicitude characteristic of the courts' application to private parties of the law. While the courts were involved with "objects unconnected with government," the executive and legislature engaged in "an exercise of sovereignty without affecting the rights of individuals." Political power was, however, at least as necessary as the courts' authority, its operation even a precondition of their existence. If the Preamble's "justice" and "liberty" require a judiciary, the "general welfare," "domestic tranquillity," "common defense," and a "more perfect union" demand the sovereign powers of the political departments. These powers alone can assure the commerce, peace, and safety without which the

[47] Speech by Marshall on the case of Jonathan Robbins, United States Congress, *Annals*, 6th Congress, 1799-1801, p. 611; Elliot, *Debates*, III, 561.

comfort, security, and gain of the individual would be impossible.[48]

Its characteristic tasks apart, political power is distinguished from its legal counterpart by broad discretion as to means. This is as true of the executive who "holds and directs the force of the nation," as of the legislature which prescribes "general rules for the government of society." That the President might "use his own discretion" in exercising "the important political powers" with which the office is endowed, was the way Marshall put it in *Marbury* v. *Madison*, and the language of *McCulloch* v. *Maryland* with respect to Congress's sphere is even more explicit. The government is indeed limited in its powers. The Chief Justice was not swayed by the ingenuity of Hamilton into affirming a plenary legislative power apart from the enumerated powers. "I have never believed," he wrote in a private letter, "that the words 'to pay the debts and provide for the common defense and general welfare of the United States' were to be considered as a substantive grant of power but as a declaration of objects for which taxes might be levied."[49] The enumerated powers, moreover, were to be interpreted in accord with their objects. They should extend, however, to all means reasonably connected with those objects. Thus Marshall is not inconsistent in holding that the leg-

[48] *Dartmouth College* v. *Woodward*, 4 Wheaton (U.S.), 634 (1819); *Ogden* v. *Saunders*, 12 Wheaton (U.S.), 334 (1827). See also *Marbury* v. *Madison*, 1 Cranch (U.S.), 164-65, 169-71 (1803). ". . . All the laws which were in force in Florida while a province of Spain, those excepted which were political in their character, which concerned the relations between the people and their sovereign, remained in force, until altered by the government of the United States." *The American Insurance Co.* v. *Canter*, 1 Peters (U.S., 544 (1828). On the political powers' subordination to the Preamble's purposes, see *Cohens* v. *Virginia*, 6 Wheaton (U.S.), 381 (1821) and *McCulloch* v. *Maryland*, 4 Wheaton (U.S.), 403-04 (1819).

[49] Letter from Marshall to Timothy Pickering, March 18, 1828 (ALS, Massachusetts Historical Society); see also *infra*, Chapter II, n. 53; U. S. Congress, *Annals*, 6th Congress, 1799-1801, p. 613; *Fletcher* v. *Peck*, 6 Cranch (U.S.), 136 (1810).

islature must keep within the political sphere apportioned by the Constitution, the great theme of the last part of his opinion in *Marbury* v. *Madison,* and in also insisting that within that extensive sphere its discretion is vast. "We admit, as all must admit," begins the well known passage in *McCulloch* v. *Maryland,"*

> that the powers of government are limited, and that its limits are not to be transcended. But we think the sound construction of the constitution must allow to the national legislature that discretion, with respect to the means by which the powers it confers are to be carried into execution, which will enable that body to perform the high duties assigned to it, in the manner most beneficial to the people. Let the end be legitimate, let it be within the scope of the constitution, and all means which are appropriate, which are plainly adapted to that end, which are not prohibited, but consist with the letter and spirit of the constitution, are constitutional.[50]

By dispensing with a concern for such disputable matters as distributive justice and cultivation of character, we may remark again, Lockean government can proceed undistracted to its more primitive tasks. The political stability or permanence which is a condition of individual self-preservation can be sought without diversion, and to that extent without limit. It is commonly known that the philosopher Hobbes' reduction of the political goal to self-preservation was accompanied by the erection of an all-powerful sovereign. Although Marshall is in no simple sense a Hobbesian, the Chief Justice is at one with the English philosopher, and his more refined and ingenious philosophic successors, in emphasizing modest ends coupled with powerful political means. Government must be great, to repeat, because in the harsh nature of things the dangers confronting the country will be great. The nation's "exigencies," to use

[50] *McCulloch* v. *Maryland,* 4 Wheaton (U.S.), 421 (1819). See also *United States* v. *Fisher,* 2 Cranch (U.S.), 396 (1804).

the term of Marshall and of *The Federalist*, require great powers and great discretion in their exercise. This is the major premise of Marshall's stern and in that way grand opinion in *McCulloch* v. *Maryland*. In what amounts to a practical dissertation on the meaning of "sovereignty" in American circumstances, he repeatedly invoked the spectre of future "exigencies" to be feared. Exigencies are crises suddenly arising, "urgent demands of the moment" Marshall elsewhere called them. Since their extent and hour cannot be predicted, although their inevitability can, the people's agents must possess sufficient authority to master them as they chance to happen. Ours is a Constitution, Marshall intoned, "intended to endure for ages to come, and, consequently, to be adapted to the various *crises* of human affairs. To have prescribed the means by which government should, in all future time, execute its powers, . . . would have been an unwise attempt to provide, by immutable rules, for exigencies which, if foreseen at all, must have been seen dimly, and which can be best provided for as they occur."[51]

It is the combination of modest ends and pervasive means which underlies Marshall's interpretation of the "great powers" corresponding to the Preamble's "great purposes." Consider the matter of trade. Marshall understood Congress's authority "to regulate commerce with foreign nations, and among the several states" as essentially a warrant to promote commerce, and thus as central to the "general welfare." No statutes positively authorizing trade were needed. Commerce was sanctioned by nature itself. "The right of intercourse between State and State . . . derives its source from those laws whose authority is acknowledged by civilized man throughout the world. . . . The constitution found it an existing right, and gave to Congress the power

[51] *McCulloch* v. *Maryland*, 4 Wheaton (U.S.), 415, 408 (1819); *Weston* v. *The City Council of Charleston*, 2 Peters (U.S.), 465 (1829). See *Cohens* v. *Virginia*, 6 Wheaton (U.S.), 387 (1821).

to regulate it."[52] Instead, the regulation of commerce required essentially the removal of "irregularities," obstacles to free trade.[53] Chief among these were the artificial barriers erected by other governments. The debility of trade under the Articles had been due to the insecurity of property and debts already noticed, and to the disruptions of war. It was also owing, however, to Britain's "rigorous commercial system," and to the restrictions the states imposed upon one another's goods. The state governments had been unable either to compel relaxation of Britain's system or to harmonize their own. It seemed to Marshall that discontent

[52] *Gibbons* v. *Ogden*, 9 Wheaton (U.S.), 211 (1824).

[53] It seems that Marshall did not read the commerce power to authorize "internal improvements." Indeed, Marshall acknowledged a certain warrant for encouraging productive facilities, especially the means of transportation which Adam Smith, the apostle of capitalism, had called "the greatest of all improvements." (Smith, *Wealth of Nations*, p. 147; see also pp. 682-90.) And clearly Marshall favored such publicly promoted improvements in his native Virginia for their commercial advantage, among others. (Marshall, *Report* [Richmond, 1816], *passim*, especially the concluding pages.) But he seemed to confine the general government to a "power to make [internal improvements] for military purposes or for the transportation of the mail." Of course, these improvements could scarcely keep from serving commerce as well. He wrote to Pickering in 1828: "I have no doubt of the correctness of your opinion that a general power to make internal improvements would not have been granted by the American people. But there is a great difference between a general power and a power to make them for military purposes or for the transportation of the mail. For these objects the power may be exercised to great advantage, and, there is much reason for thinking, consistently with the constitution; farther than this, I know not why the government of The United States should wish it, nor do I believe it is desired." Letter of Marshall to Pickering, March 18, 1828 (ALS, Massachusetts Historical Society). See also Marshall's letter to Monroe, June 13, 1822. Quoted by Charles Warren, *The Supreme Court in United States History* (Boston: Little, Brown, and Company, 1922), I, 595-96. See the report submitted by Justice Johnson to President Monroe, as "instructed" by the other justices, including Marshall. (Johnson to Monroe, undated, quoted *ibid.*, pp. 596-97.)

with this situation was perhaps the strongest motive for a national government, among both "interested" merchants, "who felt the injury arising from this state of things," and not necessarily "interested" liberal statesmen, "who were capable of estimating the influence of commerce on the prosperity of nations." What the new Constitution intended, then, was the unequivocal removal of the barriers with which the Confederation had only toyed. Marshall even reduced his foreign policy to the maxim, "We ought to have commercial intercourse with all, but political ties with none," thus echoing the Farewell Address of his great model, Washington.[54]

His judicial practice was as emphatic. In *Brown* v. *Maryland* the Chief Justice held an apparently innocuous Maryland tax on importers void as conflicting with a federal law. He reached his conclusion by finding previously undiscovered implications in an act of Congress. Ostensibly, the federal law had merely levied duties on imports. To Marshall, however, payment of the duty indicated the existence of a reciprocal and even pervasive "right to sell" the goods imported, without further hindrance from federal or state governments. Any other construction, according to the tenor of the opinion, would make the privilege stemming from payment of the import duty a mere mockery and "break up commerce" with other nations.[55]

Marshall's clearing away of hindrances to free exchange, domestic or foreign, is even better illustrated in the steamboat case, *Gibbons* v. *Ogden*. Here the Court overturned a New York state act authorizing Ogden's monopoly in particular, and the great New York State steamboat monopoly in general, by holding the act in violation of the commerce

---

[54] Marshall's Answers to Freeholder's Questions, reprinted in Beveridge, *Life of John Marshall*, ii, 576; *Brown* v. *Maryland*, 12 Wheaton (U.S.), 445-46 (1827); Marshall, *The Life of George Washington*, ii, 96. This distinction between the Constitution's supporters suggests what Marshall's reply would have been to Beardean constitutional interpretations in their usual, vulgar Marxist form.

[55] *Brown* v. *Maryland*, 12 Wheaton (U.S.), 447, 448 (1827).

power as exercised. Again, the United States law upon which Gibbons and Marshall relied seemed a rather weak reed. To all appearances its intent was only the encouragement of American shipping vis-à-vis foreign shipping.[56] Among a mass of petty regulations was a requirement for a coasting license, whose fee varied from 25 cents to $1.00, and upon possession of which Gibbons relied. Chancellor Kent, upholding the monopoly under New York law, had refused to believe that a simple "coasting license," obtained "as a matter of course, and with as much facility as the flag of the *United States* could be procured and hoisted,"[57] was sufficient to authorize any ship so equipped to contravene an act of New York's sovereign legislature explicitly granting special privileges. Marshall thought otherwise.

His achievement was to read the coasting act as if it assumed, and thus authorized, the individual right to navigate for the purpose of trade and commerce. The act does not explicitly prescribe such a liberty, said the Chief Justice, but it implies it. Privileges are granted attendant on "the right of intercourse between state and state," privileges which would be worthless if the states could annihilate the right itself. In accord with this reasoning, Marshall deduced from the license an implicit authorization of the "right to trade."[58]

The argument is typical of Marshall's judicial opinions on the government's political authority. Great and sovereign powers are granted by the Constitution to accomplish great objects. To interpret a given provision or statute narrowly would defeat the object—in this case, facilitation of free trade among the states; the words in question must be other-

[56] Act of Congress, 18th February 1793, c. 8: ". . . an act for enrolling and licensing ships and vessels to be employed in the coasting trade and fisheries, and for regulating the same." See the dissenting opinion of Justice Johnson, *Gibbons* v. *Ogden*, 9 Wheaton (U.S.), 232 (1824).

[57] *Gibbons* v. *Ogden*, Johnson's Chancery Reports (N.Y.), 156-59 (1819).

[58] *Gibbons* v. *Ogden*, 9 Wheaton (U.S.), 212 (1824).

wise construed. As Brown's "right to sell" was implied according to *Brown* v. *Maryland* by a mere duty law, so Gibbons' "right to trade" followed in *Gibbons* v. *Ogden* from the intention Marshall imputes to Congress in passing a coasting act. Marshall expanded the national sovereignty, in accord with what the natural system of liberty required and the nation's laws thus were supposed to presume.

Insuring "domestic tranquillity" required a considerably more active and subtle exercise of the political powers than promotion of commerce. The chief obstacles to Lockean law and order in America had proven to be the more democratic fringes of its dominant middle class. Here Marshall does not differ essentially from *The Federalist*. "Protection against faction" was one of the chief reasons he gave for supporting ratification. He accepted the common opinion that Shays' rebellion, despite some real grievances, was essentially a factious multitude in revolt against domestic quiet, and that the outbreak had been instrumental in arousing "a deep conviction of the necessity of enlarging the powers of the general government." The judiciary power would have much to do with securing the true peace which consists in mutual usefulness and "confidence" among individuals. "What is the service or purpose of a judiciary, but to execute the laws in a peaceable, orderly manner, without shedding blood, or creating a contest, or availing yourselves of force."[59] Stronger measures from the executive department would be required as well. While always advising conciliatory nego-

[59] Elliot, *Debates*, III, 554, 233. "There is no part of America, where less disquiet and less of ill-feeling between man and man is to be found than in [Virginia], and I believe most firmly that this state of things is mainly to be ascribed to the practical operation of our County Courts. The magistrates who compose those courts, consist in general of the best men in their respective counties. They act in the spirit of peace-makers, and allay, rather than excite the small disputes and differences which will sometimes arise among neighbours. It is certainly much owing to this, that so much harmony prevails amongst us." *Proceedings and Debates of the Virginia State Convention of 1829-30*, p. 505.

tiations, and refraining from the conspicuous enthusiasm for "energy" and "efficiency" displayed by Hamilton, Marshall too admired "vigor" in the Presidency. As Shays' uprising spread, "the lenient measures which had been taken by the legislature to reclaim the insurgents, only enlarged their demands."

It seems that Marshall wished to show the proper way of dealing with such exigencies. He gave a detailed account in his *Life of Washington* of a later outbreak, the Whiskey rebellion in western Pennsylvania, calling the affair a political phenomenon "which the statesman can never safely disregard." Again long negotiation had exacerbated rather than diminished the rebels' arrogance. This time, however, the government proceeded to muster fifteen thousand troops to overawe a countryside where perhaps seven thousand men might have been brought to the field by the opposition. The "greatness of the force" ended the whole question then and there. "Thus," concluded Marshall, "without shedding a drop of blood, did the prudent vigour of the executive terminate an insurrection, which, at one time, threatened to shake the government of the United States to its foundations."[60]

Although the federal government might use armed force to subdue extreme outbreaks of faction, it could also use lesser means, such as suppressing seditious speech, to prevent unrest from going to extremes. The state's authority to stifle dangerous opinions was more or less assumed by Marshall, as by many of his contemporaries, and his reasoning is perhaps instructive precisely because so contrary to that taken for granted at the present time. Morals generally, even the common sort that contributes to order, are "defended solely by opinion." Customs and institutions must even be "cherished" by public opinion if they are going to command any real confidence and allegiance. The good opinion of at least a portion of the people is shaken by slander, however, especially by malicious slander. Marshall did not adhere

[60] Marshall, *The Life of George Washington*, II, 340-49.

to the comforting "faith" that an invisible mind in the market-place will produce, sooner or later, opinions serviceable to the public good. He shared the belief common to Federalists and others that the Whiskey rebellion had been aggravated, if not originated, by bitter attacks in the partisan press on Washington's administration. The danger to the public peace of "calumnious" speech is reason enough for suppressing it. This conclusion formed the backbone of Marshall's constitutional defense of the Sedition Law of 1798. If the Constitution's "necessary and proper clause" authorized punishment of actual resistance to the law, did it not "also authorize punishment of those acts which are criminal in themselves, and which obviously lead to and prepare resistance"? Such acts are criminal under the common law and can be punished at the insistence of those injured—the people of the United States and the government that is their agent. This is no violation of the first amendment's prohibition of an abridgment of freedom of speech or press. Libel of the government is not freedom, but licentiousness, and in addition, the act does not punish any writing not before punishable under the common law.[61]

Neither encouragement of commerce nor maintenance of peace, however essential, formed the most important task of the general government. "Safety from abroad . . . above all" had induced the colonies to unite. Throughout his histories Marshall was led to remark on the impotency in for-

[61] Marshall, *Address of the Minority* . . . , pp. 11-14. "It is in vain to urge that truth will prevail, and that slander, when detected, recoils on the calumniator. The experience of the world, and our own experience, prove that a continued course of defamation will at length sully the fairest reputation, and will throw suspicion on the purest conduct. Although the calumnies of the factious and discontented may not poison the minds of a majority of the citizens, yet they will infect a very considerable number, and prompt them to deeds destructive of the public peace, and dangerous to the general safety." *Ibid.*, p. 11. See Marshall, *The Life of George Washington*, II, 349. Letter from Marshall to Robert Mayo and others. Printed in R. Mayo, *Political Sketches of Eight Years in Washington* (Baltimore: Lucas, 1839), p. 47.

eign relations of confederations in general, and this studied conclusion underlay his willingness to replace the Articles in particular. "United we are strong, divided we fall," he had argued in the Virginia Ratifying Convention.[62]

To the most necessary of tasks corresponded the most extensive of the general government's powers: the "great powers" involving "war and peace." Here, however, Marshall's views can only be sketched. He said nothing on the subject comparable to his pronouncements on private rights or even on commerce. As was true of his views on domestic order, his thoughts must be inferred largely from the various events he praised or condemned.

America's foreign policy, it will be recalled, would endeavor to implement "simple and natural" principles dictating commerce and peace among nations. Only "necessity, not . . . choice" would lead the country to prepare for war.[63] To a considerable extent the courts' application of the law of nations to friend and foe alike would contribute to reciprocal trade and mutual peace. Still, principal authority in foreign affairs was to rest with the executive department, especially in the actual conduct of negotiations. "The President is the sole organ of the nation in its external relations, and its sole representative with foreign nations." Occasionally, perhaps, executive discretion might be limited. Marshall is supposed to have intimated that the President's authority to dispose of United States territory was bound by judicially enforceable limits.[64] As a rule, however,

[62] Elliot, *Debates*, III, 420; see also 223, 226, 228, 231, 234. Marshall, *Address of the Minority* . . . , p. 5; Marshall, *A history of the colonies* . . . , pp. 101, 121, 124, 138, 199, 261, 301, 305, 404. Cf. 106-09, 110-12; Marshall, *The Life of George Washington*, I, 30, 47, 84, 139-41, 326, 334f., 365, 425, 427, 441; II, 27, 28, 104, 121, 289.

[63] Marshall as envoy, United States, *State Papers*, Foreign Relations, II, 487, 175; see also p. 174. *The Nereide*, 9 Cranch (U.S.), 419 (1815).

[64] Mr. Justice Story wrote that Marshall "was unequivocally of opinion, that the treaty making power did extend to cases of cession of territory, though he would not undertake to say that it could extend

the courts were to abide by the political department's principles when a treaty or the law of nations was in doubt, or when such topics as national boundaries and other "political questions" were in dispute. Even judgment as to whether an alien ought to be surrendered under an extradition treaty was for executive determination. In the area of foreign affairs, especially, the President's discretion was broad, his means extensive, and Marshall was not prone to insist on a very precise constitutional warrant. In one case he remarked that the federal authority for governing a territory of the United States might originate in the area's location within the country but not within any state. It might "be the inevitable consequence of the right to acquire territory. Whatever may be the source whence the power is derived," Marshall moved with relief from the warrant for the authority to its undoubted existence, "the possession of it is unquestioned."[65]

However peaceful its wishes, the government's expectations ought take account of the omnipresent danger of war. "Independent nations are individuals in a state of nature," Marshall remarked, and their peace is scarcely secure. A shrewd foreign policy would align the country as part of a favorable balance of power, even to the extent of such "temporary arrangements as would give us the aid of the British fleets to prevent our being invaded."[66] It would

---

to all cases. . . ." W. W. Story, *Life and Letters of Joseph Story*, II, 288. Quoted by Ziegler, *International Law of Marshall*, pp. 330-31, esp. n. 20. See E. S. Corwin, *National Supremacy* (New York: Henry Holt and Company, 1913), pp. 66, 95-98. U. S. Congress, *Annals*, 6th Congress, 1799-1801, pp. 614-15. See also Marshall's indictment as Secretary of State of practices of British courts of vice-admiralty in the territorial possessions. United States, *State Papers*, Foreign Relations, II, 489.

[65] *The American Insurance Co.* v. *Canter*, 1 Peters (U.S.), 542-43 (1828). See Ziegler, *International Law of Marshall*, pp. 334-35, and cases cited.

[66] Marshall's Answers to Freeholder's Questions, reprinted in Beveridge, *Life of John Marshall*, II, 576. To be more particular, Marshall

also look to the country's own armed strength, the necessary underpinning of negotiation as Marshall was very much aware. "To supplicating America, even discussion was denied. America armed, and immediately a different

agreed with the Federalists in not wishing to see "Europe subjected to any one power" or "the balance of Europe . . . overturned." (*The Life of George Washington*, II, n. xxii.) France's republicanism made her "no stranger to that lust for domination" (*ibid.*) which might characterize any government. In fact, France's revolutionary thirst for empire, coupled with her stature as "the most military and the most powerful nation on earth," constituted the greatest danger to Europe. (Marshall to Washington, October 24, 1797, *American Historical Review*, II [January 1897], 305. Marshall's Answers to Freeholder's Questions, reprinted in Beveridge, II, 577.)

Indeed, Marshall saw with some prescience that at least one nation besides France possessed the power to upset Europe's balance. "The policy of the world would certainly require that Russia should not be permitted to extend herself further—especially towards the center of Europe." He could not agree with Robert Harper, however, that Russia need be balanced by an enlarged France. If "augmentation of power must be given to any state for the purpose of forming a barrier against Russia, it is to Austria not to France that this augmentation may be trusted with safety." "France within her antient limits was the terror & justly the terror of Europe." (Letter from Marshall to Robert G. Harper, November 22, 1813 [ALS, Library of Congress].) Enlarged, she constituted a threat worse than ever.

That threat ought to be countered by supporting Britain, on whose fortunes depended "the independence of Europe and America." (Marshall to Washington, October 24, 1797, *loc. cit.*, pp. 302-03.) Britain, near the continent, with its navy on the Atlantic, was an essential means to America's defense from the continent. While Marshall was not one to kowtow before British insolence and threats, his concern that the United States do nothing to hinder her struggle against republican and Napoleonic France lasted as long as the Emperor. He wrote to Pickering with respect to the Jeffersonian embargo, "I fear most seriously that the same spirit which so tenaciously maintains [the embargo] will impel us to a war with the only power which protects any part of the civilized world from the despotism of that tyrant with whom we shall then be arranged." Printed in Henry Cabot Lodge's *Life and Letters of George Cabot* (Boston: Little, Brown, 1877), p. 489.

On the state of nature among nations, see *Ogden v. Saunders*, 12 Wheaton (U.S.), 346 (1827).

language was used, and the rights of an independent nation were allowed her." A fortified and spirited United States, an ocean away from the supplies of a European attacker, was an uninviting nettle. A weak and unprepared United States would only tempt the ambitions of others. "The powers of Europe are jealous of us. . . . If we invite them by our weakness to attack us, will they not do it?"[67] Throughout his life Marshall taught the hard lesson that peaceful independence depended upon a willingness to fight. To a great extent, one may repeat, Marshall's politics was one vast preparation in pursuit of peace for the trials of war.

The essence of that preparation was, of course, the matériel of fighting—"men and money to protect us," as Marshall put it. A properly regulated liberal society would generate an ever-growing quantity of both. The crop had to be reaped, however. Marshall gave considerable thought to the problems of raising revenues—the "vital spring" of government, he called them—and armies.

Most of Marshall's rhetoric on the subject of revenue was designed to disparage the Articles' reliance on remonstrances and requisitions. Again and again the reader of Marshall's histories is shown instances where pleas and requests to colonial and state governments, "in whom the vital principle of power, the right to levy taxes, was exclusively vested," were answered by too little too late, be it for war against the Dutch, French, and Indians, or against Great Britain herself. Only taxes supplemented by borrowing could do the job. Because of war's unforeseeable demands, the amount could not be defined in advance. "The people of a state . . . give to their government a right of taxing themselves and their property, and, as the exigencies of government cannot be limited, they prescribe no limits to the exercise of this right." Great means of collection were

[67] Elliot, *Debates*, III, 227. U. S. Congress, *Annals*, 6th Congress, 1799-1801, p. 254. See also the House of Representatives' *Address* to the President of 1799, which Marshall is supposed to have written. *Ibid.*, p. 296.

also legitimate. The defense of "great powers" and great discretion in the bank case, *McCulloch* v. *Maryland*, turned upon the presumption that the country must be prepared to face military situations calling for powerful financial organs to gather and dispose of the public income.

> Throughout this vast republic, from the St. Croix to the Gulph of Mexico, from the Atlantic to the Pacific, revenue is to be collected and expended, armies are to be marched and supported. The exigencies of the nation may require that the treasure raised in the north should be transported to the south. . . . Is that construction of the constitution to be preferred which would render these operations difficult, hazardous, and expensive?[68]

Besides providing immediate funds, efficient taxation would support the credit structure necessary for extensive borrowing. While on his mission to France, Marshall had been struck by the singular disadvantages, political, economic, and military, attending the Directory's inability to float loans. He had opportunity some thirty years later to pronounce authoritatively on the United States' own power to borrow. The city of Charleston had imposed a tax which applied to certain interest bearing stock of the United States Bank. Marshall declared the levy void as burdening the nation's power to borrow money, an authority whose unhindered exercise was vital in providing for the needs of war.

> No [power] can be selected which is of more vital interest to the community than this of borrowing money on

---

[68] *McCulloch* v. *Maryland*, 4 Wheaton (U.S.), 408-09, 428 (1819); Marshall, *The Life of George Washington*, II, 157: see, e.g. Marshall, *A history of the colonies* . . . , pp. 199, 301, 304, 402ff.; cf. 203, 419; Marshall, *The Life of George Washington*, I, 353, 354. It was in the context of an argument for vesting the taxing power in the general government that Marshall said, "It is, then, necessary to give the government that power, in time of peace, which the necessity of war will render indispensable, or else we shall be attacked unprepared." Elliot, *Debates*, II, 227.

the credit of the United States. No power has been conferred by the American people on their government, the free and unburdened exercise of which more deeply affects every member of our republic. In war, when the honour, the safety, the independence of the nation are to be defended, when all its resources are to be strained to the utmost, credit must be brought in aid of taxation, and the abundant revenue of peace and prosperity must be anticipated to supply the exigencies, the urgent demands of the moment.[69]

Marshall favored an organized soldiery no less than an organized revenue. He urged the establishment of both a substantial navy and a strong, disciplined, professional or standing army. The emphasis, worthy of Machiavelli's *Art of War*, was on discipline and organization. An army suddenly raised could have neither. It would be a raw militia, and Marshall's experience led him to deprecate the fighting qualities of the Revolutionary militia. Their initial ardor was insufficient; what began as enthusiasm ended in discouragement. The key to success here as elsewhere lay in the farsighted organization of vigorous means. Marshall, who had been elevated by his state to the rank of General, concluded his account of the Virginia militia's inability to overcome the French and Indians:

It adds one to the many proofs which have been afforded, of the miseries to be expected by those who defer pre-

[69] *Weston* v. *The City Council of Charleston*, 2 Peters (U.S.), 465 (1829). In a letter to Washington from Paris he wrote: "The existing government appears to me to need only money to enable it to effect all its objects. . . . There is a difficulty in procuring funds to work this vast machine. Credit being annihilated the actual impositions of the year must equal the disbursements. The consequence is that notwithstanding the enormous contributions made by foreign nations France is overwhelmed with taxes. . . . It is supposed that recourse will be had to a forc'd loan. . . ." Marshall to Washington, Paris, March 8, 1798; *American Historical Review*, ɪɪ (January 1897), 303-06.

paring the means of defence, until the moment when they ought to be used; and then, rely almost entirely, on a force neither adequate to the danger, nor of equal continuance.[70]

The fruition of all these preparations was not to be an imperial campaign. The country should nevertheless be ready for a vigorous prosecution of war. "Safety" would be obtained by a "manly resistance," not by "submission." New Englanders, he wrote in the *History of the colonies*, had been able to attend to their interests only because "they had maintained external peace by the vigour and sagacity with which their government was administered." For his part Marshall was willing to interpret all the particular war powers as a general power "to declare and conduct war," and to grant as well whatever supplementary powers were required.[71] He also clearly admired the enterprising prudence, the commanding "vigor," obtained from a single man's conduct of military operations. He lauded the "immense genius" of Napoleon, however he deprecated the

[70] Marshall, *The Life of George Washington*, i, 15. See also i, 138, Washington's judgment of the militia, quoted by Marshall, ii, 95, 106, and Adam Smith's account of why modern militia are unfitted by their occupations for soldiering, *Wealth of Nations*, Book v, Chapter i, Part i, "Of the Expence of Defence." For the connection between military preparation and the apprehension of future evils or "exigencies," we have Machiavelli's utterly characteristic remark: A prince "ought, therefore, never to let his thoughts stray from the exercise of war; and in peace he ought to practice it more than in war. . . . A wise prince . . . should never remain idle in peaceful times, but industriously make good use of them, so that when fortune changes she may find him prepared to resist her blows, and to prevail in adversity." *The Prince*, Chapter xiv.
For Marshall's remarks on the need for a navy, see Marshall, *A history of the colonies* . . . , pp. 352-53, cf. 324-25; Marshall, *The Life of George Washington*, ii, 158, 412, 413.

[71] *Worcester v. Georgia*, 6 Peters (U.S.), 546 (1832); *McCulloch v. Maryland*, 4 Wheaton (U.S.), 407 (1819); cf. *Brown v. United States*, 8 Cranch (U.S.), 110 (1814); Marshall, *A history of the colonies* . . . , p. 126; *The Life of George Washington*, i, 122, see ii, 353, 291-92.

perverted ambitions. His disposition was better shown in praise of statesmen like Pitt and that "consummate commander," Frederick the Great, leaders whose vigorous powers infused "grand plans" and "energy" into the councils and deeds of their nations.[72]

UNION

The one purpose of the Constitution's government we have yet to discuss is "a more perfect union." For Marshall union meant the uniting of individuals into the Lockean industrial empire described in Chapter I. What, however, distinguished that unity? What, that is to say, made of the individuals a nation? The individual's consent to a government, to begin with, is the answer of Marshall's jurisprudence. That consent being embodied in the Constitution, individuals are then united and ruled according to a peculiarly abstract and legal tie. This is insufficient, however important for understanding America's legalism. We have seen that a public force, rather than public agreement, is the essential condition for civil society according to Marshall. Not any common agreement will do, but only one which raises an effective government capable of doing the necessary tasks of any government. The United States was united fundamentally by the predominance of the federal powers which this chapter has discussed. The leading theme of Marshall's doctrine of "union," what we would call "federalism," is this: by the Constitution the people of America instituted a sovereign government, whose legitimate powers were to take precedence over all acts of the state governments.

The problem of "union," and especially of "a more perfect union," is considerably more complicated however, than is indicated by the chief doctrine that Marshall took every

[72] Marshall, *The Life of George Washington*, I, 18, 26, 211, 228-29. As to Marshall's opinion of Napoleon's genius, see a typed letter purporting to be a transcript of a letter from John Marshall to Henry Lee, Sept. 21, 1833 (MS New York Public Library [Miscellaneous: John Marshall]).

opportunity to expound. The very vagueness and political neutrality of the word "union" hints at difficulties concealed and perhaps intended to be concealed. "Union" connotes a whole combined of parts. "A more perfect union" may be a whole still imperfectly combined. The degree of unity intended is uncertain. The phrase as a whole thus fails to settle conclusively whether the United States is one political whole, that is, one nation, or merely a league of nations, or some combination of the two. Its ambiguity seems to rule out each of the distinct extremes in favor of an obscure middle, perhaps tending toward one or the other. For Marshall, a "more perfect union" was a mixture of nation and states which the Constitution had inclined, unequivocally inclined, toward one nation. Although one must note the American union's mixed character in order to correct the impression of Marshall's unqualified nationalism given by Beveridge and Crosskey, the Chief Justice's basic nationalism is clear.

America's political unity, according to Marshall, issued fundamentally from the subordination of individuals to a sovereign government. The nation, it will be remembered, was but an artificial whole, an invisible "corporation" comprising the web of duties and restrictions imposed by that artificial public force, government. True it is that the government's establishment, or at least its acceptance, implies the existence of "consent" or agreement to a common way of life. Marshall believed that the people of America, long ruled by common law principles governing the relations between man and man, had lived in such agreement. Yet one could not say that America's unity as a nation issued from this community. For Marshall understood that way of life as essentially apolitical. It was merely "society," an association for mutual exchange between men acting for their private interests. A national or political unit arises only with the erection of the artificial public force which moves men to act according to common political necessities. It is then but the reflection of the artificial political sovereign needed to provide for man's private interests. In this the "realistic" Marshall differed from such a more "idealistic" nationalist as Lincoln. In his redefinition of the American union, Lincoln came to find America's unity above all in a common political ideal, in "dedication" to the essential proposition of the Declaration of Independence that "all men are created equal."[73]

It is quite true that a subordinate if more noble strain of Marshall's thought on union makes far more of America's political life than that just described. The great nationalist believed that "orthodox" Americans participated in a common republican citizenship, as the next chapter will show. Following this line of argument Marshall often dated the nation from a time prior to the Constitution ratified in 1788. The new government was but an instrument to maintain an already existing country. He counted his own "devotion to the union, and to a government competent to its preservation," from the revolutionary struggle, "when patriotism and a strong fellow feeling with our suffering fellow citizens of Boston were identical—when the maxim 'united we stand, divided we fall' was the maxim of every orthodox American," when he fought beside "brave men from different states who were risking life and everything valuable in a common cause believed by all to be most precious; and where I was confirmed in the habit of considering America as my country, and Congress as my government." This powerful expression of Marshall's patriotic loyalty seems to say that the American union is constituted and distinguished by a common way of life which is "most precious," by a "spirit of liberty" which "tore the British colonies" from the empire. This view is part of a genuine republicanism in Marshall's political opinions, as we shall see, which cannot be wholly reduced to the interested liberalism characteristic of his jurisprudence. Still, it is possible to say that this opin-

[73] I am indebted to Harry V. Jaffa's searching investigation of Lincoln's understanding of the American nation, *Crisis of the House Divided* (Garden City: Doubleday & Company, 1959), especially Chapters IX, XIV, XV.

ion is not the one that dominates Marshall's political and legal thought, and certainly not his judicial practice. After all, these patriotic views are adduced only to explain the extent of Marshall's own devotion to America. They do not represent his considered reflections as to the distinguishing character of the nation or as to how that community was established. In fact, Marshall ascribes them "at least as much to casual circumstances as to judgment."[74]

It seems that in Marshall's settled judgment the nation was established by the ratification of the Constitution. After independence and before 1788, the Americans had been fundamentally members of their states or colonies. This does not mean that states and colonies had ever been completely independent. In the face of mutterings about rebellion during his later years, Marshall emphatically affirmed in a letter to his nephew that the Americans "never had been perfectly distinct, independent societies, sovereign in the sense in which the Nullifiers use the term." He is content to say, however, that "we were always in many respects one people," without declaring that we were always principally or simply one people. "In fact, we have always been united in some respects, separate in others. We have acted as one people for some purposes, as distinct societies for others."[75]

[74] Marshall, *Autobiographical Sketch*, pp. 9-10; *A history of the colonies* . . . , p. 237.

[75] Letter from Marshall to Humphrey Marshall, May 7, 1833, *New York Tribune*, February 7, 1861 (copy in Library of Congress). I am not aware that the original of this letter is extant. It follows in full:

"My Dear Sir:

I am much indebted to you for your pamphlet on Federal Relations, which I have read with much satisfaction. No subject, as it seems to me, is more misunderstood or more perverted. You have brought into view numerous important historical facts which, in my judgment, remove the foundation on which the Nullifiers and Seceders have erected that superstructure which overshadows our Union. You have, I think, shown satisfactorily that we never have been perfectly distinct, independent societies, sovereign in the sense in which the Nullifiers use the term. When colonies we certainly were not. We were parts of the British Empire, and although

Indeed, after freedom from British rule and before the Constitution, the tendency was surely toward independence of the parts, rather than unity. Marshall went so far as to call the Articles of Confederation an "alliance" of "independent," "sovereign," states. With the Constitution, however, a decisive shift occurred:

> When these allied sovereigns converted their league into a government, when they converted their Congress of Ambassadors, deputed to deliberate on their common

---

not directly connected with each other so far as respected government, we were connected in many respects, and were united to the same stock. The steps we took to effect separation were, as you have fully shown, not only revolutionary in their nature, but they were taken conjointly. Then, as now, we acted in many respects as one people. The representatives of each colony acted for all. Their resolutions proceeded from a common source, and operated on the whole mass. The army was a continental army, commanded by a continental general, and supported from the continental treasury. The Declaration of Independence was made by a common Government, and was made for all the States.

Everything has been mixed. Treaties made by Congress have been considered as binding all the States. Some powers have been exercised by Congress, some by the States separately. The lines were not strictly drawn. The inability of Congress to carry its legitimate powers into execution has gradually annulled those powers practically, but they always existed in theory. Independence was declared 'in the name and by the authority of the good people of these colonies.' In fact, we have always been united in some respects, separate in others. We have acted as one people for some purposes, as distinct societies for others. I think you have shown this clearly, and in so doing have demonstrated the fallacy of the principle on which either nullification or the right of peaceful, constitutional secession is asserted.

The time is arrived when these truths must be more generally spoken, or our Union is at an end. The idea of complete sovereignty of the State converts our Government into a league, and, if carried into practice, dissolves the Union.

> I am, dear sir, yours affectionately,
> J. MARSHALL.

Humphrey Marshall, Esq.,
Frankfort, Ky."

concerns, and to recommend measures of general utility, into a Legislature, empowered to enact laws on the most interesting subjects, the whole character in which the States appear, underwent a change, the extent of which must be determined by a fair consideration of the instrument by which that change was effected.[76]

Marshall's "fair consideration" culminated in the conclusion that the Constitution prescribes a powerful *government*, as the previous sections of this chapter have indicated. It is this sovereign power that "changes the whole character in which the states appear," as both his explicit remarks and his characteristic premises show. "The true and substantial dividing line between parties" in the United States, Marshall wrote in the uncertain political climate of 1832, amounts to the question whether "our constitution is essentially a LEAGUE and not a GOVERNMENT. One of more vital importance cannot be drawn. As the one opinion or the other prevails, will the union, as I firmly believe, be preserved or dissolved."[77]

The precise role of the general government in making

[76] *Gibbons* v. *Ogden*, 9 Wheaton (U.S.), 187 (1824).

[77] Marshall to Thomas F. Grimké, October 6, 1832 (ALS, original in the Archives Division of the Virginia State Library). The letter continues: "If a mere league has never been of long duration, if it has never been of sufficient efficacy to preserve a lasting peace between its members, we must be irrationally sanguine to indulge a hope that ours will furnish an exception to any and every thing which has heretofore occurred in the history of man. If such be the true spirit of the instrument such must be its construction, but we can not I think fail to ask ourselves for what purpose was it made? Was it worth the effort of all the wisdom virtue and patriotism of the country merely to exchange one league for another? Did the convention, did the people believe that they were framing a league and not a government?" The most thoughtful and helpful discussion of the founding generation's understanding of "union," superior to my own treatment with which I remain dissatisfied, is Martin Diamond's "The Federalist's View of Federalism," in George C. S. Benson, *et al.*, *Essays in Federalism* (Claremont: The Institute for Studies in Federalism, 1961), pp. 21-64.

America essentially one nation can be most clearly seen by examining the premises of Marshall's argument in *McCulloch* v. *Maryland*. That statement is at once the Chief Justice's most elaborate treatment of the general government's powers, and his most influential, although not his best, discourse on the relation of nation and states. The state of Maryland had imposed a prohibitive tax on the Baltimore branch of the Bank of the United States. In the proceedings which followed, Maryland not only denied Congress's power to charter a bank, but also affirmed a state's right to tax or regulate a creation of Congress—and thus to supersede the general government's chosen instruments. Marshall's reply to this assertion of state supremacy begins with his favorite argument, one of "just theory," he called it. The supremacy of the general government "would seem to result necessarily from its nature. It is the government of all; its powers are delegated by all; it represents all, and acts for all."[78] This argument is inadequate, however. The states also represent all—each represents a part, and collectively they represent all. The general government would be supreme only if it stands for the people in a manner superior to mere collective representation. As a matter of fact, Marshall immediately went on to offer a qualitative description of "all the people" as a "nation" which, "on those subjects on which it can act, must necessarily bind its component parts." That, however, begs the question at issue—whether the states are principally "parts" of a genuine nation, or principally independent nations linked by a mere confederacy. Counsel for Maryland had argued that the general government's powers had to be exercised in "subordination to the states, who alone possess supreme dominion." The Constitution was but a "compact between the states," adopted, not by the people of the United States at large, but by the people of the respective states.

Marshall agreed with Maryland's argument that the people met through representatives *in* their states. But he in-

[78] *McCulloch* v. *Maryland*, 4 Wheaton (U.S.), 405 (1819).

sisted that the ratification was that of "the people themselves," not that of the "state governments." Still, Maryland's advocate had not said that the ratification was that of the state governments, but merely that it was the act of "the people of the respective states." He was perhaps following the usage of Madison's famous *Report* of the Virginia House of Delegates, which justified the Virginia Resolutions of 1799 protesting the Alien and Sedition Acts. The Constitution's origin, said the *Report*, was to be found in "the people composing [the states], in their highest sovereign capacity."[79]

The Chief Justice's reply was as follows, and seems devastating according to the Lockean axioms that Madison himself shared with Marshall. Before the ratification of the Constitution of 1788, the people of each state had indeed granted sovereign authority to their state. Still, "they may resume and modify the powers granted to government"; that power they might not give up. In so doing they are not acting as mere citizens. "In their highest sovereign capacity" the people are not citizens of their old state governments, but sovereign individuals who may delegate their chief powers anew, to a general government if they choose. By this new subordination they are uniting beneath the general trusteeship. They become members of the union by consenting to that government. Marshall's argument assumed that the adoption of the Constitution amounted to the establishment of the "great powers" of a true sovereign government. It was an assumption whose essentials Madison always shared. The Convention, he remarked in a private letter of 1829, erected "a real Government, and not a nominal one only."[80]

[79] Virginia, House of Delegates, *Report.* Reprinted in *Resolutions of Virginia and Kentucky, penned by Madison and Jefferson* (Richmond: Robert I. Smith, 1835), p. 27.

[80] Letter of Madison to Joseph C. Cabell, September 7, 1829, *The Writings of James Madison*, ed. Gaillard Hunt (New York: G. P. Putnam's Sons, 1910), ix, 347-49; *McCulloch v. Maryland*, 4 Wheaton (U.S.), 404 (1819); *Gibbons v. Ogden*, 9 Wheaton (U.S.), 187 (1824).

Thus, America was a nation, the states united, just as far as the priority due the government's sovereign powers required. True, the people remained members of their independent states. They had subordinated themselves by distinct acts first to their state authorities, then to that of the union, and remained subject to their state governments in matters not delegated to the general government's care. They were fundamentally members of the union, however, because "the most interesting subjects" were entrusted to the general government. Hence the United States was essentially a nation, not a confederation. "That the United States form," said Marshall in *Cohens* v. *Virginia*, the most judicious and eloquent of his opinions,

> for many, and for most important purposes, a single nation, has not yet been denied. In war, we are one people. In making peace, we are one people. In all commercial regulations, we are one and the same people. In many other respects, the American people are one; and the government which is alone capable of controlling and managing their interests in all these respects, is the government of the Union. It is their government, and in that character they have no other. America has chosen to be, in many respects, and to many purposes, a nation; and for all these purposes, her government is complete; to all these objects, it is competent.[81]

Despite, or perhaps because of, the thoroughness with which Marshall established the supremacy of the union and of its custodian, there remained a perplexing difficulty in his legal reconciliation of nation and states. There was a lacuna of principle which could only be supplied by inelegant compromises. If the nation was a more perfect union, it remained an imperfect union with the states only incompletely parts of one nation. By Marshall's jurisprudence they remained for some (admittedly secondary) purposes "as distinct and perfect sovereignties" as the gov-

[81] *Cohens* v. *Virginia*, 6 Wheaton (U.S.), 419-20 (1821).

ernment "of Great Britain, or of France, or of any other nation."[82] If the states were so independent, then they might surely exercise their secondary powers in ways conflicting with one another and with, moreover, the general government's powers. Still sovereign in the modern sense—subject to no higher authority—how might their acts be measured by any law or public interest common to all? It is this problem that provoked Marshall's frequent remarks on the "complex," "novel," "rare and difficult" scheme which presented "for many purposes an entire nation, and for other purposes several distinct and independent sovereignties."[83]

The broad character of Marshall's solution has been already indicated. The state's sovereignty had been qualified, by the Constitution's acceptance, to the extent the general government's sovereignty required. Thus some harmony among the governments was established. The general

---

[82] "This Court has uniformly professed its disposition, in cases depending on the laws of a particular State, to adopt the construction which the Courts of the State have given to those laws. This course is founded on the principle, supposed to be universally recognized, that the judicial department of every government, where such department exists, is the appropriate organ for construing the legislative acts of that government. Thus no Court in the universe, which professed to be governed by principle, would, we presume, undertake to say, that the Courts of Great Britain, or of France, or of any other nation, had misunderstood their own statutes. . . . On the same principle, the construction given by the Courts of the several States to the legislative acts of those States, is received as true, unless they come in conflict with the constitution, laws, or treaties of the United States." *Elmendorf* v. *Taylor*, 10 Wheaton (U.S.), 159-60 (1825). Marshall, *Address of the Minority* . . . , p. 6. See also *Ex parte Bollmann and Ex parte Swartwout*, 4 Cranch (U.S.), 97 (1807); Elliot, *Debates*, III, 412-20; Marshall to John Pitman, Richmond, June 28 (?), 1828 (ALS, Brown University Library, Special Collections).

[83] Marshall, *Address of the Minority* . . . , p. 6; see *Barron* v. *Baltimore*, 7 Peters (U.S.), 247ff. (1834); *Sturges* v. *Crowninshield*, 4 Wheaton (U.S.), 194 (1819); *Gibbons* v. *Ogden*, 9 Wheaton (U.S.), 205 (1824); *Ogden* v. *Saunders*, 12 Wheaton (U.S.), 350 (1827); *McCulloch* v. *Maryland*, 4 Wheaton (U.S.), 316 (1819).

government's policies with respect to defense, civil order, commerce, private rights, were to predominate over those state measures which, even unintentionally, hinder them, and this very national predominance gives a unity to the collection of governments. However complicated, it was at least "*a* government, composed like ours of distinct governments."[84] It is one government because state governments have to conduct themselves within the interstices of policy and principle dictated by the general government. A difficulty remains, nevertheless. Does this mean that any deed authorized by the national authority is to prevail over every contrary act of the states? Such a view could not but sacrifice the vital core of many local projects to the trivial implications of a national measure.

Marshall's reconciliation of state and nation had to go farther than the assertion of national supremacy, and it did. He held, to begin with, that "in our complex system" the courts should not extend the national authority beyond the "object" of the power in question. He viewed, moreover, the objects of general and state governments as complementary, as parts of a larger national whole by whose common good they might be reconciled. He distinguished the "local" or "interior" objects of the smaller units from the union's "general" purposes. The former included the regulation of such matters as "internal commerce" and "domestic police," although it is difficult to be precise because no comprehensive Marshallian treatment of the states' authority exists.

Unlike Jefferson, Marshall left no very helpful reflections on the distinctive contribution local or state institutions might afford to the citizenry of a liberal republic. His most extensive remarks, in *Gibbons* v. *Ogden*, end by characterizing state power only in negative fashion—"everything within the territory of a State, not surrendered to the general

[84] *Prentiss, Trustee* v. *Barton's Executor*, 1 Brockenbrough 391 (1819). Emphasis added.

government."[85] It is probably true that Marshall's principles, as well as his office, led him to concentrate overmuch on providing for the great sovereign of the union, "the rock of our political salvation."

Its purposes included those "general in their nature, which interest all America, which are connected with the general safety." His best remarks occur in *Gibbons* v. *Ogden*:

The genius and character of the whole government seem to be, that its action is to be applied to all the external concerns of the nation, and to those internal concerns which affect the States generally; but not to those which are completely within a particular State, which do not affect other States, and with which it is not necessary to interfere, for the purpose of executing some of the general powers of the government.[86]

Insofar as Marshall presumed general and state governments to act for complementary purposes, he denied implicitly that they are independent of one another in any real sense, and especially that the state governments are in any sense "sovereign." Each government is to play a circumscribed role defined by the needs of the nation as a whole, not by what either independently may desire, and the national government, through its courts, defines finally those needs. No fundamental conflict of purposes can in principle exist, and a conflict of policy under complementary purposes can be resolved by allowing the deed which, in

[85] "Inspection laws, quarantine laws, health laws of every description, as well as laws for regulating the internal commerce of a State, and those which respect turnpike-roads, ferries, &c, are component parts of this . . . immense mass of legislation which embraces everything within the territory of a state not surrendered to the general government." *Gibbons* v. *Ogden*, 9 Wheaton (U.S.), 203 (1824); *Brown* v. *Maryland*, 12 Wheaton (U.S.), 441 (1827); cf. *McCulloch* v. *Maryland*, 4 Wheaton (U.S.), 414-15 (1819), *Ogden* v. *Saunders*, 12 Wheaton (U.S.), 252 (1827).

[86] *Gibbons* v. *Ogden*, 9 Wheaton (U.S.), 195 (1824); Marshall, *Address of the Minority* . . . , pp. 5-6, 15.

the circumstances, is most in accord with the nation's needs. This was the doctrine underlying a later Supreme Court's justly famous reflections in the case of *Cooley* v. *Port Wardens of Philadelphia.*[87]

Marshall himself, however, never did arrive unambiguously at this conclusion. His equivocations probably were due to a steady adherence to the jurisprudential doctrine distinguishing American federalism: the supposition of two kinds of governments, state and federal, not only distinct but within their sphere sovereign and independent. The *Cohens* v. *Virginia* opinion nicely reflects the ambiguity of his position. "These states are constituent parts of the United States," he said. "They are members of one great empire—for some purposes sovereign, for some purposes subordinate."[88]

Thus Marshall's understanding of the complementary purposes of these governments, each but part of one national whole ruled by the general government, was never coherently and expressly articulated. Occasionally it seemed to be altogether absent. The opinion in *Brown* v. *Maryland*, by its barely qualified doctrine of national supremacy, caused considerable difficulties to subsequent courts. Where present this understanding tended to appear as necessary but not fully articulated good sense, in the application of explicit but imperfect principles. The point is most evident in Marshall's treatment of the commerce power, which particularly encroached upon the states' domestic concerns.

In *Gibbons* v. *Ogden*, Marshall established in law the right to trade among the states, or, more precisely, the liberty of coastal navigation for purposes of trade. The tenor of his opinion, if not its words, seemed to imply that any regulation by a state of "commerce among the states" must be void. Marshall was at least tempted to say that commerce should be treated as subject exclusively to federal regulation. Presumably non-interference was as much a sign of

[87] 12 Howard (U.S.), 299 (1852).
[88] *Cohens* v. *Virginia*, 6 Wheaton (U.S.), 414 (1821).

Congress's wish as positive legislation.[89] There is a problem here, not unlike the problem in Marshall's assertion of a natural right to contract, and it is perhaps not strange that he held back. To give unqualified supremacy to commerce among the states is to eliminate all state regulations for other objects within their province—for example, health, or morals, or revenue—when these impinge, however slightly, on that trade. This was the spectre raised by counsel for Ogden, a point identical to that raised by various counsel in cases involving the contract clause.[90] Moreover, commerce among the states itself needs supporting regulations —such as inspection laws and statutes governing working conditions—varying extensively in varying circumstances. True, Marshall granted that the states can govern "completely internal" trade that does not "affect" or "concern" commerce among the states. But this regulation, no less than that originating with the states' powers over domestic police, is subordinate always to relevant national commercial regulation and hence to the freedom of commerce thereby implied. The difficulty involved in asserting unqualifiedly the supremacy of the general government's powers remains.

Marshall's solution involved two steps, each relying on practical judgment. First, the Chief Justice understood the nationally guaranteed "right to trade" in a qualified sense. It consisted only in the privileges not harmful to healthy commercial society. Just as individuals contracting were "supposed to have made those stipulations, which, as honest, fair, and just men, they ought to have made," so their commercial rights generally presumed acquiescence in the multifarious customs and obligations necessary for society and

[89] *Gibbons* v. *Ogden*, 9 Wheaton (U.S.), 209 (1824).

[90] See e.g. *Ogden* v. *Saunders*, 12 Wheaton (U.S.), 236-37 (1827); cf. *Dartmouth College* v. *Woodward*, 4 Wheaton (U.S.), 627-29 (1819). "Nothing was more complex than commerce," remarked Daniel Webster as he argued for Gibbons, "and in such an age as this no words embraced a wider field than commercial regulation. Almost all the business and intercourse of life may be connected incidentally, more or less, with commercial regulations." 9 Wheaton (U.S.), 9.

thus for trade as well. In *Gibbons* v. *Ogden*, as in *Ogden* v. *Saunders*, Marshall relied on a common-sense and hence limited notion of commerce to prevent the unlimited sway of free exchange: "The coasting trade is a term well understood. The law has defined it; and all know its meaning perfectly."[91]

The second step bears more directly on the reconciliation of general and state governments. Marshall restricted his insistence on even a qualified freedom of trade to those cases where the nation's advantage outweighed benefits from the state act in question. The common good of one nation mediated between the independent powers of the two authorities. Commerce among the states was freed from real threat, as in *Gibbons* v. *Ogden* and, perhaps less obviously, in *Brown* v. *Maryland*, but not from minor hindrances inseparable from worthy state endeavors.

No very explicit remarks exist to confirm this Marshallian manner of reconciling state and general governments. It is but a "practical insight" never expressed in "guiding analysis and luminous generalization," as Justice Frankfurter has remarked in his admirable study of *Willson* v. *The Black Bird Creek Marsh Company*, the most revealing display of Marshall's "practical insight."[92]

Willson's sloop broke down the marsh company's dam across a navigable creek in tidewater. The company sued, alleging injury to its dam, the construction of which had been authorized by Delaware law. Willson, on the other hand, pleaded his "rights of navigation," under the same coasting license act which had freed Gibbons' steamboats from the New York monopoly. It is a matter of some irony that his counsel "relied on the decision of this court in *Gibbons* v. *Ogden*, as a conclusive authority. . . ."[93]

[91] *Gibbons* v. *Ogden*, 9 Wheaton (U.S.), 214 (1824).

[92] Felix Frankfurter, *The Commerce Clause* (Chapel Hill: The University of North Carolina Press, 1937), p. 32; *Willson* v. *The Black Bird Creek Marsh Company*, 2 Peters (U.S.), 247 (1829).

[93] 2 Peters 247. It is untrue to say that "there was no specific federal legislation to which Marshall could point as a basis for showing a clash

Marshall found the Delaware law valid. His holding rested clearly, if implicitly, on the ground that the dispute between navigation rights and the act authorizing a dam was only a local matter—"an affair between the government of Delaware and its citizens." Justice Frankfurter is surely correct in denying any implicit retraction of the "exclusiveness" of Congress's power over commerce among the states.[94] Marshall expressly referred to the possibility of a conflict between a state law and the "dormant" federal commerce power.

There is a problem, however, in his treatment of the dispute as local. It involved navigation, in waters technically coastal, authorized by a federal coasting license. Since navigation for trade was a kind of commerce, according to *Gibbons* v. *Ogden*, the question would seem to have involved commerce among the states. But Marshall chose not to follow this course of argument. Instead, he affirmed that the commerce power "has not been so exercised as to affect the question." In effect, he declared that "these small navigable creeks into which the tide flows which abound throughout the lower country of the middle and southern states . . ." are not important enough in themselves to be considered routes of commerce among the states. Indeed, it appears clear that he upheld Delaware's law because he thought its purposes to accord with the authority allowed to the states by the Constitution. "The value of the property on [the creek's] banks must be enhanced by excluding the water from the marsh, and the health of the inhabitants probably improved. Measures calculated to produce these objects, provided they do not come into collision with the powers of the general government, are undoubtedly within those which are reserved to the states." Yet his final balancing was not couched as the outcome of a comparison of state and

---

between federal and state authority." Samuel J. Konefsky, *John Marshall and Alexander Hamilton* (New York: The Macmillan Company, 1964), p. 226.

[94] Frankfurter, *The Commerce Clause*, p. 29.

federal claims, in the light of a national good common to both. It emerged only beneath the bland formulation, "under all the circumstances of the case."[95]

In finding that blend of jurisprudential doctrine and shrewd judgment which the complicated combination of nation and states required, the judiciary was the key department. With Marshall's discussion of this institutional bulwark of the American union the chapter will conclude. Indeed, the courts are not government's only "means of self-preservation from the perils it may be destined to encounter" at the states' hands. Any attempt by a part to destroy the whole, Marshall remarked cryptically, "ought to be repelled by those to whom the people have delegated their power of repelling it." By its steady enforcement of national laws, however, the judiciary could perhaps contribute most "to maintain the principles established in the constitution." In *Cohens* v. *Virginia*, the Old Dominion had contended that a sovereign state might not be sued or have its judgments revised without its own consent—even when those judgments interpreted or interpreted away the national Constitution. Marshall disagreed. With the ratification of the Constitution, he argued, the states gave up their sovereignty to the extent required by a national sovereignty. A defensible and even natural requirement is the power of the national government's own judiciary to construe finally its laws. Here Marshall foresaw once again the "storms and tempests"—this time of internal dissension—which would inevitably buffet the nation in "ages to come." "We have no assurance that we shall be less divided than we have been." Thus, "exercise of the appellate power over those judgments of the State tribunals which may contravene the constitution or laws of the United States, is, we believe, essential. . . ."[96] The safety of the government and therefore of the

[95] 2 Peters 251-52. Cf. Frankfurter, *The Commerce Clause*, p. 29.
[96] *Cohens* v. *Virginia*, 6 Wheaton (U.S.), 415 (1821). The whole passage reads: "We think that in a government acknowledgedly supreme, with respect to objects of vital interest to the nation, there is

nation would depend to a considerable extent upon the
good sense of its judges.

---

nothing inconsistent with sound reason, nothing incompatible with the
nature of government, in making all its departments supreme, so far
as respects those objects, and so far as is necessary to their attainment.
The exercise of the appellate power over those judgments of the state
tribunals which may contravene the constitution or laws of the United
States, is, we believe, essential to the attainment of those objects."
See also 386, 387, 389, 422, and *Osborne* v. *Bank of United States*,
9 Wheaton (U.S.), 746-59 (1824).

CHAPTER III

THE REPUBLIC

IN common with almost all of his generation, Marshall favored a republican form of government and understood the Constitution to prescribe such. Just what that means is not easy to say, either for them or for him. One problem must be mentioned at the outset. To Marshall a republic was a political cause intrinsically precious and worthy, as well as a mere instrument, another necessary instrument, to provide for the individual's private interests. This chapter touches upon the more attractive ingredients of the Chief Justice's thought, which have been neglected perforce thus far.

A republican form was a noble end in itself. The political liberties attached to republican citizenship were even the "most precious rights," as Marshall remarked more than once. And thus Marshall's republicanism complemented and ennobled his individualistic jurisprudence. He admired for their own sake the patriotic spiritedness of the ordinary free citizen and, especially, the more rare excellences of such a statesman as Washington. There was a trace, in Marshall's character and thought, of the aristocratic republicanism more characteristic of ancient than modern writers; his liking of Cicero went deep. Still, one must not exaggerate these vestiges. They existed but precariously in the interstices of his dominant premises.

Fundamentally Marshall's republicanism fits the apprehensive empire sketched in Chapter I, sustaining the protective sovereign discussed in Chapter II. In his liberal jurisprudence the whole question of forms of government occupies a distinct but secondary place. Who rules, in the sense of what kind of man or class of men rules, is a secondary question, for the character of the country, and hence of its rulers, is a secondary matter. What is primary are the conditions of living, not the quality of life, the improvement of the human condition, to use a contemporary phrase, not the cultivation of human character.

With respect to political arrangements, then, one must concentrate on establishing a "real government," powers effectual in providing for the necessities of human life. Government is in principle to be undistracted by controversy over which men are most deserving of the offices and wealth of the country. The market distributes wealth, in principle at least, according to talent and industry. Even as to office, the matter of character loses much of its importance, although not all. Planned warily for the motives most common in men, the liberal regime relies essentially on a system of government rather than a form of government. Its elaborate checks and balances were designed, in the words of a founder of the new political science, Hume, to make it "the interest, even of bad men, to act for the public good." As avarice would check avarice in a competitive economy, so ambition would check ambition in an ingeniously arranged political system.

Still, governmental form has a place. Laws must be interpreted, powers executed, according to the spirit of the liberal political project. Laws and powers are made and interpreted by men. For a Lockean order, Lockean men must rule. At best, especially at the inception of such an order, men who deeply understand the order, like Marshall himself, are required. If enlightenment is more important than character, the inaugurating statesmen, at least, must be of such a character as to devote themselves to the public weal. Whatever the checks within government, moreover, a popular check on government is required as well. These simple and well-known necessities yield a place for Marshall's republicanism. It is a doctrine of form of *government* alone, not a doctrine involving essentially a regime, the whole way of life of a polity. It will be recalled that Marshall's kind of persuasion separates state from society. Society's character is determined, in principle at least, by its members' private strivings, not by the character of any ruling class.

There is no Marshallian treatment of the American form of government comparable in extent to the discussions of Jefferson, Madison, Hamilton, or John Adams. Still, the many remarks scattered in his *Life of Washington* and elsewhere suggest clearly enough the essential features of his republicanism. He favored a popular government by representatives, so arranged as to provide the liberties and powers discussed in Chapters I and II. Especially in the earlier years of his public life, Marshall was indeed a "votary" of popular government. It was always, however, one in which the desires of ordinary people were filtered by representation, and checked by balanced government, in such a way that the more talented and judicious might have some scope to influence public policy.

Whatever its various strands, Marshall's brand of republicanism would conflict with the infinitely various natural tendencies of any people. In America the people were coming to be of a preponderantly democratic bent, inevitably seeking greater equality in the distribution of wealth and power. Thus arose the problem of Marshall's public life second only to preserving the Union: the settling of republican arrangements upon his essentially democratic countrymen. When Marshall believed that the Americans would willingly subordinate themselves to the liberal Constitution he was a devoted republican. When that belief ebbed, his enthusiasm for popular rule receded as well. He became more "conservative," as Beveridge put it. Yet his fundamental Lockean liberalism varied not at all. All this is implied in Marshall's description, written after his political discouragement, of Washington's republicanism. Properly interpreted the passage is also the best single compression of Marshall's own principles.

116

In speculation, he was a real republican, devoted to the constitution of his country, and to that system of equal political rights on which it is founded. But between a balanced republic and a democracy, the difference is like that between order and chaos. Real liberty, he thought, was to be preserved, only by preserving the authority of the laws, and maintaining the energy of government. Scarcely did society present two characters which, in his opinion, less resembled each other, than a patriot and a demagogue.[1]

POPULAR SOVEREIGNTY
AND REPRESENTATIVE GOVERNMENT

In two distinct senses the government inaugurated by the Constitution of 1788 might be called "popular." It was raised according to general consent; it was to be conducted by the people's representatives. "That the people have an original right to establish for their future government, such principles, as in their opinion, shall most conduce to their own happiness," wrote the Chief Justice in *Marbury* v. *Madison*, "is the very basis on which the whole American fabric has been erected."[2] Chapter IV will consider the exact manner in which, according to Marshall, the Americans actually acquiesced in their new regime.

Only by virtue of its possession of representative institutions, however, might the country be called republican— the people, perhaps, could have consented to the establishment of an aristocracy or monarchy. The decisive point involved control over a government once erected. The very word "republic," and here Marshall echoes Madison in *Federalist* X, meant a government "administered . . . according to the public will by representatives chosen to administer it."[3]

---

[1] Marshall, *The Life of George Washington*, II, 447. Hume's remark occurs in the *Essays*, p. 14.

[2] *Marbury* v. *Madison*, 1 Cranch (U.S.), 176 (1803).

[3] "If it were proved," Marshall wrote to Pickering, that the French government is a government "of force impos'd on the people against

It is difficult for modern students of the Federalist era to understand how a republic could be "government by the public will," popular, and even representative, yet not democratic. We will proceed by considering Marshall's understanding of the people and their will, upon which his notions of popular sovereignty and representative government will be found to depend.

The "people" were the collectivity of individuals who had by solemn agreement and effectual subordination welded themselves into a Union. They comprised the whole population of the nation, not any particular class such as the "many" or "poor" of the ancient writers on politics, or the "proletariat" or "workers" or "little man" of more modern politics. This population was understood, however, in a modern middle-class manner. The people comprised man as man— but man as Lockean individualism conceived him. In effect the people were understood as the collectivity of liberal citizens, supposed, for purposes of political calculation, to be dominated by concern for their interests and rights.

The "people" thus understood differ considerably from their democratic equivalent. They are not unlike ordinary democrats in seeking freedom; there is a close kinship between the rise of liberalism and "the age of the democratic revolution." No man has the right to rule another without his consent, because men are basically equal. The common democrat's assertion of equality, however, turns usually on a vulgar unwillingness or inability to respect more excellent character and taste. The liberal's claim is far more subtle and calculating. Men are supposed equal not in the commonness of various opinions and desires, but in a solid

---

their will & only to be preserv'd by the armies [or] that the government is to be administered not according to the public will by representatives chosen to administer it, but according to the will of the Generals & of the armies, [then] . . . it requires no political knowledge to perceive that while the name of a republic may be preserv'd its very essence is destroy'd." Marshall to the Secretary of State, September 15, 1797. *William & Mary Quarterly*, xii (October 1955), 637-38.

passion which can be systematically regulated to secure political contentment. The spread of classical liberalism is accompanied not only by the leveling of older political hierarchies which come to be regarded as merely "social," but also by the erection of the disciplined economic hierarchies characteristic of capitalism. Liberalism demands only a limited kind of equality, "equal protection" of life, and liberty, and "equality of opportunity" to acquire property. Also, Lockean equality does not culminate in a demand for political freedom. Instead it subordinates political liberty to an effective system of collective security, especially to the sovereign government.[4] Lockean republicanism and capitalism are inseparable from a dominant and burgeoning state and bureaucracy. Be that as it may, Marshall was very careful to make plain in his biography of Washington the difference between the crude and leveling version of democratic liberty which had sprouted under the Articles, on the one hand, and the civil liberty which the Constitution was to restore, on the other.

> The restlessness produced by the uneasy situation of individuals, connected with lax notions concerning public and private faith, and erroneous opinions which confound liberty with exemption from legal control, produced a state of things which alarmed all reflecting men, and demonstrated to many the indispensable necessity of clothing government with powers sufficiently ample for the protection of the rights of the peaceable and quiet, from the invasions of the licentious and turbulent part of the community.[5]

[4] John Locke, *Two Treatises of Civil Government*, II, ii.

[5] Marshall, *The Life of George Washington*, II, 117. Consider Marshall's ironic prefatory remarks in a letter introducing a Richmond friend to Richard Peters of Philadelphia:

Dear Sir,

In democracies, which all the world confesses to be the most perfect work of political wisdom, equality is the pivot on which the grand machine turns, & equality demands that he who has a surplus of any thing in general demand should parcel it out among his

The people were then supposed by Marshall, as by Locke, to delegate in the natural course of things their sovereign powers to a government capable of protecting their interests. Popular sovereignty originated government; only in an indirect and marginal way does it conduct government. Although "the people made the Constitution, and the people can unmake it," and while the general government is "the creature of [the people's] will and lives only by their will," the people are presumed to will erection of the protecting power for which their interests call. This guardian is not to consist of the populace itself, since men generally need to be "channeled" and are bent anyway not on political life but on private advancement. Government must, instead, be entrusted to their representatives. Indeed, Marshall was not one to deny "that ultimate right which all admit, to resist despotism," the "right of rebellion" which Locke in the last chapter of his *Second Treatise of Civil Government* had made so conspicuous a bridle upon recalcitrant rulers. This was only a last resort, however. It marked the collapse of political authority, on account of the representatives' excesses. Politically speaking, "the people can act only by these agents, and . . . , within the powers conferred on them, their acts must be considered as the acts of the people."[6] Thus, the people's "real inter-

---

needy fellow citizens. It is therefore not only reasonable & just, but partial(?) to the vital principles of our excellent institutions that celebrity in any thing, especially in that which interests the community, should be burthened with the tax of communicating to all who hunt after knowledge its superabundant stores. Consequently you cannot as a good patriot, be dissatisfied if every person anxious for instruction in the great & useful science of agriculture should be desirous of availing himself of the opportunity given by an occasional visit to Philadelphia, to draw upon your vast stock, & thus enable him to show away to advantage among the smaller folks he will on his return find in his own neighborhood eager to receive the lessons he will retail to them.
Marshall to Richard Peters, July 21, 1815(?) (ALS, courtesy of the Historical Society of Pennsylvania).
  [6] *Fletcher* v. *Peck*, 6 Cranch (U.S.), 132-33 (1810); *Cohens* v. *Virginia*, 6 Wheaton (U.S.), 389 (1821).
  ". . . The true idea of government and magistracy will be found

ests" give rise to both sovereign government and representative government. The Constitution's "government of the people" is not so much of, by, and for the people as from, on, and for the people.

> The government of the Union, then, . . . is, emphatically, and truly, a government of the people. In form and in substance it emanates from them. Its powers are granted by them, and are to be exercised directly on them, and for their benefit.[7]

It follows that the popular selection of representatives, a republic's distinguishing mark, must be disposed so as to provide for the necessary functions and powers, the "natural public law," of government. This arrangement was to consist in a kind of rough division of labor between represented and representative. While the bulk of the people were to engage in electing, directly or indirectly, all of their rulers, they were to select the community's more judicious men and to leave matters of policy to their enlightened judgment. The people might defer with confidence to their betters, whose rule, after all, would not be unchecked. The republican system of election had the solid virtue so prized by liberalism of involving the interests of the legislator him-

---

to consist in this, that some few men are deputed by many others to preside over public affairs, so that the individuals may the better be enabled to attend their private concerns. . . ." William Blackstone, *Commentaries on the Laws of England*, I, 307.

[7] *McCulloch* v. *Maryland*, 4 Wheaton (U.S.), 404-05 (1819). Beveridge's statement (*Life of John Marshall*, IV, 293n.) that Lincoln's Gettysburg Address only paraphrased Marshall's opinion in *McCulloch* v. *Maryland* is surely wrong. Lincoln's democratic emphasis is different. Perhaps the great Emancipator was indeed "a profound student of Marshall's Constitutional opinions." It is significant nonetheless that not a single reference to Marshall occurs in the eight volumes of Lincoln's collected writings. Consider Lincoln's opinion of a more democratic republican: "The principles of Jefferson are the definitions and axioms of free society." Letter to H. L. Pierce and others, April 6, 1859. *The Collected Works of Abraham Lincoln*, ed. Roy P. Basler (New Brunswick: Rutgers University Press, 1953), III, 375.

self in securing the interests of his constituents. Commending to his fellow citizens a willing acquiescence in the Adams administration's firm policy toward truculent France, Marshall remarked:

> To me, gentlemen, the attachment you manifest to the government of your choice affords the most sincere satisfaction. Having no interests separate from or opposed to those of the people, being themselves subject in common with others, to the laws they make, being soon to return to that mass from which they are selected for a time in order to conduct the affairs of the nation, it is by no means probable that those who administer the government of the *United States* can be actuated by other motives than the sincere desire of promoting the real prosperity of those, whose destiny involves their own, and in whose ruin they must participate.[8]

With respect to the make-up of the electorate, Marshall's views, which may be discerned only with difficulty, seem to be of a more or less democratic kind. In the Virginia Constitutional Convention of 1829-30, it is clear that he defended a moderate property qualification which verges on the mildest oligarchy and is a sign, according to Aristotle at least, of the healthiest democracy. Marshall would never have favored universal suffrage. As we will see, he thought too much of citizenship to spread it so indiscriminately. Moreover, his principles dictated some representation of

---

[8] *General Marshall's Answer to an Address of the Citizens of Richmond, Virginia* (hereafter cited as Marshall, *Answer* . . .), reprinted in Beveridge, *Life of John Marshall*, ii, 573. In the Virginia Ratifying Convention, Marshall "conceived that, as the government was drawn from the people, the feelings and interests of the people would be attended to, and that we should be safe in granting them power to regulate the militia. When the government is drawn from the people, . . . and depending on the people for its continuance, oppressive measures will not be attempted, as they will certainly draw on their authors the resentment of those on whom they depend. On this government, thus depending on ourselves for its existence, I will rest my safety, notwithstanding the danger depicted by the honorable gentleman." Elliot, *Debates*, iii, 420; cf. 555, 560, 562.

property as well as person. In the Virginia Constitutional Convention, the aged Chief Justice replied somewhat rhetorically to such critics as imagined that "we claim nothing of republican principles, when we claim a representation for property." On the contrary, "I think the soundest principles of republicanism do sanction some relation between representation and taxation. Certainly no opinion has received the sanction of wiser statesmen and patriots. I think the two ought be connected. I think this was the principle of the Revolution: the ground on which the Colonies were torn from the mother country and made independent States."[9]

In Virginia the old Federalist fought to restrict the vote to those of at least middling property, especially agricultural property. The qualification which Marshall defended gave the vote to men owning twenty-five acres of land "with a house and plantation" upon it or fifty acres of unimproved land, as well as to certain artisans of Richmond, Norfolk, and Williamsburg. This suffrage requirement "was small enough to enfranchise nearly all white male landowners," C. S. Sydnor remarks in his excellent study of Virginia's political arrangements. "The law did not keep great numbers of small, independent farmers from voting. . . . A man did not have to be rich or even well-to-do to qualify as a voter." Chilton Williamson estimates that between 40 and 50 per cent of white males could vote in 1829. The suffrage was not oligarchic, but neither did it go to the democratic extreme of permitting the indigent, or most of those without land, to vote. Sydnor concludes that "the voters, for the most part, were neither great planters nor very poor men." The small land requirement produced what might best be called a democratic franchise, albeit of a middle-class, more-or-less-agricultural democracy.[10]

[9] *Proceedings and Debates of the Virginia State Convention of 1829-30* (Richmond: Ritchie & Cook, 1830), p. 498.

[10] Aristotle, *Politics*, 1291^b, 31-40; Chilton Williamson, *American Suffrage from Property to Democracy* (Princeton: Princeton University Press, 1960), p. 230. Cf. Charles Henry Ambler, *Sectionalism in Virginia* (Chicago: University of Chicago Press, 1910), pp. 29,

While the extension of the vote to a large and independent portion of the people would serve to "check" their governors, it was not to yield popular determination of policy. Liberal government's "policy" was fundamentally defined by the very nature of the government's powers, and its execution, shaping the long-term plans to ward off future dangers and dealing with crises as they arose, was to rest with the people's agents. A certain independence from popular control was then absolutely necessary to permit the discretion necessary for prudent action. Discretion must be taken in two senses: Marshall wished considerable freedom in the exercise of power for the country's public officials and wanted as well officials of superior judgment. Throughout Marshall's speeches at the ratifying convention there runs a presupposition that representatives are to be ". . . chosen for their wisdom, virtue, and integrity." They are supposed to be, as he said many years later, "our most virtuous and able citizens."[11] In the sequel we will show how Marshall's concern for the rulers' place led him to favor for his native state somewhat aristocratic institutions along with a more or less democratic franchise. First, however, we will consider in greater detail Marshall's respect for some of the higher human qualities. He genuinely admired a spirited independence in the ordinary citizen, and a nobility of character in the leading men.

CITIZEN AND STATESMAN

Marshall regarded citizenship in a republic, to begin with, as not simply a means of securing one's "interest." It comprised, to repeat, "the choicest rights of humanity." The status of a freeman, permission to vote in elections, and eligibility for magistracy and jury duty were, he wrote, "the most precious rights." The republican himself was to be

---

137-38; Charles S. Sydnor, *American Revolutionaries in the Making* (New York: Collier Books, 1962), pp. 38, 42.

[11] Elliot, *Debates*, III, 230-31, 236; *Ogden* v. *Saunders*, 12 Wheaton (U.S.), 352-53 (1827).

guided by correspondingly higher motives than anxious concern for selfish pursuits. Marshall urged his fellow-citizens
to aspire to "the exalted character of freemen."[12]

By "freemen" Marshall meant what was commonly meant
by the word during his time, the small and independent
landholders whose qualifications for the suffrage we have
described. The old Chief Justice struggled against the
Western democrats in the Virginia Constitutional Convention not merely for the property qualification with which he
finally had to be content, but for "our old freehold suffrage."
Marshall's regard for this agricultural qualification seems
to go hand in hand with a devotion to the freeman's "exalted
character." Although there exists no explicit consideration
of the subject in his extant writings, they at least presuppose some such connection between property tenure and
citizen character. His desire for citizens who can be called
"from their plough, . . . to defend their liberty and their
own firesides," his account of Washington as devoted to
improving his plantings and as "accustomed in the early
part of his life to agricultural pursuits, and possessing a real
taste for them," his affectionate regard for the "upper country, where I shall find near and dear friends occupied more
with their farms than with party politics"[13]—all indicate a
certain appreciation, perhaps, for the way agricultural life
nurtured sound temperament.

The common citizen at his best exhibits a kind of stout
independence—a willingness to be called "from the plough"

[12] Marshall, *Answer* . . . , in Beveridge, *Life of John Marshall*, ii,
573; Marshall, *A history of the colonies* . . . , i, 86-87, cf. 428.

[13] Marshall to Story, March 26, 1828. Massachusetts Historical
Society, *Proceedings*, 2nd series, xiv (November 1900), 32; American
Envoys to the Minister of Foreign Affairs of the French Republic
(hereafter cited, Marshall as envoy), United States, *State Papers*,
Foreign Relations, ii, 170. For a suggestion of Marshall's decisive
responsibility for the despatches in general, and this despatch in
particular, see Beveridge, *Life of John Marshall*, ii, 256, 284, 296-97,
326, but cf. 302, 328. Marshall, *The Life of George Washington*, ii,
63, 424.

to fight for his personal and especially his political prerogatives. Patriotically devoted to "the most sacred of deposits—
the right of self government," he possesses such virtues as
courage and endurance, as well as moderation, "discipline,"
and justice. Marshall was generally critical of the quality
and training of the Revolutionary army. He did not spare
praise, however, for the "patience and constancy," the bravery in battle and the moderation in peace, of segments of
the troops. Industrious and ambitious in peace, the freeman
was to be patriotic, self-reliant, and courageous in war.[14]

Whatever Marshall's admiration for the ordinary republican, he clearly reserved his highest esteem for the few capable of being gentlemen and statesmen. In his biography
of Washington he recounted at length, for example, the
chivalrous valor of Major André. André was the British staff
officer apprehended as the Americans foiled Benedict Arnold's plot to turn over West Point. His capture, confine-
ment, and hanging are described feelingly by Marshall in
disproportionate detail. The British officer was more than
spirited and courageous. He was "gallant." André stood firm
in his determination to detract in no way from the nobility
of a character not only magnanimous but even finished
with "a peculiar elegance of mind and manners." Any considerations of self-preservation were subordinated to the
high chivalry of a man of honor. "As if only desirous to
rescue his character from imputations which he dreaded
more than death," to quote Marshall's account, "he confessed
every thing material to his own condemnation, but would
divulge nothing which might involve others."[15]

[14] Marshall as envoy, United States, *State Papers*, Foreign Relations,
II, 176. Marshall, *A history of the colonies . . .* , p. 475; Marshall,
The Life of George Washington, II, 25. Marshall's praise of the ordinary republican citizen's "exalted character" reminds of the not particularly elevated kind of patriotic virtue that is, as such philosophers
as Machiavelli and Montesquieu thought, both politically necessary
and readily attainable. See David Lowenthal, "Montesquieu and the
Classics," in Joseph Cropsey, ed., *Ancients and Moderns* (New York:
Basic Books, Inc., 1964), pp. 280-83.

[15] Marshall, *The Life of George Washington*, I, 375-82. "To an
excellent understanding, well improved by education and travel, he

Marshall saw the peak of moral excellence in George Washington. The first president was a "truly great man" who, if hardly so elegant as André, was nevertheless surely a gentleman and, more important, a republican statesman of the highest type. Marshall's extended but scattered appraisals of Washington even resemble the descriptions that have come to us from classical antiquity of the best that moral and political life can attain. There is a striking similarity between the magnanimity, or the disposition "great, elevated, and despising the ordinary things happening to men," crowning the best man as Aristotle and Cicero portray him, and the "unaffected and indescribable dignity, unmingled with haughtiness," attributed to Washington by Marshall.[16] Washington was generous without being extravagant, bestowing "those donations which real distress has a right to claim from opulence." His personal courage was remarkable, his ambition restrained and dignified. The General had afforded "the highest examples of moderation and pa-

---

united a peculiar elegance of mind and manners, and the advantage of a pleasing person. It is said he possessed a pretty taste for the fine arts, and had himself attained some proficiency in poetry, music, and painting. His knowledge appeared without ostentation, and embellished by a diffidence that rarely accompanies so many talents and accomplishments, which left you to suppose more than appeared. His sentiments were elevated and inspired esteem, they had a softness that conciliated affection. His elocution was handsome, his address easy, polite, and insinuating." Marshall appended this description of André by Hamilton. *Ibid.*, I, note XVII, Appendix 38.

16 "His person and whole deportment exhibited an unaffected and indescribable dignity, unmingled with haughtiness, of which all who approached him were sensible. . . . In him, that innate and unassuming modesty which adulation would have offended, which the voluntary plaudits of millions could not betray into indiscretion, and which never obtruded upon others his claims to superior consideration, was happily blended with a high and correct sense of personal dignity, and with a just consciousness of that respect which is due to station." *Ibid.*, II, 445, 448, cf. 447; Aristotle, *Nicomachean Ethics*, trans. H. Rackham (Cambridge: Harvard University Press, 1956), II, vii, 7, IV, iii; Cicero, *De Officiis*, translator Walter Miller. (Cambridge: Harvard University Press, 1956), I, xviii, 61. Cf. III, v, 24, I, xxi, 72-73.

triotism" as he "voluntarily divested himself of the highest military and civil honours when the public interest no longer demanded that he should retain them."

The virtue Marshall most admired in Washington was practical wisdom, "sound judgment," especially perspicacity in political matters. Marshall called this "perhaps the most rare, and . . . certainly the most valuable quality of the human mind."[17] Such disparate characters as John Smith, the younger Pitt, and Frederick the Great won the Chief Justice's esteem for their practical and prudent statesmanship, and it is a quality which the biographer Marshall repeatedly noted and praised in his subject. "More solid than brilliant, judgment, rather than genius, constituted the most prominent feature of his character." Marshall even dwelled upon the various traits making up his hero's good sense. Washington had been "endowed by nature with a sound judgment, and an accurate discriminating mind." He displayed prodigious industry in endeavoring to discover the causes of events; "the lessons of experience were never lost." Events themselves did not overwhelm him. The General "was accustomed to contemplate at a distance those critical situations in which the United States might probably be placed; and to digest, before the occasion required action, the line of conduct which it would be proper to observe."[18]

Although Washington's character may resemble that of the aristocratic statesman as classically portrayed, the resemblance is not exact. He might be better described as the modern republican version of that model. The full demands of magnanimity were perhaps unsatisfied by Washington's constant repetition of an "unassuming modesty." The Virginian's expenditures were generous and liberal, by no means "magnificent." The splendor of his military accomplishments was qualified by the democratic character of the

[17] *Ibid.*, ii, 446, 129, 445-47. *A history of the colonies* . . . , xi. Cf. Cicero, *De Officiis*, i, xxii, 79-82.
[18] *Ibid.*, ii, 446, cf. 445-47 *passim*.

army only more or less under his command—" . . . an un-disciplined, ill organized multitude," its officers often without supplies or honor, impoverished and humiliated. And it is not uninteresting that Marshall failed to discuss Washington's lack of elegance, or, more precisely, the absence of wit and "genius" for philosophy or for literature, music, and other things of beauty.[19] Like the pursuits of Marshall himself, those of Washington were leavened hardly at all by these activities especially delightful and noble for their own sake. In short, as Marshall portrayed him, Washington displayed a moderation in his own demands, and a practical concern for the interests of the people generally, which befitted one devoted to a popular and commercial republic built on an assumed equality, rather than on a candid recognition of the activities and prerogatives of superior men. "In spec-ulation, he was a real republican," Marshall's description

[19] "However preeminent the antients may have been in some of the fine arts," wrote Marshall in reply to a letter from Henry Wheaton enclosing a discourse of Wheaton's, "they were, I think you very clearly show, much inferior to us, or a great way behind us, in the more solid & more interesting principles of international law;—a law which contributes more to the happiness of the human race, than all the statues which ever came from the hands of the sculptor, or all the paintings that were ever placed on canvass. I do not, by this, mean to lessen the value of the arts. I subscribe to their importance, & admit that they improve as well as embellish human life & Man-ners; but they yield in magnitude to those moral rules which regulate the connexion of man to man." Marshall to Wheaton, March 24, 1821 (ALS, courtesy of the Pierpont Morgan Library, New York City; copy in The Papers of John Marshall, Williamsburg, Virginia).
   In another letter Marshall lauded William Wirt, "alike distinguished for judgment and genius," for his "brilliant play of imagination" and "fertility of invention." He did not undertake to decide whether Wirt was wise in not foregoing the law for literature, although Marshall "would have lamented the surrender of the certain independence acquired by perseverance in professional duties, for the seductive charms of that fairy world [Wirt] was capable of adorning." Marshall to John Pendleton Kennedy (ALS, Marshall Papers, Enoch Pratt Free Library, Baltimore; copy in The Papers of John Marshall, Williams-burg). One would not wish to forget here, however, Marshall's own wit or his pleasure in the novels of Jane Austen.

of his hero's political opinions may be quoted once again, "devoted to the Constitution of his country, and to that system of equal political rights on which it is founded."[20]

If the traits of even Washington himself were less "high-toned" than those of the strictly aristocratic character, they were considerably higher than those of the better republican citizens generally. Whatever Marshall's genuine admiration for Washington's grander qualities, the "few" of whom he commonly spoke comprised simply the upper levels of the country's commercial, "professional," and agricultural occupations, a rather more gentlemanly version of what we now call the "upper middle class." Marshall habitually distinguished between the "interested" many and the "disinterested" few, or between the "greater part" whose judgment is completely controlled by the passions, and the "thinking part." In doing so, however, he does not allude to two ways of life, distinctly democratic and distinctly aristocratic. The differences are not so much of character and hence of goal, but of degree of ability in pursuing the same goals. Not the leisured gentleman, but the active upper middle-class planter, merchant, and lawyer, is to predominate. These might be called a kind of "natural aristocracy," "men of talents" as the post-Machiavellian publicists called them in England, who rose in the ordinary channels of business and politics by virtue of extra portions of drive and prudence. Marshall was perfectly satisfied with the substantial merchants and lawyers of New England such as George Cabot, Fisher Ames, Theodore Sedgwick, Jeremiah Wadsworth and Rufus King—all en-

[20] *The Life of George Washington*, II, 445-47, 25, 134; *A history of the colonies* . . . , xi-xiii. Marshall's combination of respect for the admirable traits of rare men with a fundamental orientation by the common interests of most men, is foreshadowed by the philosopher Hume. Hume sought to account for the distinctions of ordinary speech while remaining true to the epistemology, and to the "realistic" moral teaching, of his predecessors among the modern philosophers. Consider his attempt to do justice to the qualities to which praise and blame point, on the basis of a psychology involving motives solely of utility and pleasure. *Enquiries concerning the Principles of Morals*, ed. Selby-Bigge (Oxford, 1966), I, III, VI-VIII.

gaging in public life, not one a member of leisured aristocracy, some risen from very obscure origins indeed. It is this kind of man, this very dim reflection of a Washington, which Marshall's principles might be said to foster. Within a jurisprudence encouraging industrious acquisitiveness, the more substantial and settled modes of acquisition were favored, and hence the more established merchants, manufacturers, and cultivators. By preserving settled or vested property, Marshall's principles might encourage stable industry and quiet opulence rather than speculation and garishness. Similarly, one might suppose that Marshall's exaltation of the rule of law under a "sacred" written constitution would naturally draw into political prominence the lawyer, especially the great constitutional lawyer. His esteem for the Supreme Court Bar of his time needs no rehearsal here.[21]

Modified by his republicanism, then, Marshall's notion of the American polity can be redescribed as a republican as well as a commercial empire. Anxious about its safety, the nation was also to be patriotically devoted to its political freedoms. As the freeman preserved his precious rights of self-government, so the free republic would preserve its "national faith" as a repository of "the most sacred of deposits—the right of self-government."[22] And the United States was to be honorable as well as free. From the bench,

[21] See Cicero, De Officiis, II, xix, 65. ". . . Among the many admirable ideas of our ancestors was the high respect they always accorded to the study and interpretation of the excellent body of our civil law. And down to the present unsettled times the foremost men of the state have kept this profession exclusively in their own hands; but now [under the unqualified rule of Caesar] the prestige of legal learning has departed along with offices of honour and positions of dignity." Cf. Alexis de Tocqueville, Democracy in America (New York: Vintage Books, Inc., 1945), I, xvi, 282ff., II, xvi-xix; Marshall, An Autobiographical Sketch, p. 19. As to the character and aspirations of the general run of the Federalists, see Chapter I, "Federalists of the Old School," in David Hackett Fischer's The Revolution of American Conservatism (New York: Harper & Row, 1965).

[22] Marshall as envoy, United States, State Papers, Foreign Relations, II, 176, 170; cf. 177.

the Chief Justice rebuked some American privateersmen for the brutal and wanton injury they had inflicted during a search of neutral vessels; "the honor and character of the nation are concerned in repressing such irregularities." Similarly, America's repression of the Indians could be justified only until her safety from their depredations was secured. "That time, however, is unquestionably arrived," he wrote to his friend Story, "and every oppression now exercised on a helpless people depending on our magnanimity and justice for the preservation of their existence impresses a deep stain on the American character. I often think with indignation of our disreputable conduct (as I think) in the affair of the Creeks of Georgia." He was no less jealous of his country's honor when threatened by the insults of others. A conciliating moderation ought to be supplemented, he thought, by some degree of spirited daring. Free of prickly xenophobia, he always admired nonetheless those "indignant feelings which a high spirited people, insulted and injured by a foreign power, can never fail to display."[23]

[23] Marshall, *The Life of George Washington*, II, 426, cf. 427-28; *The Anna Maria*, 2 Wheaton (U.S.), 335 (1817). Marshall to Story, October 29, 1828, Massachusetts Historical Society, *Proceedings*, 2nd Series, XIV, 337-38.

Marshall's kind of patriotism is well illustrated by his special anger at the notorious "Decree of St. Cloud" perpetrated by Napoleon. This rather famous diplomatic coup contemptuously contradicted the open basis of Madison's conciliatory foreign policy, the assumption that the Emperor's Berlin and Milan Decrees had been revoked with respect to American trade before the inception of the American policy. Sick at the offensive sheet that failed to "consult the honor" of his country, Marshall showed himself even more distressed at America's "tame, unmurmuring acquiescence" which had not only occasioned the insult, but also submitted to it.

"We have submitted, completely submitted; & he will not leave us the poor consolation of concealing that submission from ourselves. . . . I cannot contemplate this subject without excessive mortification as well at the contempt with which we are treated as at the infatuation of my countrymen." Letter from Marshall to Robert Smith, July 27, 1812. Quoted by Beveridge, *Life of John Marshall*, IV, 38-39. See also a letter from Marshall to Timothy Pickering, December 11, 1813

It appears that he found this proud and honorable mien more often manifest in the deeds of Great Britain than in those of his own nation. David Hume had observed in 1742 that the British up to his time "have been more possessed with the ancient Greek spirit of jealous emulation, than actuated by the prudent views of modern politics." Marshall admired the residue of that spirit. Consider his reflections on the British declaration of war on Holland in 1789, when the Dutch were seen to favor hard-pressed Britain's galaxy of enemies. "There are situations to which only high minded nations are equal, in which a daring policy will conduct those who adopt it, safely through the very dangers it appears to invite; dangers which a system suggested by a timid caution might multiply instead of avoiding." And with England's grandeur of action went a grandeur of disposition which was a reflection of her leaders.

The British character rather wounds by its pride, and offends by its haughtiness, and open violence, than injures by the secret indulgence of a malignant, but paltry and unprofitable revenge and, certainly, such unworthy motives ought not lightly to be imputed to a great and magnanimous nation, which dares to encounter a world, and risk its existence, for the preservation of its station in the scale of empires, of its real independence, and of its liberty.[24]

(ALS, Massachusetts Historical Society), and Marshall to John Randolph, June 18, 1812 (ALS, Harvard University). On the circumstances surrounding the decree see *ibid.*, pp. 35ff; Henry Adams, *History of the United States* (New York: Charles Scribner's Sons, 1909), v, xviii, vi, xii. Twenty years later Marshall still remembered this bitter insult, regretting the absence from Webster's "Speeches" of those on the Decree. Marshall to Daniel Webster, Washington, January 23, 1831. Reprinted in George T. Curtis, *Life of Daniel Webster* (New York: Appleton, 1870), i, 110. See Oster, *Doctrines*, pp. 186-87.

[24] Marshall, *The Life of George Washington*, ii, 296; i, 393. David Hume, "Of the Balance of Power," in *Essays Moral, Political, and Literary*, 393. See also letters from Marshall to Pickering, September 15, 1797. *William & Mary Quarterly*, xii (October 1955), 637-39.

REPUBLICAN VIRTUE AND PRIVATE INTEREST

Although Marshall admired an honorable republic, it must be said that his liberal jurisprudence tended to erode the conditions needed for such a regime. Commerce and manufacturing are more profitable, manufacturing as fertilized by technology more productive, than agriculture, and they in turn dictate industrial towns and cities hardly the nursery of yeomen and country gentlemen. If the superior man despises the pettily ambitious pursuit of place and wealth through party and commerce, the entrepreneur and his lawyer tend to live that way. The gentleman may well desire an estate to sustain leisure and family. The entrepreneur desires above all that property be productive, and he turns it over for profit's sake. In short, an orientation by "interest" erodes the sense of punctilious honor, and without that what would qualify the Americans' restless striving for security, profit, and success? "What makes ambition virtue?" the younger Pitt had asked in part of a passage which Marshall quoted: "the sense of honor."[25] Even the few toiling to the top in business and law could rarely be more than anxious businessmen and politicians, the exploitative "aristocracy of manufactures" and the ambitious non-entities which the observant Tocqueville saw through. In place of freeholder and gentleman are laborer and capitalist, and more fundamentally, the enterprising, restlessly ambitious but essentially security-loving, modern middle class which Tocqueville found: "an innumerable multitude of men, all equal and alike, incessantly endeavoring to procure the petty and paltry pleasures with which they glut their lives."

There is little or no consideration in Marshall's writings of the problematic relation of modern society and excellence of character, not even a discussion comparable to that of John Adams or Thomas Jefferson. It seems that Marshall failed to reflect upon the economic and political conditions

[25] *Ibid.,* i, 211.

necessary for even his mercantile and professional gentle-men. Now and then his utterances presuppose a vague connection between agricultural pursuits and some kind of moral excellence; he never pursued that connection as a theme. Although he mentioned the effects on Washington's character of his mother and her moral and religious max-ims, the whole account of formative influences upon the young Virginian amounts to a disappointing page. There is no discussion of the small "estate" of Washington's early life, or of his extensive association with the household of Lord Fairfax, or of the proud tone still characteristic of Virginia society. One is tempted to say that Marshall took the greatness of his native Virginia for granted, just as it was being undermined by the "progress" of an interested individualism, by "a theory of manufactures more powerful than customs and laws," as Tocqueville put it, which would render even farming commerce. Marshall not only approved of that progress but thought it beneficial or at least inevitable. He would have considered deliberation on the alternatives to commerce and industry idle, as well as pernicious. His liberalism taught him not only the advan-tage, but above all the necessity, of acquiescence in the "laws of supply and demand." Marshall's best inclinations were betrayed by the new liberation of the base passions, so cleverly propagated in old forms by Machiavelli, Locke, and their successors.

Although Marshall did not examine the tensions between the character he admired and the jurisprudence he es-poused, he seems nevertheless to have sensed a certain deterioration in the American character, wondered about its cause, and mildly encouraged certain institutions and practices which tended to foster the better qualities. Mar-shall's agreement with Story that the new type of ambi-tiously partisan politician fails to live up to "those states-men of the last century" is typical. In a letter to his close friend John Randolph of Roanoke, who had evidently ex-panded upon certain mediocre tendencies in the country,

Marshall indicated that his concern was grave and searching. He seemed to wonder whether the prevailing pursuit of success, without serious concern for true character and judgment, might indeed have some deep "cause lurking beneath" the United States' institutions.

The latter part of Randolph's letter (he wrote) "treats on subjects which have often excited in my bosom the most serious doubts & serious reflections."

> To what are we to impute the disregard of those maxims which time has rendered venerable, which early impressions had surrounded with a sort of religious reverence, & whose utility has the sanction of the experience & consent of the ages? Does there exist any cause lurking beneath our institutions which so influence the education, the early habits of youth as to relax the great principles which form the foundation of national prosperity & happiness, as to substitute superficial showy acquirements for that substantial and real knowledge which is to be acquired only by labor, & which is essential to the formation of a statesman? Does the execrable doctrine that the end will justify the means derive its prevalence from temporary causes or from such as are permanent & deeply rooted in our system and habits? Does the no less execrable opinion that merit as a partisan will excuse the want of every virtue & of every moral quality belong to man in all situations or does it derive peculiar strength from particular causes in operation among ourselves?[26]

While abroad many years before Marshall had observed the precarious state of republican virtue in commercial society. In fact he had visited a nation preeminently mercantile in practice as well as principle. He had found Holland in 1797, even under France's thumb, exhibiting "a degree of wealth and population perhaps unequaled in any

[26] Letter from Marshall to John Randolph, June 26 (no year) (ALS, Virginia Historical Society).

136

other part of Europe." The inhabitants, however, generally "concern themselves less than any people in the world with politics." "Not a tenth of the freeholders assembled" for a critical vote on a long-projected constitution. Even the upper classes were detached from political activity. Some simply found the current alternatives unpalatable. Many others, however, "seem to be indifferent to every consideration not immediately connected with their particular employments." He had remarked to his Dutch informant, "a very rich and intelligent merchant," that the withdrawal of the rich might allow the success of those bent on leveling them. Marshall, who was soon to tell Talleyrand that "the right of self-government" occupied the stature of a "sacred deposit," was appalled by the Dutchman's reply: the wealthy relied on French rule to stem any democratic tide. "Very many . . . wou'd now see [France's] departure . . . with . . . regret. Thus they willingly relinquish national independence for individual safety."[27]

In light of Marshall's esteem for sturdy republicanism and his anxiety about its erosion, his encouragement of the citizenship he admired comes as no surprise. If Marshall never articulated the problem, he displayed in his deeds a definite concern for the family life, religion, and education that encourage something better than devotion to one's "interest." Indeed he worried explicitly that his country would suffer by a "carelessness in performing the great duty of impressing on the youthful mind lessons of religion and morality."[28]

[27] Marshall to Washington, September 15, 1797. Reprinted in *American Historical Review*, ii (1897-98), 296. Cf. Marshall to Edward Carrington, September 2, 1797 (ALS, Morristown National Historical Park). Thirteen years later Albert Gallatin could wonder whether it might take war to preclude "our degenerating, like the Hollanders, into a nation of mere calculators, . . . [to engender] the awakening of nobler feelings and habits than avarice and luxury. . . ." Quoted by Adams, *History of the United States*, iv, 33.

[28] Marshall to James M. Garnett, Esquire, December 17, 1830 (typescript, courtesy of Virginia Historical Society).

Understanding without special originality that men are much influenced by "the first impressions made on the youthful mind," Marshall was concerned that these be good impressions for Americans. It will be recalled that "sentiment" and "habit" had occasioned his own early patriotism —and Marshall was surely more guided by judgment than most men. In shaping the young the family was the crucial influence, and on the occasions when family matters came to his Court, the Chief Justice did what he could to preserve what he called the "sacredness of the connexion between man and wife."[29]

Marshall would have concurred in Washington's opinion that religion is an indispensable practical nourishment for "all the dispositions and habits which lead to political prosperity." "The support of religious institutions," he remarked to a correspondent, has "frequently attracted my serious attention." His views reflected not merely narrow considerations of social expediency, but also some desire for the nurture of finer character for its own sake. He noted that Washington himself had been "a sincere believer in the Christian faith, and a truly devout man" in whom "principles of religion" formed in part the very basis of his character. In a letter to his grandson the old Chief Justice indicated somewhat more fully the connection between religion and sound character.

Happiness is pursued by all, though too many mistake the road by which the greatest good is to be successfully

[29] *Sexton* v. *Wheaton*, 8 Wheaton (U.S.), 239 (1823). See also *Marbury* v. *Brooks*, 7 Wheaton (U.S.), 575-76 (1822); *Hopkirk* v. *Randolph et al.*, 2 Brockenbrough 137 (1824). The mother was particularly influential. "Precepts from the lips of a beloved mother, inculcated in the amiable, graceful manner which belongs to the parent and the sex, sink deep in the heart, and make an impression which is seldom entirely effaced." Letter from Marshall to Thomas W. White, November 29, 1824. Reprinted in James M. Garnett, *Lectures on Female Education* (Richmond: Thomas W. White, 1824), p. 8. Marshall commends the publisher of this book as dealing with a subject of the "deepest interest." *Ibid.*

followed. Its abode is not always in the pallace or the cottage. Its residence is the human heart, and its inseparable companion is a quiet conscience. . . . The individual who turns his thoughts frequently to an omnipotent omniscient and all perfect being, who feels his dependence on, and his infinite obligations to that being will avoid that course of life which must harrow up the conscience.[30]

Marshall attended the Episcopal Church in Richmond all his life, "contributing liberally," as Bishop Meade tells us, to its revival after the post-Revolutionary disestablishment. It is not impossible that part of his intent was to "set an example to gentlemen of the same conformity," as Meade described the effect of the Chief Justice's conduct. His own beliefs, in any event, were rather obscure even to contemporaries. His general thoughts on the place of religion in America's liberal polity are suggested in a letter of characteristic tact and dignity to the Reverend J. Adams, who had sent for Marshall's perusal a sermon on the relation of Christianity to civil government. Marshall agreed with Adams that in the colonial period the government had been involved in propagating Christianity, and then he continued:

No person, I believe, questions the importance of religion to the happiness of man even during his existence in this world. It has at all times employed his most serious meditation, & had a decided influence on his conduct. The American population is entirely Christian, & with us, Christianity & Religion are identified. It would be strange, indeed, if with such a people, our institutions did not presuppose Christianity, & did not often refer to it, & exhibit relations with it. Legislation on the subject is admitted to require great delicacy, because freedom of con-

[30] Marshall to John Marshall, Jr., November 7, 1834. Printed in Oster, *Doctrines*, pp. 56-57. Marshall, *The Life of George Washington*, i, 1.

science & respect for our religion both claim our most serious regard.[31]

As for the practical reconciliation of the rights of conscience with religion's salutary effect on morals, it is perfectly clear that Marshall would have favored the state governments' support of religion in general, while opposing the legal maintenance of any particular church. He vindicated a bill providing for "a small tax levied on property generally, for the support of ministers of religion, each individual being at liberty to declare the person to whom his contribution should be paid."[32]

Of more importance to Marshall than state support of religion, no doubt, was the establishment of "a good system for the education of youth," an endeavor which he placed

[31] Marshall to the Reverend Mr. J. Adams, Richmond, May 9, 1833 (copy in the William L. Clements Library, The University of Michigan).

[32] This is Marshall's account of a bill introduced into the legislature after the disestablishment of Virginia's Episcopal church. He clearly indicates the bill to be a mean between two "extremes," that of an established church in which "all were taxed for its support," and that of "individual contributions purely voluntary." "You notice towards the conclusion [of your sermons]," Marshall wrote to the Reverend William B. Sprague, "what has frequently attracted my serious attention—'the support of religious institutions' . . . Previous to the revolution we [of Virginia] had an established church and all were taxed for its support. From one extreme we passed to the other, and individual contributions purely voluntary, were substituted for those which had been imposed by law. Soon after the conclusion of the war, an attempt was made to pass a bill for a general assessment— that is a small tax levied on property generally, for the support of the ministers of religion, each individual being at liberty to declare the person to whom his contribution should be paid. This bill failed; and its supporters incurred so much popular odium that no person has since been found hardy enough to renew the proposition." Letter from Marshall to The Reverend William B. Sprague, July 22, 1828 (ALS, John Marshall Papers, Earl Greg Swem Library, College of William and Mary in Virginia). Bishop Meade, *Old Churches, Ministers, and Families of Virginia* (Philadelphia: J. B. Lippincott Company, 1900), II, 221; Marshall, *The Life of George Washington*, II, 404, 445.

"among the most meritorious efforts of patriotism." A large part of his rather un-Virginian admiration of New England was stimulated by its educational system. Education had been "engrafted . . . on their original establishments," and thus "public opinion co-operates with law to cherish their institutions." In sections less fortunate, assistance from the state legislatures ought to be inaugurated. Actually, a proper teaching of the young was "an object of national concern" as well. While no evidence survives of Marshall's support for the national university that Washington proposed, it is at least obvious that the Chief Justice went out of his way, in the case of *Dartmouth College* v. *Woodward,* to inform an unreceptive Congress that education was "a proper subject of legislation."[33]

Education served to enlighten the citizenry of a liberal republic as to its rights and interests, and especially as to the moral dispositions and duties that accord with its long term interests.[34] Necessary in any liberal regime, liberal enlightenment was especially so in a republic. "It is more

[33] *Dartmouth College* v. *Woodward,* 4 Wheaton (U.S.), 634; see 646 (1819); Marshall to Robert Mayo (and others), January 26, 1823. In Robert Mayo, *Political Sketches of Eight Years in Washington* (Baltimore: Lucas, 1839), p. 47.

[34] "Knowledge is in every country the surest basis of public happiness. In one, in which the measures of government receive their impression so immediately from the sense of the community as in ours, it is proportionately essential. To the security of a free constitution it contributes in various ways: by convincing those who are intrusted with the public administration, that every valuable end of government is best answered by the enlightened confidence of the people; and by teaching the people themselves to know and to value their own rights; to discern and provide against invasions of them; to distinguish between oppression and the necessary exercise of lawful authority; between burdens proceeding from a disregard of their convenience, and those resulting from the inevitable exigencies of society; to discriminate the spirit of liberty from that of licentiousness, cherishing the first, avoiding the last, and uniting a speedy but temperate vigilance against encroachments, with an inviolable respect to the laws." Washington, quoted by Marshall, *The Life of George Washington,* II, 176-77; see also 404, 417.

indispensable in governments entirely popular than in any other, that the mass of the people should receive that degree of instruction which will enable them to perform with some intelligence the duties which devolve on them. . . ." A widespread training of the citizenry is thus required. "I have always thought and I still think, whatever importance may be attached to our university and colleges, and I admit their importance, the primary schools are objects of still greater interest." It seems that the Chief Justice, despite the mean class interest attributed to him by the more narrow commentators, was peculiarly worried about the general debasement of vast numbers of people in "pauperism," a tendency which seemed, as Tocqueville also observed, to attend the working of the chill and unyielding laws of political economy. The price of labor would be driven down as "the supply exceeds demand." Perhaps only education could provide the useful skills enabling most men to make their way, although Marshall was by no means convinced that "famine and pauperism" could thus be always kept off.[35]

[35] "I was peculiarly struck with the melancholy picture you draw of English pauperism," Marshall replied to a letter from Charles Mercer, "—a picture which I fear is as just as it is sombre. Is this gloomy state of things to be ascribed entirely to an overflowing population, or does it proceed from the policy of the laws? The accumulation of landed property in the hands of a few individuals, and its continuance in those hands by the law of entails and of descent may contribute to this effect, but can not produce it entirely. The extremes of wealth and poverty in personal estate have perhaps more influence on the mass of the people than the extremes in real estate. The doctrines of entail and primogeniture do not reach this part of the subject. When population becomes very dense, agriculture alone will not afford employment for all the inhabitants of the country. The surplus hands must find employment in some other manner. As the supply exceeds the demand the price of labour will cheapen until it affords a bare subsistence to the labourer. The super added demands of a family can scarcely be satisfied, and a slight indisposition, one which suspends labour and compensation for a few days produces famine and pauperism. How is this to be prevented? What is the state of the poor on the continent of Europe?—Especially in Holland and Flan-

With enlightenment in mind, Marshall also commended to his countrymen such studies as political economy, as we have noted, and, more emphatically, legal philosophy in its peculiarly American vestments of constitutional law. "I wish very much," the Chief Justice wrote to the author of a "course of lectures" on America's "Constitutional Jurisprudence," "that this and similar works could be introduced into all our seminaries for education. In a government like ours, it is of the last importance that early impressions should be just." The Chief Justice of course delighted in the appearance of his protégé Joseph Story's *Commentaries on the Constitution*; and he greeted with special enthusiasm Story's abridgment intended for students of the law. "The vast influence which the members of the profession exercise in all popular governments, especially in ours, is perceived by all, and whatever tends to their improvement benefits the nation." If read by students in "all our colleges and universities," Story's massive commentary would help "in the South to remove prejudices against the national government" and would cultivate throughout the nation those political leaders whose nurture was never far from Marshall's attention. "I have finished reading your great work," wrote the Chief Justice to his friend, "and wish

---

ders? I believe with you that education—that degree of education which is adapted to the wants of the labouring class, and which prevails generally in the United States—especially in those of the north—is the surest preservative of the morals and of the comforts of human life. In the present state of our population and for a long time to come it may be relied on with some confidence. But as our country fills up how shall we escape the evils which have followed on dense population? The systems of education which have been adopted in the different states form a subject for useful reflection and will I hope attract the attention of our legislature. I have always thought and I still think, whatever importance may be attached to our university and colleges, and I admit their importance, the primary schools are objects of still greater interest." Letter from Marshall to Charles Mercer, April 7, 1827 (ALS, courtesy of the Trustees of the Boston Public Library).

it could be read by every statesman, and every would-be statesman in the United States."[36]

Marshall wanted education of the country's more talented men to include something more, however, than economics and law. He assumed that part of a good education would be given over to the ancient literature on ethics and politics. This is the inference to be drawn, at any rate, from two letters to his grandsons. Each commended the study of Cicero's works, as both models of rhetoric and reflections of "a profound Philosopher." His *de Officiis*, Marshall wrote to his namesake, "is among the most valuable treatises I have seen in the latin language."[37] Marshall was justly honored by his fellow citizens for a grave and honorable republicanism. It is scarcely susceptible of better illustration than the old Chief Justice's recommendation, to his young grandsons, of perhaps the most perfectly salutary discourse on the duties and qualities proper to the republican gentleman.

The best example of the combination of modern and classical education that Marshall favored is his own *Life of George Washington*. Almost as often as it commends the toleration and commerce of the moderns, it eulogizes austere republican statesmen of the classical mold. Always be-

[36] Marshall to Story, July 31, 1833. Oster, *Doctrines*, p. 103. Marshall to Story, June 3, 1833. Massachusetts Historical Society, *Proceedings*, 2nd series, xiv (1900), 358. See also Marshall to Story, April 24, 1833. *Ibid.*, p. 356. Marshall to William Alexander Duer, March 17, 1834. Reprinted in W. Duer, *A Course of Lectures on the Constitutional Jurisprudence of the United States* (New York: Harper & Brothers, 1844), leaf preceding title page.

[37] Marshall to John Marshall, Jr., November (December) 7, 1834. Reprinted in *The Nation*, lxxii, No. 1858 (February 7, 1901), 111-12. Marshall to James Keith Marshall, March 11, 1835. Quoted by Sallie E. Marshall Hardy, "John Marshall," *The Green Bag*, viii, No. 12 (December 1896), 489. The concluding paragraph of Story's *Commentaries* begins, "If these Commentaries shall but inspire in the rising generation a more ardent love of their country, an unquenchable thirst for liberty, . . . then they will have accomplished all that their author ought to desire."

fore the reader's eyes is the towering Washington, who had "exhibited one pure undeviating course of virtuous exertion to promote [his country's] interests."[38]

There can be no doubt that Marshall intended his work as a kind of political and moral lesson for America. At least that much truth lies in Jefferson's resentful description of it as a "party diatribe." The Federalist administration's handling of the Whiskey Rebellion was said, as we have observed, to be of a kind "which statesmen can never safely disregard." The Farewell Address was printed in full because it "contains precepts to which the American statesman can not too frequently recur." Most interesting of all, the concluding examination of Washington's character will furnish, Marshall wrote, "a lesson well meriting the attention of those who are candidates for political fame." Marshall once advised his grandson that any citizen ought to be immersed in the history of his country. To Gouverneur Morris he professed his agreement with Baron Grimm that "the inferiority of modern to antient history" exists because the former, unlike the latter, "is not written by practical statesmen. How much is it to be regretted," Marshall went on, "that some one of those who has been engaged in the great & interesting events of our country & who has talents as well as leisure, will not devote a part of that leisure to the useful object of transmitting to posterity the knowledge he possesses." Without suggesting that Marshall's original ambitions reached to the Thucididean or Tacitean heights he indicates here, it seems that he himself wished to provide for the American citizenry an authoritative, statesmanlike, and convenient interpretation of their whole history.

---

[38] When in 1798 Washington urged Marshall to enter Congress, Marshall resisted "on the ground of my situation, & the necessity of attending to my pecuniary affairs." Marshall's account continues: "I can never forget the manner in which [Washington] treated this objection. He said there were crises in national affairs which made it the duty of a citizen to forego his private for the public interest. We were then in one of them. . . ." Marshall, *Autobiographical Sketch*, pp. 25-26.

His work began with the continent's very first settlement by its colonists and culminated in the achievements—and therefore the lessons—of Washington's years. Marshall did not stop with revising the work extensively for a less cumbersome and more popular second edition. He even abridged it for a school book. He drew back from the unremitting labor for which he so admired Story. Yet he devoted considerable time after his seventy-fifth year to the tedious condensation of a work with whose original imperfections he had already long suffered. Surely a complete explanation of this dedication must take into account a desire to impress the character of Washington, and the rest of the Washingtonian political creed, upon the country.[39]

Thus Marshall sought to mingle nobility with acquisitiveness. Still, a political teaching oriented to what is most common in men finds it difficult to provide for what is best in men. Marshall's jurisprudence pointed to a materialistic individualism which depreciated religion and nobility of character as at once unreliable and unrealistic, and which inevitably eroded the ties of family and patriotism. In the same speech in which Marshall extolled the "exalted char-

[39] In a letter prefatory to the school text, Horace Binney observed that "it is quite remarkable that the Chief Justice . . . should have given a portion of his busiest days to the preparation of an abridgment, in which he was not required to exercise, to any considerable extent, the powers of his remarkable understanding. The fact must be explained, I think, by his cordial attachment to the men and principles of the Revolution, by his conscientious approval of the measures of General Washington's administration, both as a system of public policy, and as an exposition of the Constitution,—and by his paternal solicitude for the youth of our country, upon whom he desired to impress his own feelings and convictions on all these subjects." Marshall, *The Life of George Washington, written for the Use of the Schools* (Philadelphia: Crissy, 1838). This edition went through some twenty re-issues, which bespeaks a certain success. James A. Servies, *A Bibliography of John Marshall*, p. 60. Marshall to John Marshall, Jr., Richmond, November (December) 7, 1834, *loc. cit.*; Marshall to Gouverneur Morris, October 3, 1816 (ALS, John Marshall Papers, Earl Gregg Swem Library, The College of William and Mary in Virginia). *The Life of George Washington*, II, 348, 396, 448.

acter of freemen," he paid tribute to "solid safety and real security" as the liberty which America provides its freemen. Marshall made the characteristically American call for the rare to serve the common, for excellence of character to secure most men's comfort and safety. But does a preeminent concern for comfort and safety encourage excellent character?

DEMOCRACY AND THE REPUBLIC: THE CONSTITUTION'S CHECKS

Whatever the difficulty of reconciling interest and virtue, Marshall's republicanism as a whole was threatened from another direction: democracy. Insofar as Marshall had lofty hopes for the American republic, they required elevated magistrates. It is no accident that of all national characters Marshall praised most the "high-minded," "proud and brave" England. That country was ruled by a mixed regime in which the few and the many shared power, but the few predominated and set the tone. Marshall's hopes, that is to say, pointed toward a republic with a sizable aristocratic admixture, or at least toward one not unqualifiedly democratic. The equality so loved by democrats neglected "that inequality which [is found] in human nature." It would be manifestly unjust if a "superior man" such as Washington were to enjoy merely the prerogatives befitting most men. He ought to have the "opulence," the leisure, the "expensive establishment," which his dignity as well as his public service demanded. Above all he ought to have the power and hence the honors of governing. Marshall looked askance at that egalitarianism which loudly proclaimed its unwillingness to honor Washington's saving statesmanship.[40] Both Marshall's mildly aristocratic preferences, and the liberal basis of his republicanism, dictated that the people's representatives consist of the more prudent and substantial few, and, furthermore, that discretion be left to the rulers and opportunity be left to private men of talents.

[40] Marshall, *The Life of George Washington*, ii, 445, 416-19, 220; Marshall, *An Autobiographical Sketch*, pp. 20-21.

This understanding of the relation between representatives and people did not come naturally to the American people. Marshall knew that as well as the framers. The Constitution's "balance" among the governmental branches cannot be understood, he thought, except as an effort to avoid certain democratic extremes which had arisen after independence.

Marshall believed society under the Articles to have been shaken largely by democratic impulses. These showed themselves even during the Revolution. The army's discipline had been vitiated, especially in the New England regiments, when a zealous egalitarianism resulted in the election of officers by the rank and file according to their "disposition to associate with them on the footing of equality." "In some instances, men were elected, who agreed to put their pay in a common stock with that of the soldiers, and divide equally with them." As the old colonial habits weakened, and economic distress widened, democracy became pervasive as well as bold. A "party" arose, in many states constituting "a decided majority of the people, and in all of them, . . . very powerful." "Viewing with extreme tenderness the case of the debtor," opposing "harsh measure[s] which the people would not bear," this movement wherever dominant produced "the emission of paper money, the delay of legal proceedings, and the suspension of the collection of taxes." Thus the productive system of trade and industry was jeopardized. "Instead of making the painful effort to obtain relief by industry and economy, many rested all their hopes on legislative interference." Some went even further, relying not on their representatives but on their force. "Unlicensed conventions . . . arrayed themselves against the legislatures," public sentiment derided lawyers and courts, and "tumultuous assemblages of people arrested the course of law, and restrained the judges from proceeding in execution of their duty." Characteristic of these var-

148

ious movements was the "levelling principle" of more or less extreme democracy.[41]

This shook Marshall's republicanism. He had been an enthusiast for political "self-government," so long as he believed that all the citizens would model their personal and political conduct on the Lockean individual. This belief had been undermined by events under the Articles, and there is no doubt that Marshall wondered, even then, whether "man is incapable of governing himself." A famous letter of 1787, alluding to Shays' rebellion in Massachusetts and to debtor politics throughout the nation, indicates his "fear," a passion here reflecting his deep devotion to the "most precious" liberty of republican self-government:

> These violent, I fear bloody, dissentions in a state I had thought inferior in wisdom and virtue to no one in the union, added to the strong tendency which the politics of many eminent characters among ourselves have to promote private and public dishonesty cast a deep shade over that bright prospect which the revolution in America and the establishment of our free governments had opened to the votaries of liberty throughout the globe. I fear, and there is no opinion more degrading to the dignity of man, that these have truth on their side who say that man is incapable of governing himself.[42]

Whatever Marshall's doubts under the Articles, they did not then ripen to a conviction that self-government was impossible. And indeed, the Constitution of which he became the great interpreter was an "experiment" designed to prove that possibility. The new government was to prune the public will, but its pruning, like that of a good gardener upon his plants, was but the removal of excesses which kept

[41] Marshall, *The Life of George Washington*, II, 117, 118, 31, 101-02; see generally 75-128, esp. 106-09, 117-22.
[42] Letter from Marshall to James Wilkinson, January 5, 1787. *American Historical Review*, XII (January 1907), 347-48.

the populace from obtaining those long-run interests which it was supposed to want. The Constitution included means to change in degree, but not in kind, the people's strivings. Under the Articles, Marshall remarked, such contests as those between debtors and creditors had become "the more animated, because, in the state governments generally, no principle had been introduced which could resist the wild projects of the moment, give the people time to reflect, and allow the basic good sense of the people time for exercise." The Constitution was to provide that "principle." By popular means it checked popular excess; it sought "the incorporation," as Marshall phrased it, almost certainly following *The Federalist*, "of some principles into the political system, which might correct the obvious vices, without endangering the free spirit of the existing institutions."[43]

In Marshall's supposition that an essentially sound popular will need only be trimmed of secondary excesses we find the explanation of an otherwise puzzling fact: his description of the Constitution as "democratic." The Constitution's supporters, he remarked during the Virginia Ratifying Convention, "idolized democracy." This might well be thought no more than oratorical flim-flam, or a transcriber's error, were it not that Marshall himself later recalled that his views until after the 1790's were tinctured with "wild and enthusiastic democracy."[44] What reconciles Marshall's early "democracy" with his Lockean persuasion is the

[43] Marshall, *The Life of George Washington*, II, 105, 103. *The Federalist*, X, puts the Constitution's purpose this way: "To secure the public good and private rights against the danger of such a [majority] faction, and at the same time to preserve the spirit and the form of popular government, is then the great object to which our inquiries are directed."

[44] Marshall, *An Autobiographical Sketch*, pp. 9, 13; Elliot, *Debates*, III, 222. Consider also Marshall's actions with respect to the Disputed Elections Bill, recounted by Beveridge in his *Life of John Marshall*, II, 452-56. "He is disposed . . . to express great respect for the sovereign people, and to quote their opinions as evidence of truth," grumbled the Federalist Speaker of the House after Marshall's brief tour as national legislator. *Ibid.*, p. 483.

belief that the people as prodded mildly by the Constitution would confine themselves willingly to their proper interests and place. A Lockean conception of their interests and place was never absent. When as a young delegate he insisted that the Constitution's supporters "idolized democracy," he had in mind what he called in the same speech the Constitution's "well-regulated democracy." The regulations were maxims "necessary in any government, but more essential to a democracy than to any other." The precept he particularly mentions might be taken to imply vaguely the whole of Marshall's political prescription: "a strict observance of justice and public faith, and a steady adherence to virtue."[45]

He understood the Constitution's checks as two-fold, legal and political. The "legal" means—a written constitution authoritatively enforced by a Supreme Court free of direct popular pressure—occasioned the great endeavors of Marshall's life and will be discussed in a separate chapter. The "political" measures provided for a sifting of the popular will through representation and, more important, through "balanced government." These comprise two of the three political remedies foreseen by the far more comprehensive reflections of Madison and Hamilton in *The Federalist*. There is no particular mention by Marshall of the republic's large and diverse area, encompassing so many interests that no majority faction could agree on any project inimical to private rights or to the public interest.

We have already observed Marshall's wish that the people's desires might be refined by representation. He might well have thought that the Constitution's establishment afforded a happy portent of what was to come.

The Philadelphia Convention, he later said, was composed of "illustrious statesmen and patriots," and the ratifying assemblies were also made up in good part "of talents and character." It seems, moreover, that Marshall found his hopes realized when Washington's new govern-

[45] Elliot, *Debates*, III, 222, 223. Cf. Marshall, *An Autobiographical Sketch*, p. 10.

ment first met. "In the legislative, as well as in the executive and judicial departments, great respectability of character was also associated with an eminent degree of talents. . . . In both branches of the legislative, men were found who possessed the fairest claims to the public confidence."[46]

Aware, however, that under the Articles the people had misplaced their confidence, Marshall relied also upon a "balancing" of the governing departments. So far as can be known, his reflections follow those dominant in the Constitutional Convention and in *The Federalist* as well. Senate and President were by their character and their powers to check the more democratic House. Like Madison in *Federalist* LXIII, Marshall seems to have understood the upper house as "an anchor against popular fluctuations," and hence as counterweight to what he distinguishes as the "popular branch of the legislature," the House of Representatives. More essential to "balanced government" than the Senate, however, was the President. The chief executive was entrusted with some of the most important interests, including the maintenance of domestic peace and national security. With that office, moreover, rested authority for "well digested plans," especially in fiscal matters, which could direct to proper channels the energies of the people. The President, possessed of great authority and disposed to act with pervasive "vigor," was to form the decisive political check upon the populace's "passion" and "prejudices." Marshall's summation of Washington as chief executive bears quotation:

> Respecting, as the first magistrate in a free government must ever do, the real and deliberate sentiments of the people, their gusts of passion passed over, without ruffling the smooth surface of his mind. Trusting to the reflecting good sense of the nation for approbation and support, he had the magnanimity to pursue its real interests,

[46] Marshall, *The Life of George Washington*, II, 170; cf. 167-71; Elliot, *Debates*, II, 230-31. *Gibbons* v. *Ogden*, 9 Wheaton (U.S.), 202 (1824).

in opposition to its temporary prejudices; and, though far from being regardless of popular favor, he could never stoop to retain, by deserving to lose it.[47]

In his account of Washington's Presidency, Marshall praises incessantly a particular virtue: "firmness of resolution." It seems that the American President's exposed position atop a predominantly democratic order requires a rare strength of character in order that the people's interests, rather than their whims, be served. It was Washington's "invincible fortitude," displayed in standing up to pressure on domestic and foreign issues alike, that Marshall distinguished as the trait "fitt[ing] him in a peculiar manner for occupying the high place he filled in the United States in the critical times in which he filled it."

No feature in his character was more conspicuous than his firmness. Though prizing popular favour as highly as it ought be prized, he never yielded principle to obtain it, or sacrificed his judgment on its altar. This firmness of character added to his acknowledged virtue enabled him to stem a torrent which would have overwhelmed almost any other man, and did, I believe, save his country.[48]

Perhaps one may see in Marshall's remarks the traits peculiarly required, in a democratic land, of the modern and enlightened "prince" or "legislator." He is, according to such a seminal modern republican as Machiavelli, that great man who not only founds a political order but chooses to organize a free and republican system based upon the common passions, a system which henceforth, perhaps, will not require such great men. Washington supported the

[47] Marshall, *The Life of George Washington*, II, 446-47, 215, 167-68. Marshall discusses at length the dispute over Hamilton's powers vis-à-vis the legislature, 162-65, 178ff., 199ff., 203.

[48] Marshall to Timothy Pickering, March 15, 1827. Massachusetts Historical Society, *Proceedings*, XIV (November 1900), 322-23; cf. *The Life of George Washington*, II, 447.

Americans as they obtained their independence. He presided over the Convention by which they made of themselves a nation. And then, he so administered "the affairs of the Union, that a government standing entirely on the public favour, which had with infinite difficulty been adopted, and against which the most inveterate prejudices had been excited, should conciliate public opinion, and acquire a firmness and stability that would enable it to resist the rude shocks it was destined to sustain."[49]

DEMOCRACY AND THE REPUBLIC: THE PEOPLE'S POWER

The Washingtonian founding and settling of the new system proved all-important, because, as Marshall saw it, the Constitution's "political checks" turned out to be largely ephemeral, the subsequent "shocks" rude indeed. The difficulty was simple and obvious: the people refused to play the more or less deferential role for which they had been cast by Marshall, Washington, and many others who came to be called "Federalists." Any illusions as to a Lockean populace content to entrust sovereignty to its representative government were torn away by the insistent pressure of democratic demand. Marshall characterized the "extraordinary . . . sentiments" which came to be avowed by some (including Jefferson):

> . . . the people alone were the basis of government. All powers being derived from them, might, by them, be withdrawn at pleasure. They alone were the authors of the law, and to them alone, must the ultimate decision on the interpretation belong. From these delicate and popular truths, it was inferred, that the doctrine that the sovereignty of the nation resided in the departments of government was incompatible with the principles of liberty. . . .[50]

[49] "Original Preface," reprinted in *A history of the colonies* . . . , p. x.

[50] Marshall, *The Life of George Washington*, II, 281-82. Compare his remarks on France, *ibid.*, p. 250.

The mounting popular pressure upon even Washington's administration is a theme second only to the hero himself in Marshall's concluding volume. With an unwilling fascination the author portrays a developing "torrent of public opinion" capable of overruling all reason, "the physical force of [the] nation . . . usurp[ing] the place of its wisdom." There was a tide of pressures, meetings, speeches, and hasty expressions on even such a complicated matter as the Jay treaty, upon which, the moderate Federalist Marshall sadly remarked, the prudent judgment of "a statesman would need deep reflection in the quiet of his closet, aided by considerable inquiry." This "fervour of democracy" attacked hereditary arrangements of the Cincinnati, an organization of officers who had fought in the Revolution, as "an institution from which a race of nobles was expected to spring." It condemned Washington's weekly hour for receiving casual callers as smacking of the "levee days" of monarchy. It did not expend itself, however, by indulging these egalitarian effulgences. The popular movement threatened to overthrow representation itself, with violent expressions of public opinion, with resentment of secrecy in governmental proceedings, and especially with the organization of democratic societies devoted in good part to the French version of liberty, equality, and fraternity. "The manner in which that attention to the conduct of those invested with power which is essential to balanced governments, may safely be employed," Marshall remarked ponderously, "had been so misconceived, that temporary and detached clubs of citizens had occasionally been formed in different parts of the United States, for the avowed purpose of watching the conduct of their rulers."[51]

Still, representative government persisted, and the people's direct influence on government was perhaps not so great as their indirect control through the suffrage. Much to Marshall's chagrin, representatives reflected the popular

[51] *Ibid.*, ɪɪ, 269, 73, 144-46, 322, 324, 365, 447; see also 117, 171, 249-50, 256, 273-74, 281-82, 329-30, 345, 349, 353, 401-02.

temper. Increasingly the public selected men of its own stripe. It did elect Washington and even "universally" loved him, as Marshall wrote to Henry Lee. And only after the French Revolution "maddened the world" and strengthened the most radically democratic elements in the community, was that love impaired. Nevertheless, it was impaired. If the people were misled to a degree in the case of Washington, they hardly could be expected to judge accurately of others. The many incline to choose those who fit the common notion of character, judgment, and ability. "In a popular government," Marshall weighed developments in the years from 1789 to 1796, "the representatives of the people may generally be considered as a mirror, reflecting truly the passions and feelings which govern their constituents."[52]

The growth of political parties aggravated the Americans' tendency to depreciate those of statesmanlike talents. Are not the parties characteristic of modern liberal democracies essentially means by which powerful governments are rendered "responsible," that is, largely serviceable to the wants, if not the mandate, of the upper or lower parts of the dominant middle class? Of this Marshall could scarcely approve. He saw candidates chosen and elected not according to their judgment and respectability of character, but to

[52] *Ibid.*, II, 293; Letter from Marshall to Story, October 6, 1834, printed in Oster, *Doctrines*, p. 105; Marshall to Henry Lee, September 21, 1833, MS. (transcript) New York Public Library.

Martin Van Buren's not wholly accurate account of Hamilton's growing disappointment, during the late 1790's, illuminates the Federalists' problem. "[The Jeffersonian victory of 1800] presented to his mind, under circumstances the most impressive, a truth which he had overlooked in the eagerness of his pursuit after power, viz., that the people were enabled by the popular provisions of the Constitution in respect to the executive and legislative departments, to break down the greater part of such structures as those which he had reared, by dismissing from their places those who had assisted in their construction, and substituting others, who, knowing their wishes, would feel it their interest to respect them. . . ." Martin Van Buren, *Inquiry into the Origin and Course of Political Parties in the United States* (New York: Hurd and Houghton, 1867), p. 277.

their political views, their "platform." They had to fight and win under a party banner. Deference to character was on its way out. Marshall's views can be seen in his description of the election of himself, and several other supporters of the Constitution, to the Virginia Ratifying Convention. "Parties," he recounted to Justice Story many years later, "had not yet become so bitter as to extinguish the private affections. A great majority of the people of Virginia was anti-federal; but in several of the counties most opposed . . . , individuals of high character and great influence came forward as candidates and were elected from personal motives."[53]

Parties not only conveyed the people's views wholesale to their representatives; they also transmitted to the people struggles among leaders. Marshall was forcibly struck by the way a new breed of ambitious politicians, using the press and shrewd organization, managed to arouse the public prejudices and passions as well as to reflect them. "In popular governments, the resentments, the suspicions, and the disgusts, produced in the legislature by warm debate, and the chagrin of defeat; by the desire of gaining, or the fear of losing power; and which are created by personal views among the leaders of parties, will infallibly extend to the body of the nation." Like many others of his generation, Republican and Federalist alike, Marshall felt keenly the coarsening of political life which the new politics was to bring.[54]

[53] Marshall, *An Autobiographical Sketch*, pp. 10-11. See also the way in which he was elected, almost drafted, for the state legislature on two occasions. *Ibid.*, pp. 12, 15-16. See *The Life of George Washington*, II, 233, 267, 329. The Federalists' supposition of a "habit of deference" is dwelled upon by David Hackett Fischer, in Chapter I of *The Revolution of American Conservatism* (New York: Harper & Row, 1965).

[54] "Not only will those causes of dissatisfaction be urged which really operate on the minds of intelligent men, but every instrument will be seized which can effect the purpose, and the passions will be inflamed by whatever may serve to irritate them. Among the multiplied evils generated by faction, it is perhaps not the least, that it has a tendency to abolish all distinction between virtue and vice; and to

It was then inevitable, as Marshall portrayed the times in his *Life of Washington*, that the balances built into the new government should weaken as the character of its branches became more democratic. During Washington's last term the Senate itself was falling away from the Federalist party's control; the influence of the admittedly more popular House increased correspondingly. Even the executive was threatened. While Washington managed to appoint men of rare caliber to the various departments, they were in good part driven out by the steady pressures of envy, suspicion, and partisan animosity, which rendered public office a place of continual abuse and paltry reward. Men of the stamp that Marshall admired would not or could not retain office under such conditions. "It is the principal misfortune of our country," the Federalist H. G. Otis wrote with some truth to R. G. Harper in 1807, "that all avenues to great and liberal and patriotic objects are shut against the noble and high minded; and that the ardour and genius which were naturally to sway the affairs of state, are forced into a competition with mercantile and landjobbing projectors."[55]

Washington did manage to use the President's powers to "conciliate public opinion" toward the new government. Washington was, however, an exceptional President. Only his remarkable fortitude "enabled him to stem a torrent which would have overwhelmed almost any other man." And even during his terms it was doubtful whether the Chief Executive could oppose for any sustained period the onslaughts of popular desires. "In a government like that

---

prostrate those barriers which the wise and the good have erected for the protection of morals, and which are defended solely by opinion. The victory of the party becomes the great object; and, too often, all measures are deemed right or wrong, as they tend to promote or impede it." Marshall, *The Life of George Washington*, II, 348-49; cf. 378. Marshall thought the press a *sine qua non* of partisan warfare, of the mutual relation of party and populace. *Ibid.*, II, 233, 267, 329.

[55] Letter of 19 April, 1807. Printed in Samuel Eliot Morison, *The Life and Letters of Harrison Gray Otis* (Boston and New York: Houghton Mifflin Company, 1913), I, 283.

of the United States," Marshall wrote with respect to Washington's struggle to preserve American neutrality, "no firmness on the part of the chief magistrate can long resist the current of popular opinion."[56]

It was Marshall's awakening to the power and direction of the "current of public opinion" that caused him to change his mind about democracy. He kept his view of the people's interests, but, in his later years, he ceased to believe that the populace would, under light reins, voluntarily choose in its best interests. The "fears" and "doubts" about men's abilities to govern themselves, which had arisen under the Articles, had been transformed into certainties during and after Washington's administration. And the last volume of his *Life of Washington* is Marshall's record of what occasioned that transformation. It is only then that the Constitution's "balanced republic" is said to differ from "a democracy" as "order" differs from "chaos," and only much later that Marshall characterized his early beliefs in democracy as "wild and enthusiastic." Following the Constitution's framers, Marshall had desired "the incorporation of some principles into the political system, which might correct the obvious vices, without endangering the free spirit of the existing institutions." He no less than the framers might have reflected on Hamilton's speech in the Philadelphia Convention itself, a critique best summed up in Hamilton's own notes:

> Gentlemen say we need to be rescued from the democracy. But what the means proposed?
>
> A democratic assembly is to be checked by a democratic senate, and both these by a democratic chief magistrate.[57]

[56] Marshall, *The Life of George Washington*, ii, 296.

[57] Max Farrand, *The Records of the Federal Convention of 1787* (New Haven: Yale University Press, 1911), i, 310. Cf. other remarks from Madison's report of Hamilton's speech. "The members most tenacious of republicanism, he observed, were as loud as any in declaiming agst the vices of democracy." "Gentlemen differ in their opinions concerning the necessary checks, from the different estimates

In light of Marshall's reversal of judgment, it is worth inquiring why his early opinions were in a sense "democratic," or, why he failed then to consider the need for vesting in the few and wealthy a political power independent of the people generally. So far as his surviving writings indicate, this failure lasted all his life. He wrote nothing that resembles Hamilton's eulogy of the House of Lords as "a most noble institution" forming a "permanent barrier agst every pernicious innovation." Marshall did refer in the *Life* to John Adams' conviction that "balance in government" requires "distinct orders in society" distinctly represented, but he himself never explicated such a view.[58]

The Chief Justice's silence in his later years may be at-

---

they form of the human passions. They suppose seven years a sufficient period to give the senate an adequate firmness, from not duly considering the amazing violence & turbulence of the democratic spirit. When a great object of Gov't is pursued, which seizes the popular passions, they spread like wild fire, and become irresistible." I, 289.

By 1801, reports David Hackett Fischer, Fisher Ames had joined Hamilton in condemning the essential democracy of the Federalists' republicanism. "We have thought that virtue, with so many bright rewards, had some solid power; and that, with ten thousand charms, she could always command a hundred thousand votes. Alas! These illusions are as thin as the gloss on other bubbles." Ames, "No Revolutionist," Nov. 1801, *Works*, II, 205. "We are democrats; we pretend to be republicans. Experience will punish and teach." Ames to Theodore Dwight, Oct. 20, 1799, *Works*, I, 260. "Indeed it is notorious, that there was scarcely an advocate for the federal Constitution who was not anxious, from the first, to hazard the experiment of an unprecedented, and almost unqualified proportion of democracy, both in constructing and administering the government, and who did not rely with confidence, if not blind presumption, on its success. This is certain, the body of the federalists were always, and yet are, essentially democratic in their political notions." "The Dangers of American Liberty," 1805, *Works*, II, 348. All quoted by Fischer, *Revolution of American Conservatism*, pp. 20-21.

A searching examination of the framers' essential democracy is Martin Diamond's article, "Democracy and the *Federalist*: Reconsideration of the Framers' Intent," *American Political Science Review*, Vol. 53 (March 1959), pp. 53-68.

[58] Marshall, *The Life of George Washington*, II, 253.

tributed in part, no doubt, to the well-known caution of his pen and tongue. He was always the prudent politician, not least where the vastly democratic resentments of privilege were involved. By deed if not by speech Marshall surely devoted himself to that peculiar "combination of democracy and aristocracy" which C. S. Sydnor has shown to be the nurturing condition of Virginia's gentlemen statesmen. A somewhat aristocratic gentry of 300 or 400 families did manage to govern Virginia with the freemen's consent or, at least, acquiescence. The key to its rule was a self-perpetuating County Court system which Marshall greatly admired and vigorously defended.[59]

Still, these later deeds do not account for the avowedly democratic opinions of his earlier years. Nor do they fully explain the remarkable silence as to aristocratic and oligarchic institutions of his private letters no less than his published works.

It seems, to begin with, that Marshall's early experience led him to suppose that the republicanism he desired was perfectly compatible with the democracy he avowed. The sanguine years before and just after the Revolution led many sober men to this view. Colonial institutions had been popular in part, yet also tempered by aristocratic power sustained by British rule. It is noteworthy, however, that in Marshall's *History of the colonies* . . . he never diagnosed the colonial polities as a mixture of regimes in this

[59] "The county courts nominate to the Governor fit persons to fill vacancies as they arise, and he commissions them. This mode of self perpetuation has been a good deal censured, but we think its practical operation better than any other mode which has been devised. The most respectable men of the several counties are generally in the commission. Our Justices receive no fees. They have no compensation except the shrievalty which they take in succession, each Justice holding the office for two consecutive years." Letter from Marshall to Thomas W. Griffith, February 7, [18]30 (ALS, Maryland Historical Society). Sydnor, *American Revolutionaries in the Making*, Chaps. 6 and 8. See also Part three, Section 3, "The Whig Republic in Virginia," in J. R. Pole, *Political Representation in England and the Origins of the American Republic* (London: Macmillan, 1967).

sense. He did remark that "the institutions received from England were admirably calculated to prepare the way for temperate and rational republics." Throughout the work, however, that preparation was equated with only the colonists' practical experience in working free, that is, representative, arrangements. "The solid foundations of a popular government were already laid in all the colonies," he remarked at one point. "Every authority had been derived either from the people or the king. The crown being no longer acknowledged, the people remained the only source of legitimate power."[60] Whatever its benefits, practical experience alone could hardly assure the "temperate and rational" republic that he wished, as opposed to the democracy he feared. Experience may be ignored and habits thrown off as the class favoring these habits loses power. It seems, then, that Marshall took for granted the "British background of a class society," as Sydnor calls it, or what David Hackett Fischer calls "the deferential spirit of eighteenth-century Anglo-American society, in which the 'multitude' were trained from birth to 'submit to that subordination necessary in the free'est states' and the 'natural rulers of society' were accustomed to expect it." In colonial times the gentry had managed, through governors and governors' councils, not to mention the devious ways that the few must always use, to secure somewhat more than a veneer of aristocratic power in the colonies and especially in Virginia. With the shaking of foreign rule, however, there had come to light democratic tendencies which were not so "temperate and rational," tendencies which could not be checked even by the Constitution's elaborate mechanics. The democratic republic which Marshall helped erect took for granted the aristocratic arrangements which democracy, goaded on by more democratic liberals such as Jefferson, was even then eating away. Indeed, Marshall learned

[60] Marshall, *The Life of George Washington*, I, 78. See Marshall, *A history of the colonies* . . . , pp. 21, 48, 57-58, 63, 66, 68, 77, 79, 82, 85, 86, 121, 204, 318, 362, 413, 459; cf. 465.

from experience.[61] But the teachings of experience came, as is usually the case, too late.

One might go on to wonder why Marshall didn't anticipate the power and character of the democracy in America. Why, in particular, did not his reading help him to see through what was essentially a transitional time, even a revolutionary time however peaceably the domestic revolution was carried out? The answer is quite simple and brings

[61] From the vantage point of later years, Marshall ironically commented upon the early Americans' distrust of the English constitution as dangerous to a free people's morals. "The intercourse of America with the world, and her own experience, had not then been sufficient to teach her the important truth, that the many, as often as the few, can abuse power, and trample on the weak, without perceiving that they are tyrants; that they too, not unfrequently, close their eyes against the light; and shut their ears against the plainest evidence, and the most conclusive reasoning." *Ibid.*, I, 77. By 1812 Marshall could write to Randolph of Roanoke about his fears for the survival of "real genuine liberty" in the face of the democrats' clamor for liberty. "I know very little of what is passing—much less of what is in reserve for us—but the caution incident to age approaches timidity and I cannot help fearing that real genuine liberty has as much to apprehend from its clamorous votaries as from quarters that are more suspected. In popular government it is, I fear, possible for a majority to exercise power tyrannically." Marshall to John Randolph, June 18, 1812 (ALS, Harvard University Library). "If those who become citizens, and, of course, partakers of the government of their country," he wrote to William Gaston in 1832 while praising an address, "would act upon the principles you recommend, a republic would indeed be the utopia which enthusiasm has painted, but which experience has too often shown to be so coloured by the hand of the artist as scarcely to resemble the original." Marshall to Gaston, July 22, 1832 (ALS, courtesy of the Library of the University of North Carolina).

Because the colonial aristocrats were associated in Virginia with the "crown and its creatures," wrote Jefferson to Adams, "they were unpopular; and that unpopularity continues attached to their names. A Randolph, a Carter, or a Burwell must have great personal superiority over a common competitor to be elected by the people, even at this day.

"At the first session of our legislature after the Declaration of Independence, we passed a law abolishing entails. And this was followed by one abolishing the privilege of Primogeniture, and dividing

us back to our beginning. The "climate of opinion" and the books he read confirmed, rather than contradicted, his tendency to place his political confidence in the mass of men, inevitably then in the many rather than the few. The books, for example, were not concerned to nurture an aristocratic class, to put it mildly. Barely second to Christianity as the object of the attacks of Machiavelli, Locke, even Montesquieu, were the ethics and politics of aristocracy. Even in Machiavelli, who saw well the power of the outstanding man to found and destroy, there is a strong republican tendency attuned to the wants of most men. The tendency is more obvious in Locke. "There are few men of knowledge or learning," wrote David Hume, "or at least few philosophers since Mr. Locke wrote, who would not be ashamed to be thought of that [Tory or anti-republican] party. . . . [Even] the Tories have been so long obliged to talk in the republican style, that they seem to have made converts of themselves by their hypocrisy, and to have embraced the sentiments as well as language of their adversaries." What was true in Britain was by the time of the Revolution true in America, joined to the mother country in what has been well called "a great republic of Whig ideas." Marshall's own analysis of colonial institutions, according to their representative character with the people "the only source of legitimate power," is couched in Whiggish idiom. The public face of Locke's vastly influential *Second Treatise* was popular, dwelling not on the need for excellence in those ruling, but on the need for consent to rule. Locke's

---

the lands of intestates equally among all their children, or other representatives. These laws, drawn by myself, laid the axe to the root of Pseudo-aristocracy."

"You surprise me," he remarked to Adams in a later letter, "with the account you give of the strength of family distinction still existing in your state. With us it is so totally extinguished that not a spark of it is to be found but lurking in the hearts of some of our old tories." Jefferson to Adams, October 28, 1813; January 24, 1814. *The Adams-Jefferson Letters*, Lester J. Cappon, ed. (Chapel Hill: University of North Carolina Press, 1959), pp. 389, 424.

doctrine was what Marshall had called Washington's republicanism, "a speculation" counseling "equal political rights." Although not simply democratic, liberal jurisprudence was closer in its prescriptions to what most men want, than to the honorable temper of a Washington. Perhaps, then, it was a combination of Marshall's experience and the liberal intellectual temper of his time that rendered him, as well as his friends, unprepared for the majority's turbulent and leveling strength of will.[62]

THE POLITICAL TRIUMPH OF DEMOCRACY

Facing the breakdown of the representative and balanced Washingtonian republic, and not being himself so aristo-

[62] In letters quoted by Marshall, Washington and his correspondents at the time of Shays' rebellion repeatedly use the imagery of a wondrous awakening. "When I reflect upon the present aspect of our affairs, it seems to me like the visions of a dream," wrote Washington. "My mind can scarcely realize it as a thing in actual existence:—so strange, so wonderful does it appear to me." "In a word, I am lost in amazement. . . ." "This dreadful situation has alarmed every man of principle and property in New England," General Knox reported. "They start as if from a dream, and ask—what has been the cause of our delusion?" *Ibid.*, II, 224-27.

Consider Carl Bridenbaugh's comment: "To [the Chesapeake gentlemen] political and religious liberalism seemed indeed to stem directly from the law of Nature and Nature's God; to attain this liberalism they fearlessly changed from monarchical to republican principles (with their democratic implications for the future), and devoted all their political, oratorical and military wisdom and talents." *Myths and Realities, Societies of the Colonial South* (New York: Atheneum, 1963), pp. 52-53.

Again that old crustacean Fisher Ames perceived, in his rambunctious way, much that was true about his fellow Federalists: "Our good men *feel* better toward the government than they talk or reason. They really believe seven-eighths of the democratic lying theories invented and propagated to subvert all government." Ames to Gore, Nov. 10, 1799, *Works*, I, 266, as quoted by David Hackett Fischer, *The Revolution of American Conservatism*, p. 20. The remark quoted from Hume appears in *Essays Moral, Political and Literary*, p. 73. See also pp. 400-02.

cratic as to find the new order simply intolerable, the liberal Marshall tried to moderate the effects of democracy. He despised the sharp, partisan struggles for popular favor which began to characterize office-seeking. Yet he allowed himself to be prodded by Washington into active political life. He led for a term the Southern Federalists in the House of Representatives, and then he served as Adams' Secretary of State before his appointment to the Supreme Court. Occasionally his attention would be turned to his native Virginia. We have observed his struggle, in the Constitutional Convention of 1829-30, to retain freehold suffrage and the County Court system. From his election to the House in 1798, however, Marshall's major role was on the national stage.

Before elevation to the Court, his political fortunes and activities were bound up with those of the Federalist party. To understand Marshall's politics, however, one must follow such contemporaries as John Quincy Adams and Joseph Story in calling him a "federalist of the Washington School," rather than of the Hamiltonian. Marshall's respect for the powerful Treasury Secretary was very great. Yet there is no sign that it ever approached the high regard he had for Washington—"the greatest man in the world"—and his opinions and temper differed from Hamilton's in important if rarely recognized ways. Marshall shared Washington's popular republicanism. It is doubtful, as we have noted, whether he ever fully embraced the more oligarchic or aristocratic mixed regime advocated by Hamilton at the Constitutional Convention. Marshall, moreover, was a stickler for proper legal procedures, while Hamilton's temper was of a bolder cast. We have seen that the Chief Justice rejected Hamilton's ingenious evasion of the Constitution's enumeration of powers. Beveridge concluded that Marshall's constitutional scrupulosity had much to do with blocking the partisan Disputed Elections Bill, put forward by the Federalists during their moment of peril in 1800. And Marshall would never have gone behind Washington's back as Hamilton did, carrying on what Julian Boyd calls a "bold" and progressively more "devious" correspondence with a British intelligence agent, to promote a pro-British foreign policy. One might say that Marshall's liberalism was accompanied, on the one hand, by a conventionally American republicanism, and, on the other, by an almost unswerving Ciceronian respect for the moderate maxims of the decent gentleman. Hamilton was both a stronger and a more erratic man. If not a Caesar, he was an impatient, almost imperially ambitious man who had learned perhaps too well that grand designs, although they be national and not merely personal, require questionable means. Perhaps Marshall's very qualities as party leader in a democracy sum up his differences from the passionate, shrewd, powerfully articulate and marvelously energetic Hamilton. Only as Chief Justice could Marshall's talents have been fully displayed. As a party man he was too judicious and moderate; as a democratic orator he was too ponderous, deductive, and exhaustive; as an organizer he would probably have been neither aggressive nor sufficiently attentive to tedious detail. His statesmanlike and independent temper is shown by his failure to back even such Federalist measures as the Alien and Sedition Acts and, as we have mentioned, the Disputed Elections Bill.[63] Contrary to the Hamiltonian Federalists, he approved President Adams' peaceful overtures in 1799 to a chastened France.

Whatever Marshall's distaste for parties and their strife, he surely believed, in the increasingly democratic circumstances of America, that the Federalist party was a necessary means of obtaining popular support for the Constitution's republic. In considering the development of parties, he would have agreed with the modern historian Joseph Charles, who finds their emergence only well after the Constitution's ratifi-

[63] Beveridge, *Life of John Marshall*, II, 452-56; *Marbury v. Madison*, 1 Cranch (U.S.), 178 (1803). Clinton Rossiter, *Alexander Hamilton and the Constitution* (New York: Harcourt, Brace & World, 1964), p. 192; cf. pp. 240-42. Julian P. Boyd, *Number 7* (Princeton: Princeton University Press, 1964), pp. 3-85, esp. 29-31, 47.

cation, although Marshall would pinpoint Hamilton's financial program rather than Jay's treaty as the decisive event. Yet Marshall would have seen the event less as a cause than as an occasion. If the Federalists and Republicans only divided after several years of harmony beneath Washington's imposing leadership, their split merely made explicit a division which had existed close to the surface since the government's beginning. Before, during, and after ratification, Marshall found in every state "two great parties," parties which eventually ripened into Republicans and Federalists. Marshall called them "creditor" and "debtor" parties, or friends of "strong government" and "those who marked out a more indulgent course," names which indicate the distinctive commercial flavor of his politics. The Federalists had favored strict enforcement of contractual "faith as a sacred pledge," alleviation of distress by personal industry, strong administration of justice and vigorous taxation, and, "by a natural association of ideas," a strong national government. On the whole, this party tended to favor the Constitution, since "particular provisions in the constitution . . . were especially designed to counteract those views and interests" by which the opposing party was guided. Those who came to make up the Republican party were joined in different opinions. They "viewed with extreme tenderness the case of the debtor" and thus favored lax enforcement of contracts, issuance of paper money, and suspension of taxes. They generally opposed the Constitution, preferring that power be mixed with leniency as it was in the states. This debtor party was temporarily acquiescent as Washington succeeded in winning rapidly the people's affection and respect. It was rejuvenated, Marshall believed, in the struggle to defend people and states against the power and wealth coming to creditors and the federal government through Hamilton's financial program. With the *Report on Public Credit* and the assumption and funding of the war debt, provision for internal taxation, and the chartering of the first national bank, "the first regular and systematic opposition to the principles" of Washington's administration began. The bill to incorporate the bank contributed especially to the "complete organization of those distinct and visible parties, which, in their long and dubious conflict for power, have since shaken the United States to their centre."[64]

The momentous division in Congress spread to the country as the populace generally was roused by attacks on the centralizing, "monarchical," "oligarchical" tendencies of the administration. The partisan strife in Congress and country alike was then "exasperated" by the French Revolution. The establishment of a French Republic upon the old monarchy's ruins simply "maddened" the American democracy, Marshall remarked, and any doubts by the "few" as to the French people's readiness, for even an "unbalanced republic," were deemed "unpardonable heresies." Henceforth Washington's endeavor at a foreign policy essentially neutral between France and Britain only exacerbated divisions between increasingly Hamiltonian Federalists and increasingly Jeffersonian Republicans. Madison's "memorable resolutions" of January 4, 1794, managed to drive a wedge into the very heart of these domestic-cum-foreign struggles. Marshall recounted at length the progress of congressional argument, and the far more significant growth of an "irritable" popular antagonism toward England and toward an administration suspected of trafficking with the insolent and "monarchical" English.[65] The latter development culminated in the tremendous uproar over Jay's unfortunate treaty.

[64] Marshall, *The Life of George Washington*, II, 206-07, 103, 126, 181; cf. 181-92, 199-207, 212-13, 329-30. Jefferson thought that the two parties reflected the ancient distinction between the "few" and the "many." Jefferson to Adams, June 27, 1813. Lester J. Cappon, ed., *The Adams-Jefferson Letters*, II, 337.

[65] *Ibid.*, II, 299-314; cf. 227-32, 249, 419-20, 426-29, 250ff., 260, 267, 284. Cf. on Madison's Resolutions, Joseph Charles, *The American Party System* (Williamsburg: Institute of Early American History and Culture, 1956), pp. 97-103.

As Marshall told it in his *Life of George Washington*, the Federalists were doomed to defeat. The debtors had been the "more numerous and more powerful" party even under the Articles of Confederation. Ratification of the Constitution itself had been obtained only with "infinite difficulty." The majority in its favor was so small in many states as to indicate that, "had the influence of character been removed, the intrinsic merits of the instrument would not have secured its adoption." Only the combined effect of the breakdown in trade and Shays' rebellion allowed the Constitution to be proposed, and only a general "dread of dismemberment," rather than favor of the "particular system" proposed, permitted it to be passed. There was required, Marshall remarked,

> a concurrence of extrinsic circumstances to force on minds unwilling to receive the demonstration, a conviction of the necessity of an effective national government, and to give even a temporary ascendancy to that party which had long foreseen and deplored the crisis to which the affairs of the United States were hastening.[66]

The Federalists and even the Constitution itself were almost a foreign body in America's vast popular medium just emerging from the mildly aristocratic (for the most part) colonial regime. By Washington's second term the Republican party had won the House of Representatives. It was clear that the President's reputation would not sustain the Federalists much longer. The greatest caution was required, for one unpopular act might unleash the flood.

Marshall himself was prudent enough. Indeed, his conduct of the XYZ negotiations in 1798-99, with his fellow emissaries Charles C. Pinckney and Elbridge Gerry, rejuvenated the Federalists. To Marshall the credit is largely due for shepherding the mission through the most tortuous and demeaning intrigues with agents who came to be called X, Y, and Z, as the Directory, or at least Talleyrand, refused

[66] *Ibid.*, II, 77, 103, 127; *A history of the colonies* . . . , p. x.

even to negotiate without an enormous bribe. Yet Marshall managed to turn to account the mass of "open contumely, and undisguised insult," the envoys endured. He stayed not to test France further, but to make her duplicity apparent to a population at home infatuated with France. The ministers' "passiveness must search for its apology," Marshall was later to write, "in their solicitude to demonstrate to the American people the real views of the French republic. . . ." In this the envoys were successful. With publication of their despatches, "a spirit was roused on which an American can reflect with pride," wrote Marshall gravely, "and which he may consider as a sure protection from external danger." On a less elevated level, as S. E. Morison put it, "for the first and last time in its history the Federal party found itself popular."[67] The country's spirit was aroused but "for the moment," however. The Federalists' popularity lasted scarcely as long.

In the time which it took Marshall to find his triumphant way from Paris to Richmond, a popular ferment against the nation's preparations for war in general, and the Alien and Sedition Acts in particular, had already begun to prepare the Federalists' overthrow. Now Marshall thought these acts constitutional, as we have seen, and even in accord with the needs of any government. Yet they were, he also thought, impolitic in American circumstances. They opposed the dominant, if often foolish and low, democratic passion for an almost unlimited freedom from restraints, especially from restraints on speech. Plato remarked that a democratic city inclines to be "full of liberty and freedom of speech," and Marshall might have agreed. Before returning from France he had written, in one despatch, that in America the importance of no liberty "is more deeply impressed on the public mind than the liberty of the press."

[67] Morison, *Life and Letters of Harrison Gray Otis*, I, 84-85; Marshall, *The Life of George Washington*, II, 428. Beveridge, *Life of John Marshall*, II, vii-viii, describes vividly Marshall's strong direction of the American negotiations.

That this liberty is "often carried to excess," that it sometimes degenerates into "licentiousness," is true. Yet intemperate calumny and invective are "a calamity incident to the nature of liberty." Hence, an American government had better approach this liberty "only with the most cautious circumspection." This maxim the High Federalists neglected. Indeed, Marshall came to believe that the "tempest had not been raised by" the Acts: the "cause lay far deeper. Had they never passed, other measures would have been selected which would have been attacked with equal virulence." Yet the Sedition law constituted a millstone about the party's neck. "The misfortune is that an act operating on the press in any manner, affords to its opposers arguments which so captivate the public ear, which so mislead the public mind that the efforts of reason to correct false impressions will often fail of success."[68] By so conspicuously opposing the popular passion for liberty, the Federalists not only divided the country, when unity against the French danger was needed, but also dealt themselves and the Constitution a severe blow. From it and their own infighting they were not to recover. While in March of 1800 Marshall thought the chances "more than two to one in favor of the re-election of Mr. Adams," in August his remarks betrayed a premonition that old-fashioned Washingtonian Federalism was succumbing to no ephemeral whim; a "current [is] setting against us of which the force is incalculable. There is a tide in the affairs of nations, of parties,

[68] Marshall to Timothy Pickering (?), January 8, 1799 (ALS, Harvard University Library). See also a slightly earlier letter from Marshall to Pickering, August 11, 1798 (ALS, Massachusetts Historical Society). "I am entirely persuaded that with many the hate of the government of our country is implacable & that if these bills did not exist the same clamor would be made by them on some other account, but there are also many who are guided by very different motives & who tho less noisy in their complaints are seriously uneasy on this subject." Plato, *Republic*, 557b; Marshall as envoy, United States, *State Papers*, Foreign Relations, II, 196.

and of individuals. I fear that of real Americanism is on the ebb."[69]

The deep fear of Jeffersonian victory thus betrayed must seem exaggerated to us. Marshall's own defense is not easy to state, however, for the deeper reasoning behind his fears is not evident in his writings that remain. In this circumstance, we will rely upon a contrast of his political persuasion with that of Jefferson. Apart from pointing up the differences which fed the famous personal and political feud between these two statesmen, the comparison will allow us to recapitulate Marshall's own understanding from a different and illuminating American perspective.

MARSHALL AND JEFFERSON

Jefferson too reflected the influence of the modern enlightenment, notably Lockean materialism, but his was a more humanitarian and sanguine version than Marshall's. While he could praise to the skies Locke, *The Federalist*, and Adam Smith, he saw the caution of Montesquieu, Hume, Blackstone, and the Federalists, all trying to embody the radical individualism of the Lockean project in judiciously balanced institutions, as heretical trafficking with Tories, monarchy, aristocracy, and the exploded past. It seems that Jefferson was influenced by some of the more optimistic English and French followers of Locke, although not very extensively by the Rousseauan revolt from Locke.

Compared with Marshall's, Jefferson's doctrine of man's natural rights was more benevolent, yielded more discretion to individual choice, concerned itself less with protecting those who accumulated wealth and power and more with directly relieving suffering, especially through the mod-

[69] Marshall to Harrison G. Otis, Washington, August 8, 1800 (Library of Congress. Copy of an original marked as belonging to Mrs. S. E. Morison, Boston). Marshall to Reuben George, March 16, 1800 (the original is in the collection of the Archives Division of the Virginia State Library, Richmond; copy at the John Marshall Papers, Williamsburg).

ern useful sciences. The right to life was understood in more humanitarian fashion. Jefferson was very doubtful as to the rightness of capital punishment, and had a positive horror of bodily torture; generally his mind was alive with schemes for relieving bodily suffering in every form. Personal liberty was understood more extensively: Jefferson affirmed a natural right of expatriation, which, it seems, Marshall denied. In principle at least he permitted a greater latitude to political speech than did Marshall. While allowing the states to prosecute as criminal libel statements which might lead to public disorder, Jefferson wanted the connection between speech and deed to be close. As a general rule he would tolerate even inflammatory and anti-democratic speech. Marshall could never have written the following, which is a nice illustration of Jefferson's more sanguine expectations from the people and, correspondingly, for republicanism: ". . . No experiment can be more interesting than that we are now trying," he wrote to Judge John Tyler in 1804, "and which we trust will end in establishing the fact, that man may be governed by reason and truth. Our first object should therefore be, to leave open to him all the avenues to truth. The most effectual hitherto found, is the freedom of the press. It is, therefore, the first shut up by those who fear the investigation of their actions. The firmness with which the people have withstood the late abuses of the press, the discernment they have manifested between truth and falsehood, show that they may safely be trusted to hear everything true and false, and to form a correct judgment between them. As little is it necessary to impose on their senses, or dazzle their minds by pomp, splendor, or forms. Instead of this artificial, how much surer is that real respect, which results from the use of reason, and the habit of bringing everything to the test of common sense."[70]

[70] Jefferson to Tyler, June 28, 1804; in Adrienne Koch and William Peden, *The Life and Selected Writings of Thomas Jefferson* (New York: Modern Library, 1944), p. 576. In my consideration of Jefferson,

With respect to man's natural rights, Jefferson differed from Marshall most conspicuously over the place of property. Not that Jefferson disputed the crucial place of human labor in supplying the material of human progress—far from it: "The labor of man would make a paradise of the whole earth." Government was not to "take from the mouth of labor the bread it has earned." Yet the right of accumulation was somewhat depreciated. It was subordinated to a larger whole: the "pursuit of happiness." Jefferson's use of this phrase in the Declaration was neither accidental nor insignificant. Once he explicitly queried Lafayette's inclusion of property on a draft of the rights of man.[71] By happiness he seemed to mean a somewhat broader end than Marshall's property: the freedom from pain and the multiplication of pleasures. This followed Locke, whose preeminent attention to the avoidance of pain was matched by Jefferson's principal concern to relieve suffering. Jefferson was not an old-fashioned Epicurean hedonist: like Locke, he believed that people's "ideas" as to what gives pleasure and pain differ infinitely. What can be sought with almost universal approval are the bodily conditions, the comforts and conveniences, necessary for avoiding pain. It is the increase of these instruments, the "improvement" not so much of man but of the condition of man, in short, "progress," which constitutes the pursuit of happiness. The pursuit of happiness is fundamentally the improvement of one's condition, the increasing of one's freedom from want, danger,

---

I have benefited especially from Charles M. Wiltse's *The Jeffersonian Tradition in American Democracy* (New York: Hill and Wang, 1963), and Daniel J. Boorstin's *The Lost World of Thomas Jefferson* (Boston: Beacon Press, 1960). Wiltse discusses Jefferson's views on capital punishment, pp. 167-68, and on expatriation, p. 185. With respect to the latter, compare Beveridge, *Life of John Marshall*, IV, 54-56.

[71] See Wiltse, *Jeffersonian Tradition*, p. 74. Jefferson's remark on paradise occurs in a letter to Ellen W. Coolidge, August 27, 1825; in Koch and Peden, p. 721. The concern to secure the fruits of labor, not unlike Marshall's own Lockeanism, but couched in a Lincolnesque idiom of the little man, occurs in the first Inaugural Address.

and, generally, pain. For this end Locke had thought the protection of property an indispensable means: thus is stimulated the production that overcomes scarcity and builds national power. Jefferson, more sanguine about defense in particular and man's power in general, emphasized less man's right to acquire the means than that to pursue the end.

Whatever the fundamental similarity of this with Marshall's own views, it differed in important respects. The accumulation of private property, so crucial to Marshall, is subordinated by Jefferson to man's general endeavors to relieve his suffering. Marshall thought the one led incidentally to the other: acquisitiveness to progress, private interest to public gain. Jefferson too admired Adam Smith. *The Wealth of Nations* was "the best book extant in political economy," he once wrote. Yet he was also willing, if not directly to redistribute existing wealth, at least to assure that henceforth some limitation was placed upon the acquisitions of the few, in order to ameliorate the lot of the many. Jefferson's thought was considerably more solicitous of the little man's plight than was Marshall's. Unlike Marshall, Jefferson did not content himself with that equality of condition, quite striking as compared to Europe, typical of the United States at its beginning. Neither did he incline to acquiesce in the inevitable growth of the disparities which a commercial society would encourage. Whatever Jefferson's praise for *The Federalist,* he could not have written that government's first object was the protection of the "unequal faculties" of accumulating property. Marshall could. Jefferson was then far more concerned with equalizing fortunes, especially when they had left the hands of the acquirer. He erased primogeniture and entail from Virginia, and advocated laws dividing inheritances equally among children and taxing property progressively.[72]

[72] Wiltse discusses helpfully Jefferson's views on property, pp. 137-38, 151, as does Albert Jay Nock, *Jefferson* (New York: Harcourt, Brace, 1926), *passim,* esp. pp. 85, 154-55, 270-71. See Jefferson, *Notes on Virginia,* printed in Koch and Peden, *Life and Selected Writings,* p. 211; Jefferson, *Autobiography,* printed in same, p. 45.

Being more egalitarian, Jefferson's creed was far more capable of evoking popular enthusiasm than Marshall's. This quality was multiplied by the substitution of "happiness" for "property": the one connotes the most comprehensive good for man, the other (as Locke and Marshall understood it) holds up a solid but not very inspiring provision against evils. Jefferson's version promised more. By the same token, however, it went much farther toward ignoring the claims of excellent men and rare character in a homogeneous society devoted to "softening" (this most suggestive word is Jefferson's) and comforting all men. By its enthusiastic and almost unqualified egalitarian and humanitarian hedonism of the body, it verged on utilitarianism, on a contentment with "consumption" which removes even that iron in the soul caused by the primary Lockean and American virtue, industry. Although both must be held responsible, and neither fully responsible, Jefferson's humanitarianism was perhaps as much to blame as Marshall's celebration of powerful government, for the tendencies Tocqueville found so dangerous. Tocqueville conceived the possibility of a new and terrible soft slavery, a condition which "would degrade men without tormenting them. . . ." "The first thing that strikes the observation," he wrote of the tendencies of what we have called liberal individualism, and he called democracy, as he found it in America, "is an innumerable multitude of men, all equal and alike, incessantly endeavoring to procure the petty and paltry pleasures with which they glut their lives. Each of them, living apart, is as a stranger to the fate of all the rest; his children and his private friends constitute to him the whole of mankind. As for the rest of his fellow citizens, he is close to them, but does not see them; he touches them, but he does not feel them; he exists only in himself and for himself alone; and if his kindred still remain to him, he may be said at any rate to have lost his country." Then Tocqueville expressed the forebodings we have already quoted in part:

177

Above this race of men [could stand] an immense and tutelary power, which takes upon itself alone to secure their gratifications and to watch over their fate. That power is absolute, minute, regular, provident, and mild. It would be like the authority of a parent if, like that authority, its object were to prepare men for manhood; but it seeks, on the contrary, to keep them in perpetual childhood: it is well content that the people should rejoice, provided they think of nothing but rejoicing. . . .

The will of man is not shattered, but softened, bent, and guided; men are seldom forced (by the supreme power) to act, but they are constantly restrained from acting. Such a power does not destroy, but it prevents existence; it does not tyrannize, but it compresses, enervates, extinguishes, and stupefies a people, till each nation is reduced to nothing better than a flock of timid and industrious animals, of which the government is the shepherd.

I have always thought that servitude of the regular, quiet, and gentle kind which I have just described might be combined more easily than is commonly believed with some of the outward forms of freedom, and that it might even establish itself under the wing of the sovereignty of the people.[73]

For his democratic individualism the key Jeffersonian means was economic development without personal dependence. Governmental coercion need hardly play a role, for the mutual workings of an independent and industrious citizenry could be almost self-sufficient. In his natural state the individual was not afflicted with aggressive passions directed at his fellow man. Man even has a natural sympathy or compassion for his fellows. Moved indeed by self-interest, he is checked from aggression by benevolence. It was scarcity, and fundamentally over-population, that brought on aggressively hungry self-interest, and makes necessary the governments

[73] *Democracy in America* (New York: Vintage Books, 1954), II, 337.

which rapidly deteriorate into a selfish and degenerate few preying on a dispossessed and miserable many. Civilized European society exhibited unequivocally human nature's corruption, he thought, not its development. Men had been degraded from their natural rights and their natural society. Jefferson wanted to restore man's natural right to live in comfort and security, with the help of a new science to wrest from nature abundance and, supplementing the "moral sense" or natural sympathy, of popular enlightenment showing that man "has no natural right in opposition to his social duties." If Marshall's politics is a continual preparation in the cause of peace for war, Jefferson's is an unending struggle in the name of comfort against scarcity. It is a war on poverty by attacking the miserliness of nature: a war on scarcity conducted by the little man's industry and the philosopher's new science and technology. As is well known, Jefferson put Bacon and Newton with Locke in his "trinity of the three greatest men who ever lived."[74]

The Jeffersonian means for promoting this great project of ameliorating the lot of man may be reduced to three, involving America's physical lands, her people, her government. Land was fundamentally a means to be exploited for ever increasing numbers in ever more comfort. The doctrines of Marshall and Jefferson alike condone exploitation of nature, not conservation. Americans were a Lockean kind of chosen people—they were blessed by Providence with a "chosen country, with room enough," as Jefferson said in his first Inaugural Address, "for our descendants to the hundredth and thousandth generation." Besides, the continent was isolated from Europe's quarrels, and from her ludicrous, unequal, vicious habits as well. Still, Jefferson would take more. His was not the imperialism of a Hamil-

---

[74] Jefferson to Benjamin Rush, January 16, 1811; in Koch and Peden, p. 609. As to Jefferson's understanding of the relation between human nature and society, see his letter to Thomas Law, Esq., June 13, 1814; in Koch and Peden, pp. 636-40; cf. Wiltse, *Jeffersonian Tradition*, pp. 66ff.; Boorstin, *Lost World*, pp. 141-47.

ton, who admired the glory of the great and powerful. Jefferson was with Locke, against Machiavelli, in despising glory. He presumed with both the inevitability of population increase, however, and this would eventually require more land. He viewed America's destiny as manifest: spreading across the continent, encompassing not only Canada and Cuba, but even the whole of South America.[75] This was not Marshall's imperial power for the sake of defense, but imperial abundance (if of land) for the sake of security, comfort, and freedom.

Jefferson's peculiar emphasis upon agriculture rather than manufacturing as the means of production is well known, and foreign to Marshall. Manufacturing required factories, hence low and servile labor. It thus led to the great cities of degraded mobs that the Republican leader feared, and whose exploitation by the clever he feared even more. Thus he was somewhat skeptical about manufacturing, and even at times about commerce. Yet he recognized full well the connection between commerce and humanitarianism: commerce softens men and makes them serviceable one to another. He recognized also that the Americans had a commercial bent. Hence in practice he supported American commerce if only as the "handmaid" of agriculture. He granted also that when the country had filled up, its people would have to turn to manufactures. Finally, the point where his wish for amelioration rubbed most obviously against his agrarianism, he wanted the *use* of manufactures (via other countries' commerce) for both safety and improvement. He came to recognize that this required home manufactures, especially in time of war, but also for the sake of greater gain.[76] It must be said that his great desire to in-

[75] See the discussion in Wiltse, *Jeffersonian Tradition*, p. 103; Jefferson to the President of the United States, October 24, 1823, in Koch and Peden, p. 708.

[76] "I have hitherto myself depended," Jefferson wrote in 1813 on the progress of manufactures, "entirely on foreign manufactures; but I have now thirty-five spindles agoing, a hand carding machine, and looms with the flying shuttle, for the supply of my own farms. The

crease production weakened and finally overcame his reservations about commerce and industry.

With respect to the American people, all of Jefferson's prescriptions can be considered under the head of education. Education was so important because, essentially, man acquainted with his true interests and the means of satisfying them would live rightly, so long as he were not corrupted by the selfishness, idleness, licentiousness, and servility of corrupt civil society. Corruption is to be prevented by the agricultural life: hence Jefferson's famous "agricultural virtue." What is it? It differs decidedly from those qualities of the gentry which Marshall continued to respect, although not very much from the character Marshall admired in the ordinary freeman. Agricultural virtue can belong to most men, not just to the leisured few. It is part and parcel of democracy, rather than aristocracy. Moreover, it includes industrious devotion to producing—a constant concern with progressing or improving one's condition. It is the virtue of the true producer, "the producing class," and thus prepares the way for the central tenet of the "Jacksonian persuasion" which Marvin Meyers has illuminated.[77] Most important, it includes an independent jealousy of one's "rights," coupled with toleration of others and benevolence for them: a patriotic, yet humane, republicanism. Jefferson admired this for its own sake and especially for its utility. ". . . Nature has constituted *utility* to man, the standard

---

continuance of the war will fix the habit generally, and out of the evils of impressment and of the orders of council a great blessing for us will grow. I have not formerly been an advocate for great manufactories. I doubted whether our labor, employed in agriculture, and aided by the spontaneous energies of the earth, would not procure us more than we could make ourselves of other necessaries. But other considerations entering into the question, have settled my doubts." Letter to John Melish, January 13, 1813. Compare his letter to Hogendorp, October 13, 1785; in Koch and Peden, pp. 384-85. See Wiltse, *Jeffersonian Tradition*, pp. 160, 190.

[77] *The Jacksonian Persuasion, Politics and Belief* (New York: Vintage Books, 1960).

test of virtue."[78] The republican freeholder avoids the danger of scarcity by his steady industry, and of oppression by a jealous if lonely concern for his own rights. Jefferson carried political individualism, with its abstraction from the activities and thus the pleasures natural to the rational animal in society, very far. "Certain it is," Jefferson is said to have written, "that [the French peasants] are less happy [and] less virtuous in villages than they would be insulated with their families on the grounds they cultivate."[79] One gains a certain glimpse of what Grant Wood painted in his fearful "American Gothic."

Apart from agriculture's nourishing of republican character, education meant first of all getting rid of old and exploded notions which had corrupted man and kept the many in subordination to the few. While Marshall was clearly content, in the spirit of Montesquieu, Hume, and Blackstone, to insert to some extent the heady new wine in respectable old bottles, Jefferson was not. In his deeds and writings, perhaps especially in his letters, he campaigned to rid the popular mind of monarchic and aristocratic deference left over from the colonial period. The contrast with Marshall is evident. Jefferson's propaganda against religion was more subtle. In his effort to purify the Americans' Christianity of what he saw as its old, priestly, Platonic provisions, he went so far as to edit his own 40-page bible, professing his return to the true and humanitarian teachings of Jesus. One is reminded of Locke's *The Reasonableness of Christianity*, in which Lockean reason appeared in Christian guise.

Above all, education meant the spreading of enlightenment. Jefferson's elaborate plans for a selective system of education, with only a picked few emerging at the top to engage in university studies, is well known. He distinguished sharply between education for the many and the few. Yet

[78] Jefferson to Thomas Law, June 13, 1814; in Koch and Peden, p. 639.

[79] Quoted by Nock, *Jefferson*, p. 157.

both were to follow the path of utility, and teachers and books for both were to be properly republican. While sharing with Marshall a conviction that general education should be useful, showing men their duties (especially that of doing their jobs industriously), and how their duties serve their interests, he emphasized, more than Marshall, awakening men to their rights and hence to a proper jealousy of their government. For the few also, the true, the beautiful, and the good would be subordinate to the useful. Their education would be fundamentally of a kind which served "progress": the quest for truth reduced to the quest for useful truth, or the quest by a reliable method for truth: notably the new sciences. Jefferson went remarkably far in drawing the consequences of his humanitarianism. "The crown of all other sciences" is agriculture, he wrote.[80]

One's disappointment in the level of Jefferson's aspirations for the young is only partly assuaged by the thought that such an education did not produce the high tastes and character of Jefferson himself. He did indicate that the wealthy few of talents may retire to liberal studies. He himself turned to ancient authors and literature, among other things, after the Presidency. Yet his democracy and his humanitarianism render such pursuits inexplicable and irrelevant to political life. Besides, democracy and humanitarianism assault the place and the leisure of the class that most tended to do these things. There is in Jefferson an omnivorous and cultivated curiosity that is not present in the more sober and practical Marshall. Jefferson's all-embracing enthusiasm for ameliorating the lot of the many, however, probably leads him farther than Marshall in removing from the American polity the conditions nourishing excellence in intellect and character. "Preoccupation with the material and common-place human needs," the gist of Locke's counsel, goes a step farther in America with Jefferson.

In light of Jefferson's hopes from education, it is not

[80] Jefferson to Priestley, November 14, 1803; quoted by Boorstin, *Lost World*, p. 217.

surprising that government occupies a much less prominent place in his thought than in Marshall's. The law-giver or founder made but a secondary contribution to human happiness: "The greatest service which can be rendered any country," Jefferson wrote, "is to add a useful plant to its culture; especially a bread grain; next in value to bread is oil."[81] Indeed, government was even an evil since the powerful exploit the governed. Jefferson once owned that it was a problem for him that a condition without government was best. So much did he hope from plenty of land and education. While he saw that increasing population had rendered government necessary, his inclinations were always to reduce its prerogatives, and thus to reduce the opportunity of oppression inseparable from power. Hence his republicanism. While favoring a large nation with representative institutions, and even wishing the election of the "naturally" fit, he wished also and principally a government as much as possible controlled by the people. By the qualification of possibility Jefferson allowed himself a flexibility which he certainly exercised, yet the tenor of his thought went to popular control. "Every government degenerates when trusted to the rulers of the people alone," he wrote in 1782. "The people themselves therefore are its only safe depositories."[82] It was natural that Jefferson favor a militia, rather than a standing army. Instead of hierarchy, Jefferson's government amounted in principle to specialization: various bodies of the people arranged at various levels by "division and subdivision of duties," to perform just those minimum tasks the people themselves could not perform as individuals. Government was not agents ruling the people, as in Marshall's understanding. It should

---

[81] Jefferson to Miles King, September 26, 1814; in *The Writings of Thomas Jefferson*, ed. Bergh (Washington, 1907), xiv, 197f.; see Boorstin, *Lost World*, p. 216, Nock, *Jefferson*, p. 49.

[82] *Notes on Virginia*; in Koch and Peden, p. 265. See also the well-known letter to Samuel Kercheval, July 12, 1816; in Koch and Peden, pp. 673-76; and that to John Taylor, May 28, 1816; in same, pp. 668-73. See Nock, *Jefferson*, pp. 199, 312; Wiltse, *Jeffersonian Tradition*, pp. 131-32; Boorstin, *Lost World*, p. 191.

remain according to Jefferson as close to the people, and as divided among the people, as possible. Hence Jefferson's famous solicitude for "states' rights." By specialization government was by agents; by division and responsibility the agents were rendered safe. There seems to be a contradiction between Jefferson's wish for small and democratic government, and the massive empire, and efficient organization of the means of production, required for the "progress" that he also, and principally, wished.

In considering Jefferson's republicanism, it must be remembered that he supposed the people to be the sober and industrious, propertied and enlightened, American people. It does seem that Jefferson had not absolutely opposed a mild property requirement for one of the two houses in his state. Also, his draft of an education act proposed an educational qualification, literacy, for the suffrage. Jefferson even accepted *The Federalist*'s argument that a large republic mitigates the effect of faction. Still, even if the people be corrupted or misled Jefferson was disposed to avoid anything resembling "energetic" or "high-toned" government. He was not so fearful of democratic turbulence as was Marshall. Popular uprisings are less a corruption of a free people than a necessary inconvenience. "The tree of liberty must be refreshed from time to time with the blood of patriots and tyrants." Above all he feared the many's oppression by the few. Genuine corruption, greed, and servility in the people was dangerous essentially because of the opportunity for exploitation thus given the few. He wished the law to be framed to protect the peoples' lives and comfort even when their own jealous virility was dead.[83] Jefferson's humanitarianism does not merely qualify a concern for excellence with compassion for human weakness. It is governed by compassion for man, however debased.

Jefferson's judgment as to America's particular institutions

[83] See the crucial Query XIII of *Notes on Virginia*, in Koch and Peden, pp. 228-47; see also Wiltse, *Jeffersonian Tradition*, pp. 141-42; Boorstin, *Lost World*, p. 192; Jefferson, Second Inaugural Address, in Koch and Peden, p. 341.

is well known and may be briefly touched. After some doubts about the new government's extensive powers, and influenced by *The Federalist*, he approved the Constitution. His chief reservations concerned the absence of a bill of rights securing freedoms of religion, speech, and person, and trial by jury, and the continuing eligibility for reelection of the President. With respect to the structure of government itself, he seems to have understood the separation of powers as a means of checking the pretensions of the government's various branches. Marshall's characteristic concern, to check the people as well, was absent; Jefferson advocated "the right of instructing representatives, and their duty to obey."[84] He viewed the legislature as unequivocally sovereign, with the executive correspondingly subordinate. The popular House should dominate the Senate, and Jefferson seemed to feel, even in 1813, that the Senate might well be "popularized" with a shorter term.[85] He believed the Supreme Court without authority to hold other departments to its own view of the Constitution. Each department possessed authority to interpret those parts of the Constitution within its sphere. Dubious about the judges' independence, especially Marshall's independence, he would have liked some "process for the responsibility of judges, more practicable than that of impeachment."[86] The contrast with Marshall's plea for wide scope for the people's representatives is plain: "In questions of power," wrote Jefferson, "let nothing be heard of confidence in man, bind him down from mischief by the chains of the Constitution." This did not mean that laws need be permanent. Jefferson wanted to undermine in a moderate way the sanctity which Marshall was trying to attach to the Constitution. While the fundamental law should not be changed lightly, it should vary with changing conditions and especially with improve-

[84] Letter to John Taylor, May 18, 1816; in Koch and Peden, p. 669.
[85] Letter to John Melish, January 13, 1813; in Koch and Peden, p. 623.
[86] *Ibid.*

ment in knowledge. ". . . Laws and institutions must go hand in hand with the progress of the human mind."[87] Jefferson's sanguine expectations from progress and democracy qualify his nonetheless genuine adherence to fixed Lockean institutions: "only the imperishable rights of man" supply a permanent touchstone. Hence republicanism, as well as production, is much more important in Jefferson's political thought than in Marshall's. All the "order" for which Marshall stood, the rights of property, the authority of law, the energy of government, the union, the place of the few, could well appear challenged by Jefferson's endeavor to promote equality, to inspire the people with a jealous republicanism, to render responsible the government, to prevent oppression from a remote federal regime, to protect above all the "many" from the "few" through the instrument of the Republican party.[88] Such considerations, perhaps, occasioned Marshall's apprehensions.

While the choice for President between the two Republicans, Jefferson and Burr, was yet before the House of Representatives, Marshall professed himself completely indifferent as to the result. "I take no part & feel no interest in the decision," he wrote on December 28, 1800. "I consider it as a choice of evils & I really am uncertain which would be the greatest." At that time, at least, Marshall thought the election of Burr most likely. "It is not believed that he would weaken the vital parts of the constitution, nor is it believed that he has any undue foreign attachments."[89]

[87] Letter to Samuel Kercheval, July 12, 1810; quoted by Wiltse, *Jeffersonian Tradition*, p. 92. See "Jefferson's Constitutionalism," in Wiltse's Chapters v and vi.

[88] As to Jefferson's views on the difference between Republicans and Federalists, see *supra*, p. 169, note 64.

[89] Marshall to Edward Carrington, December 28, 1800 (ALS, Monroe, Wakeman, and Holman Collection of the Pequot Library, deposited in the Yale University Library; copy at The Papers of John Marshall, Williamsburg).

From the few records of his thoughts that remain, it seems that Marshall himself most feared the weakening of the general government, and with it the union, which would follow from the Jeffersonian version of the old debtor party. Marshall did not fear Jefferson as a wild and bloody Jacobin. In a well-known letter he divided the "democrats" into "absolute terrorists" and "speculative theorists" and sensibly, as one might think, put Jefferson into the latter class. Although the beginning of Jefferson's administration, especially the President's Inaugural Address, encouraged Marshall by its moderation, the Chief Justice feared nevertheless "the general cast of his political theory."[90] Two letters of the time indicate his thoughts: ". . . The tendency of [Jefferson's] administration," he predicted to Rufus King, "will be to strengthen the state governments at the expense of that of the Union & to transfer as much as possible the powers remaining with the general government to the floor of the house of representatives." Writing while Jefferson's election was in the balance, Marshall remarked to Hamilton:

> Mr. Jefferson appears to me to be a man who will embody himself with the House of Representatives. By weakening the office of President, he will increase his personal power. He will diminish his responsibility, sap the fundamental principles of the government, and become the leader of that party which is about to constitute the majority of the legislature.[91]

Marshall lived into Jackson's Presidency. The office had come full circle, from check upon the *demos* to tribune of the *demos*. Its powers had increased correspondingly to the

[90] Marshall to Charles C. Pinckney, March 4, 1801 (ALS, Charleston Library Society, Charleston, S.C.; copy at The Papers of John Marshall, Williamsburg).

[91] Letter from Marshall to Alexander Hamilton, January 1, 1801. Printed in *The Works of Alexander Hamilton*, ed. John C. Hamilton (New York: Francis, 1851), vi, 502. Marshall to Rufus King, February 26, 1801 (ALS, Free Library of Philadelphia).

point, Marshall thought, where it might "break down and trample on every other department of government." By that time Marshall favored a reduction in the executive's power. One of his letters was published, advocating limitation of the office's tenure to but a single term.[92] He feared, it seems, the partisan passions which the presidential contest engendered in "vast masses, united closely, mov[ing] in opposite directions." He would have liked "to take refuge under some less turbulent and less dangerous mode" of choosing a chief magistrate.

Nowhere are these thoughts on the Presidency, and more generally the pessimistic turn taken by his republicanism, better expressed than in a letter of 1830 to James Hillhouse of Connecticut. Hillhouse had long pressed for a number of constitutional amendments. Among them was one limiting to a year the President's term of office and providing for his election by lot, no less, from among the Senators. Seeking the old Chief Justice's judgment, Hillhouse sent to him his proposed amendments and a copy of an 1808 speech supporting them. Marshall's reply is long and revealing. He said in part:

In truth there is something so captivating in the idea of a chief Executive magistrate who is the choice of the whole people, that it is extremely difficult to withdraw the judgment from its influence. The advantages that ought to reflect from it are manifest. They strike the mind at once, and we are unwilling to believe that they can be defeated, or that the operation of choosing can be attended with Evils, which more than counterbalance the actual good resulting from the choice. It is humiliating

[92] Letter from Marshall to Alexander Smyth, January 1, 1828. *Niles' Weekly Register*, xxxv (January 10, 1829), 314. See also Marshall to Joseph Story, December 30, 1827 (ALS, College of William and Mary). See Corwin, *John Marshall and the Constitution*, p. 214; Oster, *Political and Economic Doctrines*, pp. 188-89. Letter from Marshall to Story, December 25, 1832, Massachusetts Historical Society, *Proceedings*, xiv (November 1900), 352-53.

too to admit that we must look in any degree to chance for that decision which ought to be made by the judgment. These strong, and apparently rational convictions can be shaken only by long observation and painful experience. Mine are, I confess, very much shaken, and my views on this subject have changed a good deal since 1808. I consider it however rather an affair of curious speculation than of probable fact. Your plan comes in conflict with so many opposing interests, and deep rooted prejudices, that I should despair of its success were its utility still more apparent than it is.

All those who are candidates for the Presidency, either immediately or remotely, and they are more numerous than is imagined, and are the most powerful members of the community, will be opposed to it. The body of the people will also most probably be in opposition, for it will be difficult to persuade them, that any mode of choice can be preferable to elections mediate[?], or immediate by themselves. The ardent politicians of the country, not yet moderated by experience, will consider it as an imputation on the great republican principle, that the people are capable of governing themselves, if any other mode of appointing a Chief Magistrate be substituted for that which depends on their agency. I believe therefore that we must proceed with our present system till its evils become still more obvious, perhaps indeed, till the experiment shall become impracticable, before we shall be willing to change it.

My own private mind has been slowly, and reluctantly advancing to the belief that the present mode of choosing the chief magistrate threatens the most serious danger to the public happiness. The passions of men are inflamed to so fearful an extent, large masses are so embittered against each other, that I dread the consequences. The election agitates every section of the United States, and the ferment is never to subside—scarcely is a President elected before the machinations, respecting a successor, commence, every political question is affected by it. All those who are in office, all those who want office, are put in motion. The angriest, I might say the worst of passions are roused, and put into full activity. Vast masses, united closely, move in opposite directions, animated with the most hostile feelings toward each other—What is to be the effect of all this? Age is perhaps, unreasonably timid, certain it is that I now dread consequences which I once thought imaginary. I feel disposed to take refuge under some less turbulent, and less dangerous mode of choosing the chief Magistrate, and my mind suggests none less objectionable than that you have proposed. We shall no longer be enlisted under the banners of particular men—strife will no longer be excited, when it can no longer effect its object. Neither the people at large, nor the counsels of the nation, will be agitated by the all disturbing question, who shall be president? Yet he will in truth be chosen substantially by the people. The senators must always be among the most able men of their States—tho not appointed for the particular purpose, they must always be appointed for important purposes, and must possess a large share of the public confidence. If the people of the United States were to elect as many persons as compose one senatorial class, and the President was to be chosen among them by lot, in the manner you propose, he would be substantially elected by the people, and yet such a mode of election would be recommended by no advantages, which your plan does not possess, in many respects, it would be less eligible.

Reasoning a priori, I should undoubtedly pronounce the system adopted by the convention the best that could be devised. Judging from experience, I am driven to a different conclusion.[93]

The turbulent Jacksonian democracy, however, which led the wary Marshall to seek some more quiet and certain

[93] Marshall to Hillhouse, May 26, 1830 (ALS, Yale University, Hist. MSS. Room; copy at The Papers of John Marshall, Williamsburg).

institutional machinery, only took over the fort which Jeffersonian republicanism had already reduced. The tendency of the popular will to press through legislature and executive alike faced no powerful obstacle after the Jeffersonian revolution of power and opinion. The political road was open from a more or less restrained acquisitive republic to the wide open market democracy characterized by the "Jacksonian persuasion": the combination of a leveling impulse, a respect for the laws of economics and "the sober pursuits of honest industry," and a crassly vulgar pursuit of place and gain.[94]

One reason the country did not become unequivocally democratic lay in the checks other than "political" raised by the Constitution—barriers less beset by the tides of people and party. The government was to be "balanced" by the rule of law and ultimately by the highest court. It is to these we must turn in order fully to understand Marshall's republicanism.

[94] Meyers, *The Jacksonian Persuasion.*

CHAPTER IV

COURT AND

CONSTITUTION IN THE

REPUBLIC

IT IS fitting to conclude a study of Marshall's jurisprudence by considering how the famous power of judicial review completes his liberal republicanism. Marshall's life culminated, as is well known, in a vivifying of the Supreme Court. He is rightly regarded, as we too have treated him, not as philosopher or framer, nor even as statesman in the usual sense, but as "the great Chief Justice" and as "Expounder of the Constitution." It is natural that his jurisprudence, attuned to the regime of 1788, should be rounded out in his treatment of the Constitution as fundamental law and, especially, of the Supreme Court as its authoritative interpreter. Well might the Court be dignified with the old metaphor of keystone of the Republic. It was not the most massive stone, nor the most conspicuous, but it was, Marshall thought, the crowning one that held the others in place.

This chapter completes the treatment of courts and the Supreme Court begun with the consideration of the general government's "judicial power" in Chapter II. There it was noted that the courts, to maintain their authority over strictly "legal" or "judicial" matters, had to overrule the other departments' decisions where conflicting. Even the performance of those functions "naturally" appropriate to courts was contingent on a form of "judicial review," on the judiciary's authority to revise the political departments' deeds according to its own interpretation of what a binding Constitution prescribes. This power, as extended to a general supervision of the political departments' performance of even their own tasks, is our subject here.

It will be useful to begin by clarifying a bit more the vexing question of whether the judiciary's functions are "legal" or "political." Surely the Supreme Court's correction of the nation's great political departments is itself a political deed. Present-day students of the Court commonly think so, as have some in every generation including Marshall's own. Marshall, however, did not. He vigorously and publicly denied that judges could exercise anything resembling political discretion. "Courts are the mere instruments of the law, and can will nothing." Nothing in his private correspondence suggests that he had any doubts on the matter.

Those strong words pose a problem here. It will not do to distort the Chief Justice's thoughts in the very act of arranging them in chapters, notably one elaborating the Supreme Court's service of liberal republicanism in America. To oppose Marshall's insistence with our own equally strenuous insistence will illuminate neither his understanding nor ours. How, then, can we do justice both to our impression, confirmed (to take the best example) by Tocqueville, that the courts are in some very important way engaged in politics, and to Marshall's dogged affirmation that they but follow the law?

Perhaps the resolution is by now obvious. The Americans' fundamental law, to which Marshall deferred, embraced a particular kind of politics. The Constitution of rights and powers reflected the prescriptions of liberal jurisprudence, the great means, with political economy, of applying Lockean enlightenment. Modern scholars may view this as one among several kinds of politics. Hence we see the judges' interpretation of the fundamental law, in the light of that politics, as involving not only discretion but will or bias. What we now see as but one variety of politics appeared to Marshall, however, as the private law, and the public law, dictated by nature itself. Marshall viewed the Lockean political understanding as the true political perspective. From that point of view courts simply follow the law, or at least guide their discretion according to the appropriate "general principles of law."

This reasoning, which explains Marshall's views with respect to "legal power," is not quite sufficient to make intelligible his treatment of judicial review. No philosopher of classical liberalism had suggested such authority for the courts. Marshall's argument contains additions to liberalism's typical views, then, although additions in the spirit of liberalism, serving liberal objects in America's democratic conditions. Judicial review is inseparable from Marshall's, and for the most part the framers', liberal republicanism.

WRITTEN CONSTITUTION
AS REPUBLICAN IMPROVEMENT

According to Marshall the Constitution of 1788 was to be an effectual guide to government, not merely a blueprint. It was fundamental law no less than fundamental plan. The permanence and authority of the charter played an integral part, in fact, in the whole scheme of government. It guaranteed the continued working of that ingenious system of public powers and private energies introduced by the "enlightened" philosophers. In accord with one of Locke's more technical distinctions, the Americans' charter of 1788 might be said to correspond to the second contract whereby a people proceeds to erect governing arrangements through the "original constitution" of a legislature. This "legislature is not only the supreme power of the commonwealth," Locke wrote, "but sacred and unalterable in the hands where the community have once placed it." "The power of the legislature," Locke dwelled on his lesson once again, "being derived from the people by a positive voluntary grant and institution, can be no other than what that positive grant conveyed. . . ."

By the very nature of the institutions thus established, the government erected is a limited government. Chapter II indicated how the legislature's sovereign powers were to be interpreted according to fixed and narrow, if nonetheless demanding, purposes. And in several opinions on domestic and international law, notably that of *Fletcher* v. *Peck* which has been already noted, Marshall indicated that "general principles of law" might restrain political authority even in the absence of express provisions.

The distinguishing excellence of the Americans' basic law, however, was explicit definition and limitation of governmental powers. It was this written document that had been "deemed" by Americans, as Marshall interpreted their thoughts, "the greatest improvement on political institutions." Again the Americans were following in their political improvements the spirit of Locke, and perhaps even the letter. At the establishment of a new government, the liberal philosopher had advised, the people should insist on "express conditions limiting or regulating" governmental powers. The Americans did so, according to Marshall's terse account in *Marbury* v. *Madison*.

> This original and supreme will [of the people] organizes the government, and assigns, to different departments, their respective powers. It may either stop here; or establish certain limits not to be transcended by those departments.
>
> The government of the United States is of the latter description. The powers of the legislature are defined, and limited; and that those limits may not be mistaken, or forgotten, the constitution is written.[1]

Once established the Constitution was not to be varied in its fundamentals. This no doubt sounds strange to those educated in sociological jurisprudence, who believe society is always changing, or rather progressing, and that the

[1] *Marbury* v. *Madison*, 1 Cranch (U.S.), 176 (1803); John Locke, *Two Treatises of Civil Government*, ii, 134, 141, 112; *Fletcher* v. *Peck*, 6 Cranch (U.S.), 135, 136 (1810).

law too must constantly vary to keep up with society. Marshall was not unaware of the development of industry and population which the country was about to undergo. Yet he thought this in good part the product of the Constitution's unchanging fundamentals. Development followed from sound laws; it was not a "historical process" to which man is inevitably fated. Hence the importance in Marshall's eyes, apart from the intrinsic worth of man's rights, of making permanent the framers' sound laws.

It is quite true that Marshall affirmed "we must never forget that it is a constitution we are expounding." But this Marshallian maxim so well known to modern jurists has been grossly, if perhaps necessarily, twisted by commentators from the meaning Marshall gave it. It means, as he said in *McCulloch* v. *Maryland*, that the government's powers are to be interpreted in accord with the tasks posed by its objects. Marshall's emphasis upon the great "exigencies" which the government must confront in providing, say, for the national defense, need not be rehearsed. Subordinate objects, like a national bank, and powers, like that to charter a national bank, may be deduced from the "great objects" of the chief powers. But this in no way implies that the objects themselves, or the basic kinds of powers, may change or "evolve." Flexibility there is, but flexibility as to only the means in accord with the spirit of a Lockean Constitution. "Its means are adequate to its ends," wrote Marshall, and he intended to say no more. The famous passage that we have already quoted must be taken in all its parts: "Let the end be legitimate, let it be within the scope of the constitution, and all means which are appropriate, which are plainly adapted to that end, which are not prohibited, but consist with the letter and spirit of the constitution, are constitutional." Marshall's understanding of the Constitution's powers must be interpreted, as in Chapter II, according to the view of the country's objects considered in Chapter I. ". . . Should Congress," he wrote a bit later in the McCulloch opinion, "in the execution of its powers, adopt measures which are prohibited by the constitution; or should Congress, under the pretext of executing its powers pass laws for the accomplishment of objects not intrusted to the government, it would become the painful duty of this tribunal, should a case requiring such a decision come before it, to say that such an act was not the law of the land." We need repeat that there is no contradiction between Marshall's opinion in the McCulloch case, elaborating Congress's political powers, and that in *Marbury* v. *Madison*, defining the obligation of the President to obey strictly a congressional act upon which individual rights depend. There is only the difference of tenor which accords with liberalism's generous supply of power for the political departments' indirect sustenance of individual rights, and with its jealous protection of the rights themselves. In both cases, it is presumed that the Constitution's public law and private law is to endure.

Marshall's supposition that law so serviceable to the people's interests must be supposed permanent is perfectly visible in his treatment of the amending power. Apart from the last resort of revolution, that provision is the sole legitimate way that the ultimately sovereign people could vary the fundamentals of the government to which they had delegated so many of their sovereign powers. "A state without the means of some change is without the means of its preservation" is a good Burkean maxim. Marshall's interpretation of the amending power amounts to scarcely more. The provision is but another mode, he wrote, of assuring "immortality to [the framers'] work." It allows the variations in detail which changing circumstances might require. So long as their government is not oppressive, the people are supposed to have essentially exhausted their own exercise of sovereignty with the authoritative, and even presumptively immortal, expression of their will embodied in the Constitution.

That the people have an original right to establish, for their future government, such principles as, in their opinion, shall most conduce to their own happiness, is the basis, on which the whole American fabric has been erected. The exercise of this original right is a very great exertion; nor can it, nor ought it to be frequently repeated. The principles, therefore, so established, are deemed fundamental. And as the authority, from which they proceed is supreme, and, can seldom act, they are designed to be permanent.[2]

If a written constitution was "the greatest improvement on political institutions," in America this improvement would inevitably be republican in character. Any rule of law tends to moderate government and thus the preponderant political force of the community governed. That force belonged in the United States to the democratic majority. Thus the American constitution tended to moderate the American democracy with the elaborate liberal mechanism of rights and powers characteristic, together with popular institutions, of Marshall's republicanism. "With the exceptions . . . of Connecticut and Rhode Island, whose systems had ever been in high degree democratic," commented the historian Marshall on the spread of the "improvement" through the first state constitutions, "the hitherto untried principle was adopted, of limiting the departments of government by a written constitution, prescribing bounds not to be transcended by the legislature itself."[3]

Indeed, the Constitution's somewhat undemocratic character was apparent in its very origin. The document had been framed not by the many, but by the "enlightened," "illustrious," "statesmen and patriots" of the Federal Convention. Marshall always interpreted the instrument according to their intentions, not in light of the opinions expressed in the Ratifying Conventions. The people generally had only consented to what the few had proposed. Strictly speaking,

[2] *Marbury v. Madison*, 1 Cranch (U.S.), 176 (1803); Marshall, *Address of the Minority* . . . , p. 2.
[3] Marshall, *The Life of George Washington*, II, 78.

the many, the people in a democratic sense, did not even consent to it. The Constitution was ratified by "the best talents of the several states," natural if indeed elected representatives of the "people" understood in Marshall's republican sense. "Had the influence of character been removed," it will be remembered, "the intrinsic merits of the instrument would not have secured its adoption" in the face of popular distrust.[4]

JUDICIAL REVIEW

To be more than weak pretensions the Constitution's claims to permanence obviously had to be enforced. Just as obviously, Marshall thought, the task was principally the Supreme Court's. With the nation's highest judicial authority rested the chief responsibility for preserving a republican fundamental law in a country strongly tending towards democracy. No doubt "the maintenance of the principles established in the constitution" was the duty of all the departments. Still, the judiciary's role was first in dignity and authority, for it was to determine the principles to be guarded. While the Americans were to be ruled by a fundamental law, the courts alone, according to Marshall, authoritatively expounded the law's meaning and application. In effect the judiciary ruled the political departments by defining the outlines of their duties.

Although the Court's predominance over the political branches is a necessary implication of Marshall's famous argument in *Marbury* v. *Madison*, it is by no means the obvious theme. Marshall never asserted that the Court could rule the other departments in their political tasks. He even rejected indignantly the imputation to the Court of

[4] *Ibid.,* II, 127; *Gibbons* v. *Ogden*, 9 Wheaton (U.S.), 202 (1824). "A great majority of the people of Virginia was anti-federal; but in several of the counties most opposed to the adoption of the constitution, individuals of high character and great influence came forward as candidates and were elected from personal motives." Marshall, *An Autobiographical Sketch*, pp. 10-11.

any such view. "Questions in their nature political, or which are, by the constitution and laws, submitted to the political departments, can never be made in this court."[5] There is, however, a catch in this statement that we have noted. It is, according to the Marbury opinion, the judiciary that decides finally which questions are "in their nature political," or which are indeed, "by the constitution and laws," submitted to the political departments. While the courts might not meddle in the political sphere, they alone determine how far the forbidden sphere extends. By their authority to interpret the Constitution and laws they can limit law-maker and law-executor alike. The national courts thus not only judge under the laws but magisterially preside over them.

The Marshallian reasoning which supports this authority, then unique among great nations, is not only as magisterial but as obscure as his statement of the authority itself. With a diffidence which has emboldened his friends and exasperated his enemies, the Chief Justice declared the questions involved "not of an intricacy proportioned" to the interest which had somehow been aroused. "It seems only necessary to recognize certain principles, supposed to have been long and well established, to decide it." And then Marshall read his countrymen a terse primer on the "theory . . . essentially attached to a written constitution."[6]

Before we show the dependence of this theory on Marshall's republicanism, it is necessary to caution the reader against another kind of political explanation so common in this age of reductionism: the tendency to reduce Marshall's thoughts to his politics in a narrowly partisan sense. The doctrines of *Marbury* v. *Madison* are sometimes treated as the Chief Justice's last minute expedient to foil the onrushing Jeffersonians. That he wanted to foil the Jeffersonians is undoubtedly true. That he manipulated the case of *Marbury* v. *Madison* to arrange an ingenious opportunity to affirm judicial review is probably true, although the per-

[5] *Marbury* v. *Madison*, 1 Cranch (U.S.), 170 (1803).
[6] *Ibid.*, pp. 176, 177.

suasive inferences of Corwin and others have yet to be accompanied by other evidence. Whatever doubts may surround the occasion for his remarks, however, the convictions expressed are those which he had long held. In 1798 he had presumed that it was the "province" and "duty" of "the judges of the United States" to construe the fundamental law. In his first public deliberations on the Constitution at the Virginia Ratifying Convention, long before Jefferson and his Republicans were a source of anxiety, Marshall had said, "If [the government of the United States] were to make a law not warranted by any of the powers enumerated, it would be considered by the judges as an infringement of the Constitution which they are to guard. They would not consider such a law as coming under their jurisdiction. They would declare it void."[7]

Considering the settled nature of Marshall's convictions on the judiciary's authority, it is proper to understand his defense of judicial review not as mere partisan maneuver but in the perspective of his whole jurisprudence. This explanation conforms to the confident manner in which Marshall himself argued along lines "supposed to have been long and well established." It is confirmed as well by the conclusions of Corwin in the most assiduous investigation of judicial review. "The power rests upon certain general principles thought by its framers to have been embodied in the Constitution."[8] These principles underlie Marshall's argument in particular, as well as the framers' views in general. It is true, however, that the skimpy and sanguine shape of the argument in *Marbury* v. *Madison* cannot be fully explained by Marshall's deeper premises. To understand the argument's peculiarities of form, one is compelled to return once again to the political circumstances of the time.

The discussion which follows does more than elaborate the basic and explicit doctrines of the Chief Justice's argument. Corwin has already done that. I wish to show that

---

[7] Elliot, *Debates*, III, 553; Marshall, *Address of the Minority* . . . , p. 14.

[8] E. S. Corwin, *The Doctrine of Judicial Review*, p. 10.

those doctrines presuppose a republican role for the Court. In unearthing these political premises I have found nothing more helpful than the biting criticisms of Justice John B. Gibson of Pennsylvania. The conclusion of constitutional scholars that Gibson's opinion in *Eakin* v. *Raub* contains the most compelling analysis of *Marbury* v. *Madison,* is not matched, so far as I know, by any thorough confrontation of Marshall's reasoning with Gibson's rebuttal, finally measuring the one by the other. The Pennsylvania judge offered the careful and systematic dissection that the more influential Jefferson never made.

To begin with, Gibson's opinion helps to tear away the puzzling persuasiveness resulting from the very order of Marshall's argument. The Chief Justice turned to consider the Court's authority to void legislation as unconstitutional only after he had adjudged unconstitutional a certain section of the Judiciary Act of 1789. He then divided the rest of his opinion into a discussion of two questions. First, "whether an act, repugnant to the constitution, can become the law of the land," and, second, whether an unconstitutional act does, "notwithstanding its invalidity, bind the courts, and oblige them to give it effect." Gibson showed that this procedure begs the question. At every step Marshall assumed the propriety of an independent judicial appraisal of an act's constitutionality, whereas the Court's authority to engage in such a judgment is precisely the issue in dispute. In his formulation of the first question, for example, the Chief Justice assumed that the Court can take cognizance of conflict between law and Constitution. As Gibson remarks, "to affirm that the Judiciary has a right to judge of the existence of such a collision, is to take for granted the very thing to be proved. And that a very cogent argument may be made in this way, I am not disposed to deny; for no conclusions are so strong as those that are drawn from the *petitio principii.*"[9]

To insist that Marshall's arrangement of his discussion

[9] *Eakin* v. *Raub*, 12 Sergeant & Rawle (Pa.), 348, cf. 347 (1825); *Marbury* v. *Madison*, 176, 177.

begs the question, however, is not to show that his opinion is devoid of relevant discussion. This Gibson realized full well. Whatever the mere prejudices which existed on the subject generally—and by 1825 Gibson considered the doctrine of judicial review "a professional dogma" which "universally has been assumed by the *American courts*"—the Chief Justice at least could be depended upon to offer an argument. "Although the right in question has all along been claimed by the judiciary, no judge has ventured to discuss it, except Chief Justice Marshall. . . ." The Marshallian syllogism supporting judicial review has been long familiar. The laws of a country are to be construed by its courts; the Constitution is a law of the United States; therefore, the Constitution is to be interpreted by the courts of the United States and finally by its highest court.

It is emphatically [Marshall wrote in *Marbury* v. *Madison*] the province and duty of the judicial department to say what the law is. Those who apply the rule to particular cases, must of necessity expound and interpret that rule. If two laws conflict with each other, the courts must decide on the operation of each.

So if a law be in opposition to the constitution; if both the law and the constitution apply to a particular case, so that the court must either decide that case conformably to the law, disregarding the constitution; or conformably to the constitution, disregarding the law; the court must determine which of these conflicting rules governs the case. This is of the very essence of judicial duty.

If then the courts are to regard the constitution; and the constitution is superior to any ordinary act of the legislature; the constitution, and not such ordinary act, must govern the case to which they both apply.[10]

Now there is a certain difficulty in this beguiling syllogism which Gibson brings out very clearly indeed, a difficulty according to Marshall's own liberalism. The Pennsylvania

[10] *Marbury* v. *Madison*, 177-78; *Eakin* v. *Raub*, 341, 346.

judge agreed with Marshall's major and minor premises—but only with a significant qualification. Granted that it is "emphatically the business of the judiciary to ascertain and pronounce what the law is"; this business, however, is limited as a rule to "civil," and does not include "political," law. Indeed, the Constitution is a law of the United States, but it is not "an act of ordinary legislation, by the appropriate organ of the government." It is instead "an act of extraordinary legislation, by which the people establish the structure and mechanism of their government, and in which they prescribe fundamental rules to regulate the motion of the several parts." The Constitution is "political law" *par excellence.* Thus, Gibson concluded, the judiciary is by no means an appropriate interpreter of the Constitution.[11]

The force of Gibson's argument is not difficult to see, and it has been popularized by such students of the Court as Charles Grove Haines. The Pennsylvania judge was like Marshall in being a Lockean liberal, if, as we will see, of a somewhat more democratic type, and he strikes with the Chief Justice's own liberal weapons. Neither Locke nor Hume nor even Montesquieu had ever recommended a power in the courts comparable to judicial review. In Chapter II we saw Marshall himself limit the judiciary's authority to "legal" rather than "political" matters. He granted on many occasions, moreover, that certain matters in form legal, such as treaties among nations, were in fact political. The success of Marshall's once-famous speech in Congress on the Jonathan Robbins affair turned upon a distinction between legal questions reserved to the judiciary, and questions involving points of law which were nevertheless "questions of political law, proper to be decided by the executive, and not by the courts." Although Marshall never called the Constitution itself a political law, he certainly distinguished it very forcefully indeed, in *McCulloch* v. *Maryland,* from "an ordinary legal code." The whole point of the now familiar remark, "We must never forget that it

---

[11] *Eakin* v. *Raub*, 345-48.

is a constitution we are expounding," depends upon the peculiar character of the fundamental law. The Court's opinion, he wrote in *McCulloch* v. *Maryland*, might "essentially influence the great operations of government." After all, in *Marbury* v. *Madison* itself, Marshall had deemed a fixed Constitution the greatest improvement in "political institutions."[12] To repeat, Gibson's critique strikes home in Marshall's own liberal premises.

If Gibson's argument has great force, however, it is by no means decisive. For he himself admits exceptions, both express and implied, to the judiciary's obligation to obey the political departments' constructions of the Constitution. The judiciary might engage in review of legislation, albeit only by "producing a direct authority for it in the constitution, either in terms or by irresistible implication from the nature of the government. ..."[13]

Through such holes it might seem that Marshall could drive his whole argument. Indeed, the Chief Justice relied chiefly on implications of the government's nature, rather than express provisions. Only at the conclusion of his discussion did he refer to several explicit limitations upon the national government, and these are but "illustrations" by means of which his "theory" of government is "confirmed" and "strengthened."

The gist of the theory Marshall finds "essentially attached to a written constitution" is the necessity for effectual limita-

[12] *Marbury* v. *Madison*, 177-78; *McCulloch* v. *Maryland*, 4 Wheaton (U.S.), 400, 407 (1819); see also Marshall, *Address of the Minority* ..., p. 7. "When the gentleman has proved that these are questions of law, and that they must have been decided by the President, he has not advanced a single step towards proving that they were improper for Executive decision. The question whether vessels captured within three miles of the American coast, or by privateers fitted out in the American ports, were legally captured or not, and whether the American government was bound to restore them, if in its power, were questions of law; but they were questions of political law, proper to be decided . . . by the Executive, and not by the courts." U.S. Congress, *Annals*, 6th Congress, 2nd session, 1800.
[13] *Eakin* v. *Raub*, 347.

tion of the legislature. At every crucial point in Marshall's reasoning, when he is establishing that a law contrary to the Constitution is void, or when he insists that a void law must be ignored by the judges, the spectre of an unchecked legislative department is brought forth to justify Marshall's alternative. The judges, to quote the most illuminating passage, must follow the Constitution in preference to conflicting law, or else they "would be giving to the legislature a practical and real omnipotence, with the same breath which professes to restrict their powers within narrow limits." That "or else" provides the key to Marshall's argument and to his rhetorical skill, in *Marbury* v. *Madison*. It is the Court's role as "balancer" that is used to justify judicial review. Marshall's argument proceeds by pointing to the horrors of "legislative omnipotence," elevating judicial potency only (as it might appear) inadvertently and hence inconspicuously.[14]

It is, however, just such an elevation of the Court's power that Gibson believed unjustifiable. While he admitted exceptions to his maxim that courts can't overrule the other departments, he showed himself disposed to limit the exceptions to those authorized by explicit provisions, and to confine such provisions to those expressly applicable to the Judiciary Department. Gibson would emphatically restrict the courts to "civil" affairs, and allow them to overrule other departments only where the Constitution assigns civil duties directly to the judiciary. There is a manifest difference from Marshall, who had taken the Constitution's limits on every department as indicative of the Court's authority to enforce the whole Constitution. Either the Courts enforce, "or else. . . ."

The difference as to the Court's sphere is occasioned by Gibson's very different theory of the government's nature, a theory exalting the legislature rather than fearing it. Again Gibson's doctrine reminds us of Marshall's own liberalism, in this case the account of separation of powers which we

[14] *Marbury* v. *Madison*, 176-80.

considered in Chapter II. All the organs of government "are of equal capacity; or, if not, each must be supposed to have superior capacity only for those things which peculiarly belong to it. . . ." And hence the limits on each department are to be interpreted by that department. "Legislation," to take the key case, "peculiarly involves the consideration of those limitations which are put on the law-making power. . . ." The legislature's peculiar capacity, moreover, makes it superior to that of any other department. In the law-making branch is vested the power to *command*, whereas the other departments are but "governed by prescribed rules and exercise no power of volition." "The very definition of law, which is said to be 'a rule of civil conduct prescribed by the supreme power in the state,' shows the intrinsic superiority of the legislature."[15] For Gibson as for Locke, the legislature was not merely one department but the "sovereign" department.

Yet a reply to Gibson is possible on liberal grounds, if not in a conventionally liberal manner. Sovereign legislative power is granted, it will be recalled, not as an end in itself, but as a means to the security of life, liberty, and property. Suppose that in America's robustly popular circumstances the liberal means do not fit the liberal end, that an unchecked legislature does not protect the rights of persons and property but endangers them. Might not a judicial supervision of the legislature be introduced? One of Corwin's early articles demonstrates that it was precisely the post-Revolutionary democratic excesses of popular state legislatures that led to a gradual public acceptance of judicial correction of their acts, although not quite to the unambiguous devotion to judicial review exhibited by the classic *Federalist* 78 and by Marshall. Judicial review, not recommended by the philosophers of liberalism, nevertheless emerged in popular America as a revision required by liberal ends.[16]

[15] *Eakin* v. *Raub*, 351, 348-53.

[16] Note the remark of Hume, who was always concerned to moderate the dogmatism endemic to Lockean liberalism's natural public

It is quite clear that such judicial supervision would involve a certain amount of judgment as to matters of "policy," as to the legitimacy of the political departments' exercise of their powers. Courts perhaps lack the "superior capacity" of the legislature for such judgments. Yet this difficulty does not dispose of the matter. For the broad outlines of political policy were defined, as Marshall thought, by natural public law, an integral part of that liberal jurisprudence with which Courts educated by Blackstone were familiar. Particular details were to be left in any event to the discretion of executive and legislature. Thus the original premises of Marshall's argument can be more deeply appreciated. Although the Constitution was a political law, its politics were to be guided by natural public law. The judges' training in liberal jurisprudence made them at least as fit as the legislature, the more democratic legislature, to discern the natural constitution behind the written Constitution. Thus the Courts were competent to play the ambiguously political checking role which the "theory" of American government demanded from them.

It is with respect to those demands that Gibson finally differed. The Pennsylvania judge even agreed that some counter-balancing power was needed to render the Constitution's written limitations more than vain admonitions.

---

law. He pointed to a "remarkable custom" indicating "that all general maxims in politics ought to be established with great caution." The ancient Athenians relied upon prosecutions in a "court of judicature" of those legislators proposing laws which appeared "to the court unjust, or prejudicial to the public." Hume treated this judicial control over laws and law-makers as a salutary check upon the "Athenian Democracy" and its "tumultuous government." Were "it abolished or neglected, it were impossible for the Democracy to subsist." "Of Some Remarkable Customs," in David Hume, *Essays, Moral, Political and Literary*, pp. 372-75. The article of E. S. Corwin's mentioned in the text is "The Progress of Constitutional Theory between the Declaration of Independence and the Meeting of the Philadelphia Convention," *American Historical Review*, xxx (April 1925), *passim*, esp. 514-32.

That check should be provided by the people, however, not by the judges. "The notion of a complication of counter checks has been carried to an extent in theory," Gibson remarked, "of which the framers of the constitution never dreamt." An error by the judges in interpreting the Constitution could be corrected only by "the extraordinary medium of a convention," whereas "an error by the legislature admits of a remedy . . . in the ordinary exercise of the right of suffrage." "It rests with the people, in whom full and absolute sovereign power resides, to correct abuses in legislation." It is finally Gibson's democracy, the active role which he found assigned to the people in the constitutional system, that caused his objection to judicial review. "It is a postulate in the theory of our government, and the very basis of its superstructure," he wrote when his argument had reached its crucial turn, "that the people are wise, virtuous, and competent to manage their own affairs."[17] Yet this "postulate" was not shared by the dominant framers. Their experience under the Articles had left them with less than Gibson's confidence in the people. Indeed they had feared especially the more democratic legislatures. Assuming a basically popular country, the framers set forth a liberal separation of powers arranged so as to trim out the people's excesses. They sought balanced government, balanced against the more democratic legislature especially. For Marshall, as for the framers, the judiciary was an integral part of a government designed in good part to minimize the people's vices, not merely to depend upon their virtues. It was because of Marshall's republicanism, then, that he was able to blithely ignore the "implications for democracy" which bother many now and bothered Gibson then.

I have tried to show the essential presuppositions underlying Marshall's argument in *Marbury* v. *Madison*. Yet the brief and even skimpy form which the argument takes has yet to be explained. In good part, the deeper and more re-

[17] *Eakin* v. *Raub*, 355.

publican assumptions never appear. Marshall was instead content to set forth in memorable sentences only the most obvious principles justifying judicial review. Why did he not probe deeper? Surely the reason lies not in his ignorance. He knew *The Federalist*. In *78* Hamilton had made explicit enough the connection between independent judges, judicial review, and the suppression of those "ill humours which the arts of designing men, or the influence of particular conjunctures, sometimes disseminate among the people themselves, and which . . . have a tendency . . . to occasion dangerous innovations in the government, and serious oppressions of the minor party in the community." The superiority of what Corwin justly calls *The Federalist*'s "classic" discussion is precisely owing to its development of the connection between judicial review and the Constitution's liberal republicanism. Why did not Marshall himself develop this connection, which makes intelligible the weight he puts upon "certain principles, supposed to have been long and well established"? His abilities were not wanting, nor was the judiciary's place as he wished it perfectly appreciated in the Jeffersonian climate of 1803.

Perhaps the reason lies in Marshall's caution in the face of the democratic inclinations of his audience. One does not preach democracy's limitations to democrats and expect thus to leaven democracy. The more likely effect in Marshall's own situation would have been the Court's overthrow. The effect of *Marbury* v. *Madison* was in fact far different. Charles Warren showed that, while Marshall's discussion consoled and encouraged the Federalist press, it failed to arouse a reciprocal reaction even in "the most bitterly partisan Republican papers."[18] Jefferson himself was repeatedly to bemoan the acceptance of Marshall's argument among bench and bar. Part of the reason for its appeal surely lay in the moderate American public's devotion to many of the moderating principles on which Marshall

[18] Charles Warren, *The Supreme Court in United States History* (Boston: Little, Brown, and Company, 1926), i, 248; cf. 231-73.

relied. Yet that is insufficient. The public had displayed other tendencies, which dragged law and legal principles in other than Marshallian directions. An adequate explanation must then take into account the rhetorical skill of Marshall's own opinion. The Chief Justice's ingenuity lay in building his doctrines into the susceptible side of the Americans' dispositions, thus reducing the other in spite of itself. Marshall did not, like Justice Samuel Chase, cast the republican judiciary into the teeth of the democrats. Not one express criticism of democracy can be found in the Chief Justice's judicial opinions. Instead he insinuated his judiciary into their minds. The task did not call for an exhaustively enlightening discussion. It demanded a prudently cautious inculcation in memorable phrases of only those principles necessary for public belief in order that judicial review be sustained. Unlike Hamilton, Marshall wrote not for the "best talents of the several states" who were considering the Constitution, but for the considerably more democratically inclined public of Jeffersonian America.

The discussion comes full circle, then. Beginning with a search for the Marshallian reasoning which is intellectually necessary but not apparent, we understand from the argument's character why it had to be left implicit. For a politics better than the common wish, or even instrumental to the common desires, neither true speech nor wisdom, to say nothing of free speech, is sufficient. Statesmanship employing rhetoric is still required. It must be of a kind that constructs the political edifice on the foundations provided by common opinion, and thus is able to shape the public mind. Such was Marshall's achievement in establishing judicial review.

GUARDIAN OF THE REPUBLIC

As keeper of the Lockean scrolls in a popular polity, the national judiciary enjoyed the peculiar advantage of selection and tenure considerably removed from the democratic voice. The justices were not elected by the people but appointed by the President, and were removable only for breach of good behavior—which meant only personal corruption after the unsuccessful impeachment of Justice Chase. They thus enjoyed an enviable independence from the pressures that beset the other branches. However they might follow the election returns, their tenure did not depend upon the result. Marshall's concern for the judiciary's "independence in office, and manner of appointment" has already been observed. It is this independence, rather than the incumbent's "interest" in satisfying his constituents, that assures, Marshall said, his "wisdom" and "virtue," no less than his "impartiality" and "candor." While the elective branches increasingly adopted the dispositions and views of the majority, the judiciary at least could remain a haven for distinguished citizens unable and sometimes unwilling to brave popular election. The judiciary furnishes the "offices of honor and places of dignity," as Cicero put it, which provide one haven for excellence. The courts could also harbor correct constitutional principles. Jefferson once observed with bitterness and with some truth that the Federalists, defeated at the polls, "have retired into the judiciary as a stronghold . . . and from that battery all the works of republicanism are to be beaten down and erased."[19] What were to the more democratic republican Jefferson "English" and "monarchical" heresies, however, were to the Washingtonian Federalist Marshall the very outlines of the Constitution's rights and

[19] Quoted by Beveridge, *Life of John Marshall*, iii, 21; Elliot, *Debates*, iii, 552, 556, 557, 559. "The judges of the United States are as independent as the judges of the state of Virginia, nor is there any reason to believe them less wise and less virtuous. It is their province and their duty to construe the constitution and the laws, and it cannot be doubted, but that they will perform this duty faithfully and truly. They will perform it unwarped by political debate, uninfluenced by party zeal." Marshall, *Address of the Minority . . .*, p. 14; Cicero, *De Officiis*, ii, xix, 65. See also C. Herman Pritchett, quoted in Walter F. Murphy and C. Herman Pritchett, *Courts, Judges, and Politics* (New York: Random House, 1961), p. 693.

powers, outlines which the Supreme Court was charged, not by the Federalists but by the framers, to preserve.

Marshall was perfectly aware that his Court, and the Constitution itself, could only with difficulty maintain its place in the nation of Jefferson and Jackson. "The harmony of the bench will, I hope & pray, never be disturbed," he wrote to his friend Story in 1821. "We have external & political enemies enough to preserve internal peace." Beveridge concluded that a number of cautious and even timid measures of conciliation taken by Marshall, at the onset of Jefferson's rule, can be traced to the Chief Justice's prudent appraisal of his "enemies'" strength. We have noted the wariness of Marshall's opinion in *Marbury* v. *Madison.* His circumspection during the Burr trials seems owing to the same cause.[20]

It is quite possible that the Chief Justice chose the occasions for some of his great judgments on prudential grounds. Most of his grand constitutional opinions grew from cases of proportional scale. *McCulloch* v. *Maryland, Cohens* v. *Virginia,* and *Gibbons* v. *Ogden,* come to mind. Some clearly did not. Marshall prided himself on his ability to avoid by "construction of the act" an issue of constitutional principle, which had involved Justice William Johnson in "a democratic snag on a hedge composed entirely of thorny States-Rights." He was, however, fully as capable of developing an issue of constitutional principle from a problem which might have been solved by the same kind of statutory interpretation. *Marbury* v. *Madison* has been described with reason as the supreme example of his art. "[Marshall's Court] took the engaging position of declining to exercise power which the Constitution withheld from it," E. S. Corwin remarked, "by making the occasion an opportunity to assert a far more transcendent power."[21]

[20] See *infra,* Appendix II; Marshall to Story, July 13, 1821. Printed in Massachusetts Historical Society, *Proceedings,* second series, XIV (November 1900), 328; Beveridge, *Life of John Marshall,* III, 176-79, 192-96.

[21] E. S. Corwin, *The Doctrine of Judicial Review,* pp. 10, 3-17. Cf. Marshall's remarks to the justices on the serious consequences of

The bulk of Marshall's efforts was given, however, to strengthening and shaping the Court itself, not to conciliating its potential enemies. He was not unwilling to intercede deferentially with Presidents, at least with John Quincy Adams, in favor of a suitable candidate for associate justice. He surely wished to postpone his own retirement until someone more congenial than Jackson occupied the White House.[22] As is generally known, Marshall put a stop to the justices' custom of delivering their opinions *seriatim.* Henceforth, occasional dissents were permitted, but, by Marshall's example, discouraged; the Court spoke with one strong voice. Usually the voice was that of Marshall. Contemporaries and commentators alike acknowledge his awesome sway over his associates. The causes were various: his winning ways, forceful and steady character, great intellect, industry; the age, incompetence, laziness, and deference of some of his colleagues; the Court's close and common way of life; the justices' common perception that the times were indeed not propitious for disrupting the "harmony of the bench." The effect was striking. In his first five years as Chief Justice, Charles Grove Haines reported, Marshall wrote the opinion of the Court in every case in which he participated. In the next seven years, he delivered the Court's opinion in 130 cases, leaving but thirty to associates. Those like Donald G. Morgan who depreciate Marshall's role are compelled to admit that he was at least conductor of the orchestra.[23] The analogy is still insufficient.

---

declaring unconstitutional the Republicans' Circuit Court Act of 1802. Warren, *The Supreme Court in United States History,* i, 268-69. Letter from Marshall to Story, September 26, 1823. Quoted in Warren, i, 626. Marshall's remarks to Story were occasioned by Justice Johnson's failure in South Carolina to avoid the snag which Marshall had eluded in Virginia. *Ibid.,* 620-28; Beveridge, *Life of John Marshall,* iv, 382-84.

[22] Letter from Marshall to Story, October 12, 1831. Reprinted in Massachusetts Historical Society, *Proceedings,* 2nd series, xiv (November 1900), 347; Letter from Marshall to Henry Clay, Richmond, November 28, 1828, printed in Oster, *Doctrines,* p. 42.

[23] Donald G. Morgan, "Marshall, the Marshall Court, and the

One must credit him also with the role of soloist and almost of composer at the bulk of the orchestra's performances and especially at the grander concerts. Marshall's influence was particularly important in cases involving constitutional law, where the Court's opinions were most often the "fruits of his own unassisted meditation," as Story phrased it.

These constitutional discourses can only be properly appreciated, as we have seen in the case of *Marbury*, as means of molding the legal opinion of the country, and thus, of molding the nation itself. In a republic like the United States, Marshall once remarked, "much of the public happiness" depends on "rescuing public opinion from those numerous prejudices" with which it tends to be surrounded. We have remarked more than once on the importance Marshall attached to "enlightenment." The United States was not to be supported fundamentally by sound habits and hence by ancient ways, but by a liberation of private interest and by an enlightened appreciation in its citizenry of the economic and political system that worked for their mutual interest. Marshall's opinions were meant in good part to supply that enlightenment. Our previous discussion of his views on "education" is incomplete until we consider the place of his grand commentaries on the Constitution.

Indeed, his rhetoric was hardly of the lively sort, filled with striking language and figures of speech, that appeals to the general public. Yet it exhibited a tenacious grasp of liberal premises, a constant clarification of basic words, a great power of deducing with appropriate limits all relevant implications, and a confident openness in confronting, using, and exposing opposing points of view. All were guided by astute judgment and an obvious and painstaking devotion to the public good. At times, moreover, Marshall's

Constitution," in Jones, *Chief Justice John Marshall*, pp. 168-85; Charles Grove Haines, *The Role of the Supreme Court in American Government and Politics, 1789-1855* (New York: Russell & Russell, 1960), p. 630, esp. n. 58; cf. p. 404, n. 93.

discourses reached a solemn grandeur. The Marshallian persuasion was then fitted to reach the more respectable American citizens already influenced to a large extent by the Lockean persuasion. At the very least Marshall could not but move, or at least confound, the legal profession and its peak, the judges. Corwin quoted a remark of Randolph of Roanoke which is perhaps too good to be true: "All wrong, all wrong," he cried despairingly after one of Marshall's judgments, "but no man in the United States can tell why or wherein."[24]

Apart from the particular doctrines which we have discussed, perhaps the most obvious message in the Chief Justice's opinions is the authority, even the sanctity, of law. He endeavored to inculcate a lesson which men of almost all capacities might grasp, a devotion to law and *a fortiori* to the supreme law, the Constitution. "Let reverence for the law, be breathed by every American mother . . . , let it become the *political religion* of the nation," Lincoln was to say when he saw some evils of America's democratic individualism coming out.[25] If Marshall's sobriety would never let him recommend a "political religion," his judicial endeavors went toward much the same instruction.

It seems that Marshall understood deeply the problems involved in establishing a liberal nation which was, according to its own tenets, but an artificial instrument of the natural individuals of which it was composed. It is striking that his great opinions never depended solely or even chiefly upon "natural" principles alone. He came closest in his judgment for the Court in *Fletcher* v. *Peck*. Georgia's revocation of her grant was

[24] Edward S. Corwin, *John Marshall and the Constitution*, p. 124. See Marshall's letter communicating the Supreme Court's approval of a bill providing for reports of its decisions. Letter from Marshall to the Hon. Dudley Chase, February 7, 1817, reprinted in Oster, *Doctrines*, pp. 80-81.

[25] "The Perpetuation of our Political Institutions: Address before the Young Men's Lyceum of Springfield, Illinois," January 27, 1838. Roy P. Basler, ed., *Abraham Lincoln, His Speeches and Writings* (New York: Grosset & Dunlap, 1962), p. 81.

void "either by general principles, which are common to our free institutions, or by the particular provisions of the Constitution of the United States." Note that Marshall relied not merely on general principles, but on "general principles common to our institutions." Moreover, he left his answer at an alternative. It was Justice Johnson who, in a concurring opinion, chose to rest his decision unqualifiedly and solely upon "a general principle, on the reason and nature of things." Marshall chose the more restrained, but also the more politic and permanent course, of building natural rights into the law, and, at the same time, of retaining the authority of the law to overrule natural rights when necessary. Similarly, Marshall did not content himself in *Ogden* v. *Saunders* with exhibiting the true meaning of the phrase "obligation of contracts," according to "writers on natural and national law."[26] He felt the necessity of demonstrating as well that this was the meaning that controlled the Constitution's framers. Not the genius of publicists, nor even that of nature, but "the genius of our laws" was to rule.

The Chief Justice's mode of construction, "adhering to the letter of the statute, taking the whole together," also tended to engender close respect for law. And the style of his writing had a similar effect. Story remarked that Marshall followed Lord Bacon's suggestion, with which the conduct of Justice Holmes might be instructively compared, that "judges ought to be more learned than witty; more reverend than plausible; and more advised than confident."[27] The gravity of the Chief Justice's style is proverbial.

---

[26] *Ogden* v. *Saunders*, 12 Wheaton (U.S.), 347, 354 (1827); *Fletcher* v. *Peck*, 6 Cranch (U.S.), 139, 143 (1810). Consider Marshall's views on the legal status of slavery, *infra*, Chapter II, and his remark in *Hepburn and Dundas* v. *Ellzey*, 2 Cranch (U.S.), 445 (1804): "the word State is used in the Constitution as designating a member of the Union and excludes from the term the signification attached to it by writers on the laws of nations."

[27] Joseph Story, *A Discourse upon the Life, Character, and Services of the Honorable John Marshall*, p. 54.

While it dulls the *Life of George Washington*, it yields an appropriate dignity to the judge. Marshall rose to a kind of magisterial reverence when he treated the fundamental law. By no means, his whole manner indicated, was the Constitution to be confused with the hurly-burly of politics. It was to be venerated, not controverted. It seems, as the more flippant and unreflective commentators have not hesitated to point out, that Marshall dealt not merely with a constitution framed by unusual men, but with a sacred law made by sainted men. The reverence of Americans for their law and for the "cult of the robe" has not gone unnoticed. It is certain that the great Chief Justice's endeavors have something to do with this. Apart from the tone of his opinions, he repeatedly called the Constitution "sacred." Perhaps the best illustration of his treatment occurred when in *United States* v. *Maurice* he was faced with a rather ambiguous provision of the fundamental law. He wanted so badly to shield Constitution and framers from any imputation of error, that he ascribed to the flaw itself responsibility for its own appearance. "I feel no diminution of reverence for the framers of this sacred instrument, when I say that some ambiguity of expression has found its way into this clause."[28] In his own way Marshall too tried to found a "political religion."

There is a deeper lesson in Marshall's opinions. It comprises the whole tightly knit web of liberal principles. These were intended to form a kind of shield defending the Constitution, so far as rhetoric can, from interpretations prejudicial to its genuine purport. The point has been anticipated in our discussion of *Marbury* v. *Madison*. Dwelling upon the respect to be paid the Constitution as law, the Chief Justice pointed beyond the law to the justice and system of government in light of which the law needed to be construed. America's fundamental law was the first of the liberal or Lockean constitutions to rule a great nation.

[28] *United States* v. *Maurice*, 2 Brockenbrough 100 (1823); *Marbury* v. *Madison*, 1 Cranch (U.S.), 158 (1803).

Marshall's efforts, analogous to those of *The Federalist* and other commentators, produced the elaborately deduced and comprehensive umbrella of protective opinions which this study has endeavored to reproduce. Samuel Konefsky says quite rightly that Marshall tried always "to deal with [a] question with a patience and spirit of elucidation that might have been bestowed on it had it been raised for the first time." Such thoroughness is one sign of the founder, and Marshall is properly called the founder, not indeed of the Constitution, but of American constitutional law. He wanted to make his foundations as sure from challenge as possible. Hence he relied not on precedent, whose justice and appropriateness might always be challenged, but on "safe and fundamental principles" self-evident to Americans and indeed drawn from nature itself. Marshall's judicial opinions are comprehensive beyond their genre. They approach the treatise. Yet their intent was clearly practical, and the conclusion of *Gibbons* v. *Ogden* sums up their purpose in an America so influenced by the Jeffersonian variant of liberalism:

> The Court is aware that, in stating the train of reasoning by which we have been conducted to this result, much time has been consumed in the attempt to demonstrate propositions which may have been thought axioms. . . . But it was unavoidable. The conclusion to which we have come, depends on a chain of principles which it was necessary to preserve unbroken. . . .
>
> Powerful and ingenious minds, taking, as postulates, that the powers expressly granted to the government of the Union, are to be contracted by construction into the narrowest possible compass . . . may . . . explain away the constitution of our country, and leave it, a magnificent structure, indeed, to look at, but totally unfit for use. They may . . . obscure principles, which were before thought quite plain, and induce doubts where, if the mind were to pursue its own course, none could be perceived. In such

a case, it is peculiarly necessary to recur to safe and fundamental principles to sustain those principles, and, when sustained, to make them tests of the arguments to be examined.[29]

Of these little practical discourses on liberal government the only rival of *Cohens* v. *Virginia* is *Marbury* v. *Madison* itself. That opinion amounts to a brief essay on what the rule of law is to mean in the United States. Surely its intent was not just the reading to Jefferson of "a lecture on his legal and moral duty to recent Federalist appointees to judicial office." It is only apparently tough historical "realism" to believe that Marshall's cautious judgment, in the face of Jefferson's popular backing, would allow him to engage in such puerile and partisan sniping. It appears from what the opinion says, and from what it leaves unsaid, that the Chief Justice was after far bigger if less conspicuous game. He sought to establish in the nation generally, and especially in the minds of its judges, the authoritative place of a liberal Constitution kept authentic by the courts. This was the starting-point of Marshall's judicial endeavors, and the key to his achievement.

With its authority to interpret the Constitution established, the Supreme Court could not but influence profoundly the Americans' political life. In good part this would issue from its "legal power" alone. The very make-up of the "people" would be conditioned by the Court's protection of private rights, especially that to acquire property. While the position of old wealth would not be directly threatened, the rise of those with acquisitive and productive talents to wealth and even to great riches would be encouraged. Political power would follow economic power. The power of the upper middle class would be multiplied by the rapid organization through corporations of the means of production. It is well known that the Court's

[29] *Gibbons* v. *Ogden*, 9 Wheaton (U.S.), 221-22 (1824); Konefsky, *John Marshall and Alexander Hamilton*, p. 170.

opinion in the Dartmouth College case[30] encouraged this process, affording to corporate charters the protected status of private contracts. In that case Marshall and his fellows were concerned to keep legislatures out of colleges and their curricula, rather than out of companies and their franchises. The larger implications were clear, however. The protection of private rights made way for inequality—of education or of acquisitions. The Court encouraged an approximation among the American people of Marshall's kind of republican hierarchy.

Besides influencing the American people, the Marshallian Court could moderate the government which the people had raised. A consequence of judicial protection of the "individual" was the removal of a vast sphere of human life from the purview of the political departments. Life, liberty, accumulations of property—the chief activities and things pertaining to what we call "society" and "economy"—were in good part transferred from political control to the more reliable hands of the judges.

Supported by the power of judicial review, the Courts' supervision of the other departments did not depend merely on implication and hence on sufferance. *Marbury* v. *Madison* provided for review of executive and legislature alike, measuring their deeds against statutes, the Constitution, and finally the "general principles" of law. The opinion thus forms a comprehensive plan for limiting American government. Unless the President was subjected to the Court's judgment as to when the law obliges him to act, our government would not deserve "that high appellation, a government of laws." If the legislature was not subjected to the Supreme Court's view of the constitutionality of its laws, we would possess no "fundamental and paramount law." And judicial interpretation of law and even of the supreme law would follow "general principles of law," on the one hand, and "certain principles, supposed to have

[30] *Dartmouth College* v. *Woodward*, 4 Wheaton (U.S.), 644-50 (1819).

been long and well established," on the other.[31] Popular government was moderated toward republican government, the protector of Lockean liberalism.

The Supreme Court was indeed the crucial stone in the framers' liberal edifice. It provided for the "tenderness" to individuals and their property that constituted the very object of government. By its patronage, the laws of commerce were allowed to work on unhindered, silently piling up wealth and contributing to union, thus providing for safety and peace as well as comfort. The Court, moreover, adjusted the spheres of general and state governments, being specially solicitous to guard the new general authority from its older and well-established rivals. And, not to be forgotten, it provided a place where the community's finer men might govern free of political harassment, where judgment might sway community affairs without any more concern for popularity than a cautious prudence might dictate.

GLOOM AND PROMISE

Whatever the contributions of the judiciary might be in theory, Marshall came to believe that its efforts were doomed to failure. If a keystone, the Supreme Court was only a keystone. It presupposed an adequate support. It could not by itself stem the spread of democracy and the erosion of the Union. The Supreme Court might expound Congress's powers. It could not ensure their exercise. Whatever its opinion in *McCulloch* v. *Maryland*, for example, it could not force the President to maintain the national bank. It certainly was unable to ensure that "Old Hickory" would imitate the dignified Washington's search for men of character and talent to fill the executive branch. The Court could hardly prevent the growth of parties, an attendant change in the legislature, the transformation of the Presidency from a Washingtonian check upon democracy to a Jacksonian tribune of democracy. Furthermore,

[31] *Marbury* v. *Madison*, 1 Cranch (U.S.), 163, 176-80 (1803).

all its elaborations of constitutional principle would never sway the South. Far from convincing Virginia, Marshall's efforts in *McCulloch* v. *Maryland* and *Cohens* v. *Virginia* were "grossly misrepresented" by the "democracy" there and were threatened by principles that would transform the Constitution into the old confederation and, ultimately, as Marshall thought, bring on "dismemberment."[32]

Even Marshall's hopes for the Supreme Court itself seemed doomed. The Court was insulated from popular pressures—but it was ultimately at their mercy. The appointments by a succession of Republican and then Democratic presidents could only push the judiciary from Washingtonian Federalism. Marshall found it increasingly difficult to exercise his accustomed dominance over the Court's decisions involving contracts, bills of credit, and commerce.[33] To say that his Court had been inundated by democracy or Jeffersonian states' rights would be rash, but the Court itself had changed.

As sectionalism and democracy waxed during Marshall's declining years, he grew ever more gloomy about the prospects for the Constitution. It appears that Marshall died knowing full well that to a considerable degree he, and in a deeper sense the Constitution, had failed. It had proven impossible to unite in a republic cemented by mutual in-

[32] Letters from Marshall to Story, May 27, 1819; July 13, 1821; September 18, 1821. Reprinted in Massachusetts Historical Society, *Proceedings*, xiv, 325, 329.

Story's *Commentaries* would not be read in Virginia. "I greatly fear that south of the Potomack [*sic*], where it is most wanted, it will be least used. It is a Mahomedan rule, I understand, 'never to dispute with the ignorant,' and we of the true faith in the South abjure the contamination of infidel political works. It would give our orthodox nullifyer a fever to read the heresies of your Commentaries." April 24, 1833. *Proceedings*, xiv, 356.

J. Q. Adams had been too sanguine. "Marshall has cemented the Union which the crafty and quixotic democracy of Jefferson had a perpetual tendency to dissolve." *Memoirs*, ed. Charles Francis Adams (Philadelphia: Lippincott & Co., 1874-77), ix, 243-44.

[33] See E. S. Corwin, *John Marshall and the Constitution*, pp. 224-25.

terest the great popular American community still divided by state and section. "I yield slowly and reluctantly to the conviction that our constitution cannot last," Marshall wrote to Story during the dark days of 1831.

I had supposed that north of the Potowmack [*sic*] a firm and solid government competent to the security of rational liberty might be preserved. Even that now seems doubtful. The case of the south seems to me to be desperate. Our opinions are incompatible with a united government even among ourselves. The union has been prolonged thus far by miracles. I fear they cannot continue.[34]

The foundering of Marshall's Constitution is not simply incidental to our theme, although the responsibility of its defects, as opposed to external causes, must not be exaggerated. It cannot be held responsible for the old divisive loyalties and interests. To a degree, however, the practical failure reflects the deepest problem in Marshall's own understanding, the difficulty of reconciling good government with popular government. The attacks on the Union and its government were supported in good part by the democracy. The people were familiar with their states, lacked foresight to adopt the strong measures required for union, suspected "internal improvements," the "banking power," and other manifestations of a general government trying to grease the channels of mutual interest. Moreover, the Constitution's wavering reflects the problem within Marshall's understanding of good government itself. Fine men and perhaps even patriotic men are not easily nourished by an interested individualism. Before Lincoln, however, the best that the nation could hold up to its best citizens, in office and on the battleground, was their "interest" in "union." How strange to fight for "Union!" Is it not deeply significant that, in the nation's great moment of peril, Lincoln

[34] Letter of Marshall to Story, September 22, 1832. Reprinted in Massachusetts Historical Society, *Proceedings*, XIV (November 1900), 352.

redefined the Union, as Harry V. Jaffa has shown, "dedicated" it to a "proposition," elevated it so that among other things it might inspire men?

These difficulties ought alone make us wary of applying uncritically Marshallian jurisprudence to the problems of the modern Supreme Court and country. From this point of view Marshall's constitutional understanding is not a plan to be executed, but an object lesson, exhibiting the characteristic pitfalls which a popular country based on a liberation of private acquisitiveness must ever face.

Marshall's constitutional understanding is more, however, than its defects. It is not our present task to say how much more, to compare the merits of his views and ours. One might say, nevertheless, that Marshall failed at a level higher than that at which we succeed. His jurisprudence was the work of rare talent in a unique opportunity. His was a fine intellect guiding a practical Court compelled to articulate the peculiarly theoretical basis of the first "new nation." The result affords an unusual chance for a comprehensive appreciation and diagnosis of this American nation and its ills. In John Marshall's political and legal views, moreover, there was a respect for excellence, and a loyalty to a grand tradition of judges, that can always elevate the jurisprudence of his heirs.

APPENDIX I

JUSTICE HOLMES AND

CHIEF JUSTICE MARSHALL

IN THE course of my inquiry into Marshall's jurisprudence, I soon found it necessary to consider the very influential appraisal of him and his legal thought made by Justice Oliver Wendell Holmes. This appendix contains the essence of that consideration: an account of Holmes' critique (for it is nothing less) of Marshall, an exposition of the point of view in light of which the critique is made, and a weighing of Holmes' point of view, chiefly by comparing its advantages with those of Marshall's own jurisprudence. Two caveats are appropriate here. I am content to characterize succinctly Marshall's own doctrines, relying upon the fuller elaboration in the text. And, while examining the gist of Holmes' legal thought, I do not pretend to do justice to its many sides, or to the wit, eloquence, and a certain grandeur of manner that captured for him the loyalty of many admirable men of the law.

This topic appeals to the great interest naturally attaching to these judges, the two most famous in our country's history. Its importance is more considerable and more serious, however. For the jurisprudence of these two men represents different and powerful trends in American law, especially among the thoughtful people of bench, bar, and law schools, whose views guide to some extent the country's law. By no means do these two represent all shades of opinion; yet they represent very powerful views. It was Holmes who chiefly began in this country the jurisprudential revolt from natural rights, the assertion of social expediency as the standard of judicial decision, the doctrine of judicial deference, the change from the primacy of property rights to that of free speech, the rise of moral skepticism, sociological jurisprudence, legal realism, and many other things now widely taken for granted. "The effort of the modern science of law," wrote Mr. Justice Frankfurter of Holmes' influence, "is to investigate problems in the perspective in which he has set the problems of law." This Holmesian victory, however, came at the expense of the older jurisprudence, and it is not unreasonable to take Marshall's thought as symbol of the old legal understanding. One would not wish to make him responsible for all the legal narrownesses against which Holmes to some extent reacted, but one may say that the "great Chief Justice" represented the older point of view at its best. Here we can refer again to Holmes' own authority: ". . . If American law were to be represented by a single figure, sceptic and worshipper alike would agree without dispute that the figure could be one alone, and that one, John Marshall."[1]

An investigation, then, of Holmes' critique of Marshall illuminates the basic principles of American law, both in their original form and as stamped by Holmes. Such a study may also have for the reader the practical effect it had upon me: a gradual yet compelling realization that what seemed to be a great step forward in the name of social advantage is not so obviously superior, that we have been misled about the quality and character of the country's original jurisprudence, and, generally, that the struggle between what Holmes urged and what Marshall stood for needs to be reconsidered without prejudice.

[1] "John Marshall," *Collected Legal Papers* [to be cited as *CLP*] (New York: Peter Smith, 1952), p. 270. Felix Frankfurter, *Law and Politics*, ed. A. MacLeish and E. F. Prichard (New York: Harcourt, 1939), p. 48. See also Frankfurter, *Mr. Justice Holmes and the Supreme Court* (Cambridge: Harvard University Press, 1961), p. 112; Lon Fuller, *The Law in Quest of Itself* (Evanston: The Foundation Press, 1940), pp. 116-17.

The character of that struggle is best revealed by Holmes' only considered remarks expressly on our topic, his little essay, "John Marshall." This is a short but vivid sketch originally delivered in 1901 from the bench of the Supreme Judicial Court of Massachusetts. The occasion was the centenary of Marshall's accession to the Chief Justiceship. The tribute conveyed by the sketch was no trite gesture. It raised, as Holmes' excellent biographer, the late Professor Howe, put it, "some rather disturbing questions." Holmes himself indicated that he was "conscious, perhaps, of some little revolt from our purely local or national estimates, and of a wish to see things and people judged by more cosmopolitan standards."[2] We must first understand his estimate of Marshall, and "the more cosmopolitan standards" underlying his estimate, before considering the appropriateness for American law of these standards, and thus the adequacy of his estimate.

Holmes' sketch is not without praise of Marshall. ". . . But when I consider his might, his justice, and his wisdom," he began the passage from which we have already quoted, "sceptic and worshipper alike" would agree that Marshall would be the one man to represent American law. Still, this praise is introduced as a qualification of the fundamental tenor of the sketch. It finds its place, as is well known, in a portrait largely questioning the stature given Marshall by "our purely local or national standards." Holmes' new and "cosmopolitan" standard is indicated by the last and culminating paragraph of the sketch. This characterizes Marshall's significance as that of "symbol" from four points of view: from that of the Virginian, the patriot, the lawyer, and, crucially, the thinker, the "one who lives in what may seem to him a solitude of thought."

To the citizen of Virginia Marshall may symbolize the glories of his state, to the patriot he represents "the fact

[2] "John Marshall," *CLP*, p. 268. Mark DeWolfe Howe, *Justice Oliver Wendell Holmes* (Cambridge: The Belknap Press of Harvard University Press, 1957), II, 118.

that time has been on Marshall's side" and his theory of union victorious. "To the more abstract but farther-reaching contemplation of the lawyer," Holmes then made a characteristic and astute estimate of Marshall's efforts, the day's commemoration "stands for the rise of a new body of jurisprudence, by which guiding principles are raised above the reach of statute and State, and judges are entrusted with a solemn and hither-to unheard-of authority and duty." Above all these, however, Holmes put the perspective of the solitary thinker, the perspective which concludes Holmes' essay and controls his appraisal of Marshall. To such a thinker, Marshall's accomplishments symbolize "the fact that all thought is social, is on its way to action; that, to borrow the expression of a French writer, every idea tends to become first a catechism and then a code; and that according to its worth his unhelped meditation may one day mount a throne, and without armies, or even with them, may shoot across the world the electric despotism of an unresisted power. It is all a symbol, if you like, but so is the flag. The flag is but a bit of bunting to one who insists on prose. Yet, thanks to Marshall and to the men of his generation—and for this above all we celebrate him and them—its red is our lifeblood, its stars our world, its blue our heaven. It owns our land. At will it throws away our lives."

We need take time here simply to grasp the meaning of this remarkable prose. We need especially to understand the thinker's culminating view. From such a perspective the significance of Marshall is the power of his thought (not, to mention the obvious alternatives, the prudence and justice of his deeds or the wisdom of his thought). That power is "social," which Holmes immediately equates with "tending to action." Marshall is interesting because his thought moved society. Marshall's greatness symbolizes the fact that ideas may mount a throne or "may shoot across the world the electric despotism of an unresisted power." Ideas are but symbols, Holmes writes, yet he also writes: "We live by symbols." We live especially, evidently, by social symbols. The flag comprises for "us" our blood, our whole world, even, as Holmes said, our heaven. The thinker judges Marshall according to the power of his thought in winning a society's allegiance. We must note, however, that Holmes indicated the power of a thinker's ideas to depend upon their merits: only "according to its worth" may "his unhelped meditation one day mount a throne." In short, Holmes finally judged Marshall by the standard of the thinker who wants his ideas to rule people, rather than by that followed in the text, of the statesman who rules them.

From this overarching perspective the particulars of Holmes' sketch are intelligible. Holmes began by dwelling upon the inseparability of human action and "circumstances." He characterized Marshall's acts as but a part of the movement of society, of a great stream of social action through time that the thinker evidently sees. "A great man represents a great ganglion in the nerves of society," goes the best-known sentence of the sketch, "or, to vary the figure, a strategic point in the campaign of history, and part of his greatness consists in his being *there.*"

This, indeed, is almost unexceptionable. Surely Holmes was correct if he meant that the circumstances for greatness must be propitious, the opportunity must be there. If Adams had not appointed "a Federalist and loose constructionist to start the working of the Constitution," as he said, Marshall, probably at least, would not be famous. Still, is the formulation quite right? Is just being there "part of his greatness?" Is it not necessary to distinguish between having the opportunity to be great, and being great? Many have the chance—and muff it.

John Jay, the first Chief Justice, had in considerable measure the chance attributed to Marshall by Holmes, "to start the working of the Constitution." Yet he gained no great reputation from his office. More telling, Jay even declined reappointment to Marshall's very opportunity. "I left the bench perfectly convinced," he wrote in reply to Adams' offer, that a judiciary "system so defective," could never obtain "the energy, weight, and dignity which are essential to its affording due support to the national government, nor acquire the public confidence and respect which, as the last resort of the justice of the nation, it should possess."[3]

Holmes, it seems, overestimated the extent to which favorable circumstances contribute to great deeds. He even overestimated the favorableness of Marshall's circumstances and thus failed to note the extent to which a great man can turn even unpropitious circumstances to account. One wonders, in short, whether Holmes does not take the "inevitability" of what Marshall did too much for granted when, after dwelling on the importance of circumstance, he wrote: "When we celebrate Marshall we celebrate at the same time and indivisibly the inevitable fact that the oneness of the nation and the supremacy of the national Constitution were declared to govern the dealings of man with man by the judgments and decrees of the most august of courts." We will return to Holmes' depreciation of a statesman's efforts in favor of a society's supposedly inevitable development. But there is no need to quibble over what here may seem to some a minor point. For Holmes too recognized that some credit, some place of honor, belonged to Marshall's "personal" qualities.

Yet these excellencies of Marshall's character are praised in a rather disparaging manner. "I should feel," Holmes wrote in an often quoted passage, a "doubt, whether, after Hamilton and the Constitution itself, Marshall's work proved more than a strong intellect, a good style, a personal ascendancy in his court, courage, justice and the convictions of his party."[4]

Let us for the moment suppose Holmes' doubt well-founded. One still must raise the question: why the disparagement? No one ever claimed Marshall to be a framer of the Constitution: he was, however, celebrated as the founder of the country's constitutional law. Similarly, no one ever thought Marshall an original political philosopher,

[3] Jay to Adams, Jan. 2, 1801, quoted by Beveridge, *Life of John Marshall*, III, 55.
[4] "John Marshall," *CLP*, p. 269.

even of a kind comparable to Hamilton. Yet his deep understanding of the Constitution and of the needs of this first "new nation" gave birth to those grand judicial expositions of the Constitution, and of international law, for which he is best known. Marshall was, as is generally agreed, chiefly a statesman of a peculiar kind, a judicial statesman whose talents were peculiarly fitted for expounding and reconciling the principles of America's variant of modern constitutionalism. It was as such a statesman that his accession to the Chief Justiceship was being celebrated. Why does Holmes belittle this?

The answer is connected with the one error in Holmes' listing of Marshall's qualities that we will take up here: Holmes omits Marshall's statesmanlike judgment. Marshall's quiet judiciousness was famous. It discomfited even the prince of diplomats, Talleyrand, in the XYZ imbroglio. It discomfited Jefferson, no mean political intellect, in *Marbury* v. *Madison*. According to Beveridge it made Marshall known as a kind of natural judge among his young peers in the army.[5] It yielded him success in private law practice and in every one of the long string of offices he filled. It was the key to his success as Chief Justice. A little later in his sketch, in the flourish of praise that we have already quoted, Holmes himself acknowledged Marshall's "wisdom." Why then, to repeat, the disparagement? The reason lies in Holmes' more cosmopolitan perspective of the "thinker," which depreciates the merely practical judgment of a Marshall.

"My keenest interest is excited, not by what are called great questions and great cases, but by little decisions which the common run of selectors would pass by because they did not deal with the Constitution or a telephone company, yet which have in them the germ of some wider theory, and therefore of some profound interstitial change in the very tissue of law. The men whom I should be tempted to commemorate would be the originators of transforming thought. They often are half obscure, be-

[5] Beveridge, *Life of John Marshall*, I, 119.

cause what the world pays for is judgment, not the original mind."[6]

We must try to make crystal clear the bearing of Holmes' comment. Judgment, even the judgment necessary to settle great cases involving great national questions, is less admirable in judicial decisions than "transforming thought." If Holmes were belittling practical judgment because it did not embrace some of the higher activities of the human intellect, perhaps one could agree. Philosophy, the fine arts, science, may involve more noble and delightful qualities than the judiciousness characteristic of the statesman and required by his tasks. Yet Holmes does not put his argument on these grounds. Even in the statesman's tasks the transforming thinker is to be preferred; he is the standard of measurement. In celebrating thinker over statesman Holmes was not talking philosophy, poetry, or science, to philosophers, poets, or scientists. He was talking about law to lawyers, not about law in general but about American law to American lawyers, and especially about the founder of the constitutional law under the essentials of which they continued to live. In such a context, then, he depreciated not just an ordinary statesman but one who had many marks of the founder, in favor of "the transforming thinker." That is Holmes' final perspective, to repeat, not just for man, or for a man of the law, but for the man of American law. Why? Why should one measure American statesmen of the law by the standard of a "transforming thinker"? Fundamentally, why is the best thing for American law this thinker, governed by a desire to see his thoughts in power?

Answering these questions will involve some appraisal of Holmes' own legal philosophy. For the views guiding the sketch of Marshall are those characteristic of his whole philosophy and, indeed, of his practice. Marshall's typical posture on the bench was that of judge or judicial statesman, soberly judicious, subordinate to the law and to its framers' intentions. Appropriately, he called the statesman's "sound judgment

[6] "John Marshall," *CLP*, p. 269.

. . . certainly the most valuable quality of the human mind."[7] Holmes' posture was that of thinker, transforming and thus frequently dissenting thinker, if thinker in the thick of practical affairs. It is not unjust to believe that he too pursued what he called "the secret isolated joy of the thinker, who knows that, a hundred years after he is dead and forgotten, one who never heard of him will be moving to the measure of his thought." "The law is the calling of thinkers," he told law students.[8] In weighing the reasons for these very theoretical views of Holmes I shall rely chiefly on his *Collected Legal Papers* and on *The Common Law*, his only book. His judicial opinions will also be used, although I can make no pretense of rivaling Professor Yosal Rogat in penetrating the many sides and implications of his practical decisions.[9] Professor Rogat's analysis of a part of Holmes' practice provides, I think, a useful corrective for any distortions arising from my own concentration on Holmes' theory. I believe our findings to be complementary.

It will be well to sum up the argument that follows since Holmes' jurisprudence is complicated. That complication originated, it seems to me, in an elaborate philosophy of history, the well-known "social Darwinism" that formed the basis for his thought. This is a very theoretical basis for a country's legal practice. As such, it will explain a certain abstractness in the discussion which follows. This basis explains Holmes' emphasis on the thinker: because he knows the direction of history, his is the counsel which all others need to follow. Let us then make clear the direction of history as the thinker Holmes understood it.

History was one long development of society. It was an

---

[7] John Marshall, *The Life of George Washington*, II, 446.

[8] "The Profession of the Law," *CLP*, pp. 29-30, 32; see also *CLP*, pp. 105, 159 end. "If I haven't done my share in the way of putting in new and remodeling old thought for the last 20 years then I delude myself." Holmes, in a letter to Sir Frederick Pollock in 1902, upon his accession to the Supreme Court. *Holmes-Pollock Letters*, ed. Mark De Wolfe Howe (Cambridge: Harvard University Press, 1941), I, 106.

[9] "Mr. Justice Holmes: A Dissenting Opinion," 15 *Stanford Law Review* (December 1962, March 1963), pp. 3-44, 254-308.

evolution from primitive individual beginnings to civilized society, "from savage isolation to organic social life."[10] This process was usually understood, as the notion of "development" would imply, as a growth toward maturity. History's evolution was in crucial respects a "progress." There is a problem in this evaluation, since Holmes rejected all "absolutes." He occasionally denied that the historical process was progressing, even if it was moving.

In any event this historical process was not a knowing or intelligently guided one, Holmes thought, until very recently. Then man had become "conscious" of his development and hence able to "consciously" affect it. Until that change, the process had been "spontaneous growth." Man's moral development through history occurred with the submission of his individual desires to the laws of society. Society was itself developing automatically by virtue of the Darwinian "struggle for life" among its members. Hence Holmes could characterize Marshall's efforts as but "a ganglion in the nerves of society," or as but a point following more or less inevitably from Marshall's circumstances in the "campaign of history."

There is then a link between Holmes' positivism and his evolutionary account of society and morals. The positivism which saw law as the will of society or as the deeds of its judges, went together with an understanding of law as the agent of man's moral development toward an "ideal." His realism, one is tempted to say, is inseparable from his idealism, the link being given by a real history whose movements (in the form of society's developing will) take man toward an ideal condition.

Here, it seems to me, the difficulties come galloping in herds. The suppositions that history moves for the best, that societies generally act for their members' expediency or even out of motives of social expediency, that law can be simply identified with will, and that the better solution always emerges, or at least always emerges out of conflict, seem historically and politically naive, to say the least. To return to our special concern,

10 "The Law," *CLP*, p. 27.

Holmes underestimated the role, and hence the preciousness, of great statesmen—of a national founder like Washington and even of a lesser law-giver like Marshall.

Be these problems as they may, Holmes quite obviously thought that the historical process had in his time reached a key point. Finally men could know their fate and shape it: the difference is attributable to the coming of modern science. Therefore the thinker's transforming power: he can bring the true account of history and above all science itself to the service of the law. Conversely, he can turn American law toward the law's true development, which is to be henceforth guided by science. Thus the importance, according to Holmes' sketch of Marshall, of "some profound interstitial change in the very tissue of law." It will be recalled that the power of a thinker depended on the worth of his thoughts. For Holmes worthy thought was scientific thought. Holmes went so far as to speak of his "ideal" as "a commonwealth where science is everywhere supreme."[11] Because law reflects the growth of society, and society's moving forces can now be measured by science, old-fashioned judgment must take a back seat in the law itself to the transforming thinker who brings the new legal science. As for that science itself, Holmes seems to have had in mind something like what we call social science. Its prescriptions, he seemed also to think, will have an exactitude far surpassing the recommendations of mere statesmen. We must consider eventually whether Holmes' hopes for science were well-founded, the implications of that for his jurisprudence, and, then, on this and other grounds, whether indeed the judicial statesman deserves disparagement and displacement.

The whole tenor of Holmes' jurisprudence was controlled by his own endeavor to be "scientific" in all his "thinking about the universe." This meant, he wrote in "The Path of the Law," that one supposed "a fixed quantitative relation between every phenomenon and its antecedents and conse-

---

[11] "Law in Science—Science in Law," *CLP*, p. 242; see p. 195.

quents."[12] All is determined, i.e., has fixed causes and effects, and anything "outside the law of cause and effect" is not the concern of human reason. The task of science was then to trace cause and effect. This was true also of legal science. "The first call of a theory of law," Holmes wrote in *The Common Law*, "is that it should fit the facts. It should explain the observed course of legislation."[13] To adopt a loose contemporary distinction, Holmes' science tried to be "descriptive," not "normative." "When properly taught," he said in "The Bar as a Profession," "jurisprudence means simply the broadest generalization of the principles and deepest analysis of the ideas at the bottom of an actual system."[14]

At this point we must note a difficulty: Does not Holmes here presuppose what cannot be taken for granted? He assumes, not merely the existence of a "legal order," but of one ordered consistently, according to "principles" and "ideas." This seems to presuppose as a matter of fact what is in fact a rare, chancy, and precious commodity, one requiring great human endeavor to begin, nourish, and preserve.[15]

However that may be, Holmes himself supposed that "generalization" and "analysis" will eventually come to the basic "force" which moves and shapes any legal system, the basic "cause" or, to continue our previous distinction, the basic "is." His thought focuses upon discovery of "the forces which determine [the law's] content and growth."[16] Here the necessary presuppositions are provided by the philosophy of history that we have noted. All societies are assumed to be in a process of growth, and therefore basically healthy. Professors Howe and Rogat have pointed out how Holmes was influenced by German scholarship that presumed the inevitable "growth" of the common law

---

[12] *CLP*, p. 180.

[13] Holmes, *The Common Law*, ed. Mark De Wolfe Howe (Cambridge: Harvard University Press, 1963), p. 167.

[14] *CLP*, p. 157.

[15] Consider Fuller, *The Law in Quest of Itself*. See also the works cited in this Appendix, n. 24.

[16] "The Path of the Law," *CLP*, p. 179; compare p. 167.

through history, beginning with certain far-off Teutonic tribes.[17] That is why Holmes could suppose societies to have legal systems of a kind that have ideas to be deeply analyzed and principles that can be extensively generalized. Moreover, he needn't take the generation and preservation of these for his concern—because "inevitable" history has done so. "The development of our law has gone on for nearly a thousand years, like the development of a plant, each generation taking the inevitable next step, mind, like matter, simply obeying a law of spontaneous growth. It is perfectly natural and right that it should have been so."[18]

Some defend Holmes as a tough-minded skeptic, a man too strong to have to lean on such reeds of the weak as natural rights and natural law. Whether the Marshallian view of natural rights is such a weak reed is a question we have considered in the text. The important thing to note here is that Holmes himself tended to bow acquiescently to all legal history as "natural and right."

In this development of law through history the basic force was the will of society, or, as Holmes often formulated it, social expediency or considerations of social advantage. Quite clearly Holmes sought to avoid the deficiencies of certain philosophies which sought to deduce the law systematically from the presumed will of an assumed sovereign, or from the "will" or rights or "interests" of individuals.[19] Holmes decried the notion that "a given system, ours, for instance, can be worked out like mathematics from some general axioms of conduct."[20] Like all law our law reflected "considerations of social advantage," and in any community "experience," rather than "logic," determines these. His famous passage beginning *The Common Law* goes as follows: "The felt necessities of the time, the prevalent moral and political theories, intuitions of pub-

[17] Howe, *Holmes*, II, 135-59. Yosal Rogat, "The Judge as Spectator," 31 *University of Chicago Law Review* (Winter 1964), pp. 218-19.
[18] "The Path of the Law," *CLP*, p. 185.
[19] Howe, *Holmes*, II, 151-55.
[20] "The Path of the Law," *CLP*, p. 180.

lic policy, avowed or unconscious, even the prejudices which judges share with their fellow men, have had a good deal more to do than the syllogism in determining the rules by which men should be governed. The law embodies the story of a nation's development through many centuries, and it cannot be dealt with as if it contained only the axioms and corollaries of a book of mathematics."[21]

It is not easy to say which of these (felt necessities, theories, intuitions of policy, or prejudices) Holmes thought more important and which less, which determinative of society's will, which derivative. It seems, however, that the first mentioned, the "felt necessities of the time," were basic, even if the others (such as theories of philosophers to which Holmes attributed great influence) may exercise some independent power. Elsewhere, Holmes indicated that the experience fundamental to a society's view of social advantage is that of "the interests of life." More precisely, it is that experience of "the interests of life" possessed by the dominant interests within a society, by "a dominant class" or "the predominant power in the community."[22] If I interpret correctly Holmes' several remarks in the *Collected Legal Papers*, the "interests of life" or "necessities of the time" as felt by the dominant social groups, or classes, have determined the law's "content and growth."

There is much good sense in this view of law as the will of society, but there are also difficulties. No doubt the laws of a country usually reflect the views of the man or men dominant there—else the law would not be instituted, preserved, or enforced. Does it follow, however, that such law is to be deemed *ipso facto* socially expedient or necessary, or even as arising from "considerations of social expediency?" Holmes tended to identify the will of society, or the laws factually existing, with that society's advantage, or at least with its "considerations of social advantage." It is quite possible, however,

[21] *The Common Law*, p. 5.
[22] See "The Path of the Law," *CLP*, p. 186, and pp. 126, 128, 130-31.

that many laws extant are not expedient or, at least, reflect private wishes or group selfishness (even at the expense of the society). In short, it seems optimistic to sanction with the word "expedient" the law, even the fundamental law, of all nations through history, and to sanction with the word "social" the motives which originated them. Holmes again seems to take for granted as given by history the political efforts and virtues which originate just laws. Holmes himself acknowledged the importance of a kind of wisdom and virtue. He referred to the "good sense at every stage of our law" which adjusts laws to the needs of society or of the times.[23] He mentioned often the "reasons" which lead one time to dispose of an out-dated policy while retaining only the forms. One might question Holmes' suppositions that the "needs" of society or of "the times" are somehow self-evident to the judge, and then go on to wonder whether the notion of "adjustment" is not then an inappropriate belittling of the judge's tasks. However, our question here is this: can one take "reason" and "good sense" for granted as inevitably attending the law's "stages" or "the times"?

There are other difficulties in the notion of law as the will of society. It seems to be not only a naive reading of history, but also an unjustifiable elevation of society. Why *ought* we, as Holmes exhorted, restrict our conception of law to what society wills? As Professor Fuller has shown with clarity and grace, society might not desire laws.[24] Law implies at least a rule, a principle of reason governing similar cases similarly. But it is quite evident from this very statement that not all rulers govern themselves thus. Tyrants do not like to bind themselves by laws, as the expression goes; they decree, dictate, act without legal warrant, act under cover of law but not in the spirit of the law, ignore the law, and so on. In short, Holmes takes for granted the rule of law when he as-

[23] *The Common Law*, p. 22.
[24] Lon L. Fuller, "Positivism and Fidelity to Law—a Reply to Professor Hart," 71 *Harvard Law Review* (1958), 644-57; see also Fuller, *The Morality of Law* (New Haven: Yale University Press, 1964), pp. 33-91.

sumes that societies "will" laws. The same sanguine supposition appears in Holmes' positivist definition of law as "prophecies of what the courts will do in fact." This assumes that the courts will in fact "do" law. Professor Howe quotes a suitable illustration of Holmes' assumptions:

> The only question for the lawyer is, how will the judges act? Any motive for their action, be it constitution, statute, custom, or precedent, which can be relied upon as likely in the generality of cases to prevail, is worthy of consideration as one of the sources of law, in a treatise on jurisprudence. Singular motives, like the blandishments of the emperor's wife, are not a ground for prediction, and are therefore not considered.[25]

Supposing that society wills laws, moreover, why must they be regarded as, *ipso facto*, sufficiently good to oblige obedience? By presuming the social advantageousness of law, as well as the necessity of society for men, Holmes implies the obligation of all laws. He sometimes says that we should obey law because it brings us civilization. This remark, of course, is true only of civilized laws. Similarly, he was wont to say that society will kill the disobedient or the dissenter. Even if the fact were true, it wouldn't prove any obligation. The fact is doubtful: in civilized societies whose better parts take seriously the rightness of what they do, disobedience of law may not in itself occasion punishment, to say nothing of death. Sometimes the claims of justice, equity, or of a higher law, are considered. It is striking that in Holmes' two chief endeavors to reduce the study of law to that of the will of society, *The Path of the Law* and *The Common Law*, he excluded from consideration that branch known as "equity."[26]

Perhaps a contrast with Marshall's analogous doctrine will make the point more clear. In the text I have sketched Marshall's answer to the question why laws oblige: by just laws men's interests are served. Holmes denied that "logic,"

[25] Howe, *Holmes*, II, 74.
[26] *CLP*, pp. 175-76; *The Common Law*, "Preface."

deduction from individual interests, determined the law: law follows policy and policy felt necessities of the time. But the objection doesn't meet Marshall's kind of liberalism. For that did not pretend to describe how the factual polities of history, liberal and illiberal, primitive and civilized, actually made their law. His jurisprudence explained man's obligation to just laws. Beginning with an understanding of the basic interests or rights which law was to protect, it went on to recommend *sound* laws.

The point is of obvious importance and can be briefly elaborated. Like Holmes' theory, Marshall's jurisprudence begins "realistically" from a basic force. It issues in a realistic recommendation, however, not in a realistic description. The force, as indicated in Chapter I, is "interest": the desire to avoid danger and to acquire the means of life and pleasure. Marshall's thought, influenced by Locke and his various followers, was concerned to turn this force to political account. The natural force of interest was understood by the liberal philosophers as a useful foundation for justice. Private interest, public gain, when the private passions were ingeniously channeled and regulated by elaborate economic arrangements, by a massively powered yet artfully balanced government, and by a public thoroughly reconciled by "enlightenment" to its interests and the instruments needed to serve them. With all its concern for social unity, public order, and national power, the end of Marshall's jurisprudence was the security and comfort of the individual. It was, we have argued, fundamentally humanitarian, if not quite to the same degree as the thought of, say, Jefferson. Both law and society were then measured by their service to man.

In Holmes' jurisprudence that measurement disappears with the legitimation of all actual societies, and the corresponding if paradoxical obscuring of the particular powers and limits of any society. One is tempted to say that Marshall's sanctification of the Constitution, setting forth a government and its limits, is replaced by Holmes' celebration of society's will, assumed to be always progressing. One might also say that Marshall's moral and political guidance of the law is replaced by Holmes' assumption of "the path of the law"; private law is assumed to be following a historical trail to the public good. Not a single important article or book by Holmes is devoted to constitutional law: his attention is fixed on private law. Holmes' readings turned him, in the formulation of Professor Howe, "towards a view of law and its history, not towards a philosophy of government and its destiny."[27]

Yet we must not push too far this "positivist" side of Holmes' thought, which sees law as simply society's or the court's will. For in this as in any definition of law there is implicit a selection of "true" as opposed to merely "apparent" law, and hence a notion of "good" (e.g., that which keeps up with the times or society's advancing will) as opposed to bad law. Within Holmes' complicated doctrine there was, as there had to be, a notion of justice or right, which sustained or justified the society and the law he wished merely to describe, but in so doing inevitably defended. That notion has already been noticed slightingly: society or its dominant part doesn't will just anything. Its will is attuned to its experience, and the fundamental experience is that of "the interests of life." We must now consider the meaning, the basic moral and political stance, which that cryptic phrase hides. To do justice to Holmes' whole "descriptive" orientation, however, one must say that this stance is less the starting point of Holmes' reasoning than the presuppositions which permit his reasoning to proceed: the moral judgments presupposed by his views that history is development, and law and society are justifiable. Professor Howe's great familiarity with Holmes led him to a perfect characterization of the spirit we try to set forth: "May one discover," he wrote, "behind the juristic principles

[27] *Holmes*, II, 150. Rogat, in "The Judge as Spectator," pp. 214-16, shows how Holmes "characteristically solved constitutional law problems by using common-law formulas."

and historical propositions of *The Common Law* an outline
or an intimation of a political philosophy?"[28]

It is not surprising that this "intimation," not the theme
of Holmes' thought but presupposed by the theme, should be
most apparent in Holmes' earliest major work, *The Common
Law*. It occurs even there as scattered remarks rather than
as considered discussion. Again Professor Howe has noted
the essential premise. ". . . At the bottom of all private relations," Holmes wrote in Lecture II, "however tempered by
sympathy and all the social feelings, is a justifiable self-
preference." Holmes spoke, as Professor Howe remarked,
"not merely descriptively, but defensively."[29] Not merely the
force of self-preference, if one may so speak, but a "justifiable
force."

This reminds one very much of Marshall's own individualism. That originated, as we noted in the text, in Locke's
legitimation of certain basic passions. We are not too surprised to see that the things Holmes presumed the self to
prefer echo Marshall's concern for life and property. The
"object of the [criminal law]," Holmes wrote, "is to prevent
human life being endangered or taken."[30] The place of
property is apparent in a paragraph of Lecture VI, "Possessions." Perhaps this passage is most remarkable, however,
as exhibiting Holmes' willingness to rest content, for the
sake of social peace and comfort, with a "morality that is
generally accepted" (as he elsewhere put it). It is a morality
attuned to "actual forces," like the desire to protect one's
property, that do not set high and difficult goals for the law.
"Those who see in the history of law the formal expression
of the development of society will be apt to think that the
proximate ground of law must be empirical, even when that
ground is the fact that a certain ideal or theory of government is generally entertained. Law, being a practical thing,
must found itself on actual forces. It is quite enough, there-

[28] *The Common Law*, p. xxiv.
[29] *Ibid.*, pp. xxv, 38.
[30] *The Common Law*, p. 47, cf. p. 86.

fore, for the law, that man, by an instinct which he shares with the domestic dog, and of which the seal gives a most striking example, will not allow himself to be dispossessed, either by force or fraud, of what he holds, without trying to get it back again. Philosophy may find a hundred reasons to justify the instinct, but it would be totally immaterial if it should condemn it and bid us surrender without a murmur. As long as the instinct remains, it will be more comfortable for the law to satisfy it in an orderly manner, than to leave people to themselves. If it should do otherwise, it would become a matter for pedagogues, wholly devoid of reality."[31]

At bottom Holmes too began with the realistic moral basis fathered by Lockean individualism. Social Darwinism presupposes the original choices made by earlier and greater political philosophers. The task of government and society was essentially that of merely protecting men's lives and properties against the impinging passions of other men. Holmes sanctified the will of society, but considered unrealistic any society which didn't "will" policies in accord with the low but powerful motives of human nature. He sanctified society, but, as is well known, had no use for socialism. We must note some of the problems involved in Holmes' adherence to such a moral and political viewpoint.

There is surely a difficulty in reconciling this outlook with Holmes' well-known indictment of all "absolutes." In particular, Holmes committed himself to the essence of just that natural rights thinking he elsewhere disavowed. How could he reconcile his position with his criticism of old-fashioned liberalism like Marshall's, the "simple philosophizing" which he rather condescendingly attributed to Story?[32] Whether or not it is true that the "instinct" for possession is universal, it was the liberal philosophers who taught men to concentrate upon that and similar basic passions as alone "justifiable," and to disregard for political purposes the distinctively human inclinations unknown to the dog and the seal. If low and

[31] *Ibid.*, p. 168.
[32] "The Uses of Law Schools," *CLP*, p. 41.

contemptible, these common passions were at least capable of serving as touchstones of a reliable, of a more certainly safe, of what Holmes calls a "more comfortable," political life. Chapter I discusses this basic premise, the acceptance of which has much to do with the spread of classical liberalism, and with the tendencies now summed up under "modernization." Here we need only note that Holmes' belief in a progressive history merely sanctified with the mantle of inevitability the kind of development which the modern philosophers began. His understanding of "progress," involving ever more peace, commerce, production, multiplication of human power with the application of science, and ever more completely collective "organization of the world," as he put it, encompassed a good part of the recommendations of Bacon, Locke, Descartes, Montesquieu—and Hamilton, Marshall, Story, Madison, and Jefferson. The critic of "simple philosophizing" is in good part its child.

Again, however, we must not push too far one part of Holmes' complicated understanding. We have considered the manner in which law develops through history, its vehicle being the will of society. We have also seen that this descriptive account presupposes a rudimentary moral and political orientation fundamentally similar to the liberal individualism which Holmes at times affected to despise. Here, however, we must put Holmes' account back together again: his emphasis upon the "will of society" developing through history is different from classical liberalism, even if it borrows a crucial premise. The individualistic basis pops out only occasionally, it will be remembered, and, as it might appear, incidentally. There is absent from Holmes' thought Marshall's clear deduction of Lockean government and society from Lockean man's needs. Holmes, having supposed on liberal grounds the necessity of law, is disposed then to lend legitimacy generally to any society and to any law. The reason lies in the peculiar form of Holmes' philosophy of history.

Social Darwinism assured him that man's interests are

automatically ever better served. By the omnipresent "struggle for life" the most fit men and institutions survive. Thus the means for satisfying the "real interests of life" are continually improved. In "Law and the Court" Holmes deplored attacks upon the Supreme Court as protector of the wealthy and the monopolists, and went on to deplore as well the misrepresentation of those classes of society. "We are apt to think of ownership as a terminus, not as a gateway, and not to realize that except the tax levied for personal consumption large ownership means investment, and investment means the direction of labor towards the production of the greatest returns. . . . The function of private ownership is to divine in advance the equilibrium of social desires—which socialism equally would have to divine, but which, under the illusion of self-seeking, is more poignantly and shrewdly foreseen."[33]

Holmes' debt to liberal individualism is seen in this invocation of the invisible hand. Yet his own views on free markets and the deeds of monopolists were more sanguine than those of Smith or Marshall. Moreover, they reflected but one part of his willingness to permit the stronger to dominate. Not solely the economic master, but the victorious social group generally, and especially the victorious ideal, was to have its way. Holmes seemed willing to throw society completely open to struggle. Is it with him that there originates the unpleasant characterization of society as an "arena"? Behind Holmes' willingness to sanction struggle lay his Darwinian supposition of progress by struggle. Surely there is a problem here. Marshall and classical liberalism are often condemned for belief in the invisible hand. Holmes seemed to suppose an invisible mind governing all of history.

In the light of this elaborate and abstract theory of law in general was cast Holmes' understanding of American law in particular. The country was seen through a filter comprised of a realistic description of law as the majority's will, mixed

[33] *CLP*, pp. 293-94.

with a supposition of evolutionary development; of admiration for the social organization serving the individual's interests, combined with an assumption that gloves-off struggle was the means to further progress. We will attend chiefly to Holmes' interpretation of America as a free market of ideas, and then contrast his views on specific constitutional rights and powers with those of Marshall. First, however, it is necessary to treat the best-known ingredient of his more practical views, the doctrine of judicial deference. Involved in Holmes' own posture as judge, it is perhaps the best illustration of the way an esoteric philosophy of history underlay his recommendations for the American judge and lawyer.

The doctrine was essentially this: defer to the dominant force that arises from society's struggle for existence. It was thus a peculiar mixture of manifest deference and implicit presumption. If the judge was to defer to the stronger, this standard was itself a transformation of the American judicial role. Besides, it was thus made the judges' task to distinguish the stronger, which in doubtful cases would mean prophesying the future course of history, and to conceive of the country as a great arena of struggle. The Holmesian "detachment" that Rogat rightly pointed out went hand in hand with the exhortations to change so characteristic of Holmes' judicial opinions.

Let us look at the ambivalent character of Holmes' counsel of deference in another way. He dwelled upon the judges' inadequacy in appraising the will of society, in placing their merely individual values or "absolutes" in the way of a developing history. Yet this presupposed, as we have seen, the justice of history. Holmes' famous skepticism had a peculiarity not always perceived: while questioning the judgment of individuals, it presupposed the truth of that of majorities, and future majorities at that. "I used to say, when I was young," wrote Holmes with characteristic self-dramatization, "that truth was the majority vote of that nation that could lick all others. . . . Our test of truth is a reference to either a present or an imagined future majority in favor of our view."[34] What is taken from the judge's mind is bestowed on that of history. Beneath the skepticism was a dogmatism; with the practical recommendation of deference went a far-reaching transformation for judges to press upon America.

The United States was to be understood fundamentally as a great competitive market, "a struggle for life" as Holmes phrased the notion by which he would replace the "free competition" of classical liberalism. Justice Holmes' preferences here are well known. He would let the "majority" have its way in the political arena, the economically powerful dominate in the market-place of business. Above all, he believed "that the best test of truth is the power of the thought to get itself accepted in the competition of the market . . ."[35] The crucial part of the social struggle was that of ideas or ideals for dominance. Men live by ideals, equated by Holmes with symbols. Consider that Holmes thought Marshall's significance chiefly symbolic. The true symbol or ideal is, however, the one that wins. Hence the winner in any part of the great struggle for life is chiefly significant as embodying the ideal of the future and hence the truth. America and its fundamental law are to be interpreted in the light of this fundamental law of social progress. "If in the long run the beliefs expressed in proletarian dictatorship," Holmes wrote in a famous dissent from the bench of the Supreme Court of the United States, "are destined to be accepted by the dominant forces of the community, the only meaning of free speech is that they should be given their chance and have their way."[36]

Although contrary and more attractive ingredients existed within Holmes' thought, they entered hardly at all into his jurisprudence. The Boston Brahmin displayed occasionally a rather aristocratic contempt for the pervasive American

[34] *CLP*, p. 307.
[35] *Abrams* v. *U.S.*, 250 U.S. 630 (1919).
[36] *Gitlow* v. *N.Y.*, 268 U.S. 673 (1925).

spirit of "success," especially business success. He favored, for example, legal education of a kind teaching "law in the grand manner" and making "great lawyers," rather than that exalting "smartness, as against dignity of moral feeling and profundity of knowledge."[37] On the other hand, he discounted the importance of a university education for the American lawyer, defending himself against the criticism of the Lord Chief Justice of England with the remark that he was "speaking only of [a university education's] importance for what I may call a fighting success."[38] Holmes' view of the community as a gloves-off arena, in which all must fight not for honor but for survival, qualified his devotion to "nobility" of character. It dominated his understanding of the law itself.

This law of social struggle involved a paradox which is evident throughout Holmes' interpretations of the Constitution. There are no fundamental constitutional principles, but the principle that wins in the market is to be regarded as fundamental. The deference implicit in the principle, no absolutes, is contradicted by that absolute and its supporting absolutes: the premises sustaining Holmes' supposition that the free market in ideas is *the* means to ever truer principles. Holmes favored the victor, but only the victor by a certain process. He favored basically the free struggle for existence, as his remark on the "proletariet" indicates. There was a tension here. While Holmes was wont to defer to the will of majorities and legislatures and generally to the government's claims, he is also well known for his decisions favoring unbridled economic competition and, especially, a free arena of competition for ideas. In one paragraph of a judicial opinion he might say that a constitution "is made for people of *fundamentally* differing views." In the next paragraph he could indicate that the word "liberty" in the Fourteenth Amendment might "prevent the natural out-

[37] "The Use of Law Schools," *CLP*, p. 37, *passim*. As to Holmes somewhat aristocratic manner, see also *CLP*, pp. 33-34, 153, 273-75.

[38] "Postcript" to "The Bar as a Profession," *CLP*, p. 163; cf. pp. 162 and 153-59.

come of a dominant opinion" when that outcome could properly be said to "infringe *fundamental* principles as they have been understood by the traditions of our people and our law."[39] The Constitution, according to Holmes, did not embody Herbert Spencer's *Social Statics*. Nor did it contain any "particular economic theory." It did, however, enact Holmes' understanding of the free market in ideas. "But when men have realized that time has upset many fighting faiths, they may come to believe even more than they believe the very foundations of their own conduct that the ultimate good desired is better reached by free trade in ideas—that the best test of truth is the power of the thought to get itself accepted in the competition of the market, and that truth is the only ground upon which their wishes safely can be carried out. That, at any rate, is the theory of our Constitution."[40]

The practical implications of Holmes' general views on American law become more evident when contrasted with the Marshallian constitutionalism discussed in the text. Marshall supposed fixed rights and powers. Holmes supposed social progress in the person of the victorious group or idea, together with fixed social conditions of competitive conflict whereby the victor arises. Marshall's old Lockean natural rights are subordinated by Holmes to the will or expediency of society. "Manifestly, therefore, nothing but confusion of thought can result from assuming that the rights of man in a moral sense are equally rights in the sense of the Constitution and the law." With occasional qualifications Holmes was proud to have emphasized "the criterion of social welfare as against the individualistic eighteenth century bills of rights."[41] Still, Holmes' own Darwinism alleged the natural necessity, if not the natural right, of each to struggle. Holmes' variation from Marshall is more in tenor than in kind. Crucially, the right to acquire property, while defended as

[39] *Lochner* v. *New York*, 198 U.S. 75-76 (1905), italics added.
[40] *Abrams* v. *U.S.*, 250 U.S. 630 (1919).
[41] "Ideals and Doubts," *CLP*, p. 307; "The Path of the Law," *CLP*, pp. 171-72, cf. p. 168.

in society's advantage, is somewhat depreciated in favor of
unbridled free speech. "If there is any principle of the
Constitution that more imperatively calls for attachment than
any other it is the principle of free thought—not free thought
for those who agree with us but freedom for the thought
that we hate."[42] The quotation suggests another difference.
When Holmes did protect private liberties, including property and the management of businesses, his doctrines tended
to be less restrained, more in tune with a no-holds-barred
struggle, than Marshall's. On the other hand, Holmes was
much more inclined to respect legislative acts which impinged
on private rights, especially that to acquire property. The
legislature represented the will of society. At times, it must
be said, Holmes' insistence on the right of the stronger to
act through its legislative will seemed to display a certain
disdain toward minorities and the weak generally. "The
legislature," he was willing to affirm openly, "has a general
power to make a part of the community uncomfortable by
change."[43] It is hard to believe that Marshall would have
ranked among constitutional authorities such a power, however he might have recognized the inevitable incidental effects
of government action. Professor Rogat has called "harsh" and
even "callous" Holmes' judicial opinions treating such vulnera-
ble classes as aliens and Southern Negroes.[44] These might
profitably be compared with the Marshallian equivalent dis-

[42] *U.S.* v. *Schwimmer*, 279 U.S. 654-55 (1929).

[43] *Tyson Bros.* v. *Banton*, 273 U.S. 446 (1927).

[44] Rogat concludes his two articles thus: "Nowhere in any of the
cases we have considered did Holmes help in framing a remedy to
secure a constitutional right. He did not develop further any inchoate
right or liberty, or broaden the scope of those which were already
established. . . . Instead, he habitually upheld government action by
pointing to the most general powers that government had already
exercised, giving little indication of how the Court might determine
the limits of those powers, and sometimes leaving it unclear whether
any such limits existed. It is not accidental that future courts sometimes found unacceptable the implications of Holmes' terse, permissive
opinions and had to provide . . . the qualifications that he had omit-
ted." "Mr. Justice Holmes: A Dissenting View," pp. 305-06.

cussed in Chapter II of the text: the Chief Justice's views on slavery and his magnanimous as well as judicious treatment of the Cherokee Indians.

With respect to the workings of government, Holmes continued to presuppose liberal government's various departments. He tended to interpret them, however, in a manner permitting the dominance of the strongest force in the community. This he identified with "the majority," for reasons not perfectly clear. "If the welfare of the living majority is paramount, it can only be on the ground that the majority have the power in their hands."[45] Holmes favored the legislative department as best reflecting the majority's will. In obvious contrast to Marshall's desire to restrain the legislature, Holmes did not think judicial review absolutely necessary.[46] He did, however, strongly support the union against the states and the federal judiciary's power over the states and their legislatures. Indeed, in so sanctifying national power and loosening constitutional restraints, his nationalism went farther than the Marshallian doctrine discussed in the last section of Chapter II.

As for the government's judiciary department, Holmes' doctrines would tend to reduce the courts' supervisory role over American life. This must be understood. The introduction of these new doctrines, by Holmes especially, supposes a judicial transformation of American institutions on a grand scale. In themselves, however, those doctrines cut down the courts' powers extensively. Marshall understood the federal judiciary as responsible for enforcing upon the country the public law and private law implicit in the Constitution—the natural constitution behind the written law. Holmes was languid as to judicial review of the political departments, and he made great efforts to evict anything resembling "natural private law" from the courts.

[45] "Masters and Men": The Gas-Stokers' Strike, 7 *American Law Review* (1873), quoted by Max Lerner, ed., *The Mind and Faith of Justice Holmes* (Boston: Little, Brown and Company, 1943), p. 51.
[46] "Law and the Court," *CLP*, pp. 295-96.

It is true that his positivist definitions seemed to give final word as to what is law to the courts. "The object of our study, then, is prediction, the incidence of the public force through the instrumentality of the courts."[47] "The prophecies of what the courts will do in fact, and nothing more pretentious, are what I mean by the law."[48] Law is what the courts say it is ("in our kind of society," Holmes occasionally alluded *sotto voce* to the political decisions taken for granted by his descriptive science)—not, as Marshall said, what the legislature makes.

The issue is not so simple. While Marshall said that "Courts are the mere instruments of the law," he also said that they alone construed the law as applied to individuals. In following in their constructions those Blackstonean "general principles of law" which secure individual rights, courts gain in effect tremendous authority to lay down the law. "The question whether a right has vested or not is in its nature, judicial, and must be tried by the judicial authority."[49]

Holmes made a famous attack on this doctrine, which Mr. Justice Story had used, in *Swift* v. *Tyson*,[50] to establish a national common law jurisdiction for federal courts. "The common law is not a brooding omnipresence in the sky," Holmes countered in *Southern Pacific Co.* v. *Jensen*,[51] "but the articulate voice of some sovereign or quasi-sovereign that can be identified." "If there were such a transcendental body of law outside of any particular State but obligatory within it unless and until changed by statute," went his dissent in the *Black and White Taxi* case,[52] "the Courts of the United States might be right in using their independent judg-

47 "The Path of the Law," *CLP*, p. 167.
48 *Ibid.*, p. 173.
49 *Marbury* v. *Madison*, 1 Cranch (U.S.), 87 (1803). As to Marshall's views, see the discussion in Chapter II, "Legal Power: Private Rights Secured."
50 16 Peters (U.S.), 1 (1842).
51 244 U.S. 222 (1917).
52 *Black and White Taxicab Co.* v. *Brown and Yellow Taxicab Co.*, 276 U.S. 533 (1928).

ment as to what it was. But there is no such body of law." Holmes' dissent on this point became the doctrine of the Supreme Court in *Erie R.R. Co. v. Tompkins*.[53] The whole question, involving the possibility of a uniform national commercial law among other things, remains alive.

Holmes himself had asserted in his sketch that Marshall's significance to the lawyer consisted in "the rise of a new body of jurisprudence, by which guiding principles are raised above the reach of statute and State, and judges are entrusted with a solemn and hitherto unheard-of authority and duty." What Marshall had raised, Holmes sought to destroy. The natural constitution behind the written constitution, characteristic of Marshall's jurisprudence and the object of the courts' solicitude, was to give way to the will of society and the competitive conditions for its appearance. Hence the two chief parts of Holmes' recommendation to lawyers and judges in *The Path of the Law*: first, an exhortation not to decide according to their merely moral convictions; second, an exhortation to decide according to social policy. Holmes turned courts from a solicitude for private security to a concern to follow social policy. He was more responsible than any other single man for turning American jurisprudence toward a study of judicial decision-making, for destroying the old Lockean standards of decision, and for dwelling on social expediency as the new standard. Hence the problem which has troubled his heirs ever since: how to know what is socially expedient, or, what is the will of society?

To some degree the problem was solved by the whole practical recommendation that we have been considering: lawyers and, especially, judges were to defer, indeed, but to the path of the law as Holmes presented it; to the progressing will of majority and legislature; and generally to the struggle for life in America. To that degree, however, Holmes' solution is subject to this difficulty: does not it deserve his powerful slur, "brooding omnipresence," more than Marshall's own doctrine? It is just as much a standard for judges. Holmes'

[53] 304 U.S. 64 (1938).

slur connotes moreover, a guiding force that is everywhere—
"omnipresent"—and, in addition, self-moving or at least itself
alive and thinking—"brooding": traits more characteristic of
Holmes' progressively developing historical process than
Marshall's own doctrine of rights and powers. Besides, this
brooding something is not essentially oriented to human
benefit, also truer of Holmes' historical process than Marshall's rights and powers. It is true, of course, that Marshall's
doctrine is more "in the sky" than Holmes'. That seems,
however, but a necessary consequence of Marshall's rather
sounder initial assumption: that legal institutions must be
made by men to accord with just and reasonable aspirations,
and do not have their purposes and shape bestowed by a
historical process.

More serious than the irony attending Holmes' standard
for judicial decision are the difficulties corroding it. Suppose
we agree, as to some extent Marshall would have agreed, that
courts affect the nation's "policy" in their ordinary civil
and criminal tasks, as well as when engaging in review of
legislation. Is it sufficient to say: judge according to what
is socially expedient? Is it not necessary to indicate what
is socially expedient, i.e., what is good or wise for the country and the law? Marshall did this. Holmes did not, or he
did it only equivocally. He denied his ability, or that of any
judge, to provide "absolutes," to say what is good and wise.
The reason is that the historical process upsets old truths in
providing better ones. Therefore, defer to the process. But
that presumes knowledge of truths: that there *is* a historical
process, that new truths are truer than old ones. Holmes'
deference, it will be remembered, was built on a dogmatism. Holmes was constantly recommending to his audience his version of what was good and wise. The difficulty
is that his version is beset with a fatal flaw. Its test of truth
is in the future, and we can not know that. Truth is what
wins. What any majority thinks now is subject to the will
of "an imagined future majority." True law is not what
courts do in fact but "*prophecies* of what the courts *will* do

in fact." But the future is not known. And thus, according to Holmes' own standard, truth cannot now be known. What is good and wise for society can't be known. How can judges decide now if they have to know the unknowable future?

In fact, we must carry our argument as to the difficulties in Holmes' doctrine one step further. For Holmes believed that in the decisive respect the future was knowable. The good for society, if not *now* known, could be *then* known and will be then known by science, modern natural science applied to the law. At least one knew now that science could provide the answers not yet known. Holmes knew there was a historical development, and he knew therefore its maturity: modern "consciousness." "The time has gone by when law is only an unconscious embodiment of the common will. It has become a conscious reaction upon itself of organized society knowingly seeking to determine its own destinies."[54] The light of that modern consciousness is science. To change the metaphor, it is "the root from which comes the flower of our thought."[55] It is not easy to say more about Holmes' understanding of science than its attention to "the quantitative relation between cause and effect" that we have mentioned before. As his biographer Professor Howe reported, Holmes did not investigate very deeply Comte and others of the positivists on whom he relied. He knew, a scientist friend of Holmes has remarked, "of science only by hearsay, so to speak . . . ," and on the subject was "extraordinarily trusting and uninformed."[56]

Holmes' trust took the form of seeing science as the key to discovery of true law, socially advantageous law. Law is the will of society, and science will enable us to know that

[54] "Privilege, Malice, and Intent," *CLP*, pp. 129-30. "We are only at the beginning of a philosophic reaction, and of a reconsideration of doctrines which for the most part still are taken for granted without any deliberate, conscious, and systematic questioning of their grounds." *CLP*, p. 185.

[55] *Holmes-Laski Letters*, ed. Mark De Wolfe Howe (Cambridge: Harvard University Press, 1953), i, 210.

[56] *Holmes*, i, 222.

will. To know the law's past a scientific history could perceive the motives of policy which have given birth to legal forms. Perhaps *The Common Law* was meant to be part of that endeavor. To know what the will of society is at present, however, requires more than a scientific history. "I think, as other people do," Holmes wrote in an essay, "Law in Science—Science in Law," "that the main ends of the subject are practical, and from a practical point of view, history, with which I have been dealing thus far, is only a means, one of the least of the means, of mastering a tool."[57] Not scientific history but social science is the true mastery of the "tool": "An ideal system of law should draw its postulates and its legislative justification from science."[58] The "ultimate question" is "worth," that is, potential strength. The will of society could be truly known by an accurate measurement of the will, "the intensity of desire," as Holmes called it, behind competing policy alternatives. Thus a proper study of the law does not consist in individualism's "logical development as in mathematics, or only in a study of it as an anthropological document from the outside [Holmes' scientific history]; an even more important part consists in the establishment of its postulates from within upon accurately measured social desires instead of tradition."[59] Science will yield recommendations as well as descriptions. Through such means, it seems, Holmes expected a kind of scientific utopia to be established. From "postulates" based on accurately measured desires might be deduced comprehensive practical corollaries. Functionaries could then be trained to carry out these policies in the modern and progressive way, with "the substitution of quantitative for qualitative judgments."[60] While recognizing this procedure to be not without difficulties, Holmes thought that it should nevertheless form the "ideal" of jurispru-

[57] *CLP*, pp. 224-25.
[58] "Learning and Science," *CLP*, p. 139.
[59] "Law in Science—Science in Law," *CLP*, pp. 225-26; cf. p. 242.
[60] *Ibid.*, p. 231.

dence. "Very likely it may be that with all the help that statistics and every modern appliance can bring us there never will be a commonwealth in which science is everywhere supreme. But it is an ideal, and without ideals what is life worth?"[61] The "ideal" of jurisprudence is the replacement of the old-fashioned jurisprudence and statesman by the transforming thinker's quantitative social science and its practitioners, men fed by the statistician aware of quantitative methods, modeled after the economist accustomed to weigh comparative costs. "The man of the future is the man of statistics and the master of economics," as Holmes put it in *The Path of the Law*.[62] This is the capstone of the cosmopolitan "thinking" in light of which, according to Holmes, are to be judged the achievements of mere judicial statesmen like Marshall. This is both the reason for the depreciation of mere judgment and the promise for America of the thinker's transformation.

But what a capstone and what a promise. Let the reader just consider that the goal held out for jurisprudence, the only explicit suggestion approaching a political utopia in Holmes' thought, is this chill, purely methodological, ideal. There is no discussion of the excellences and necessities of man, justice, economic plenty, political arrangements, civilization. It is not strange that, in many remarks on eugenics, and in some judicial decisions, Holmes was willing, with an absence of moral feeling and of politic caution, to justify a scientific or pseudo-scientific manipulation of humans.[63] We will return shortly to this primary consideration. Let us first reflect on the sufficiency of Holmes' science in providing what his own system requires: knowledge of the social will.

The difficulties again are several. What needs to be measured is a tendency, the tendency of an idea to be stronger, to win in the future. But his science cannot measure tendencies, which are not discreet and manifest facts to be quantitatively

---

[61] *Ibid.*, p. 242; cf. p. 195.
[62] *CLP*, p. 187; cf. p. 195.
[63] The classic example is *Buck* v. *Bell*, 274 U.S. 200 (1927).

added up. Suppose it might measure the stronger at any given time. That is not necessarily identical with that tending to be stronger. Indeed, by Holmes' supposition of progress by struggle, often a new and weaker ideal will tend to surpass a stronger one whose time is past.

Second, his science can't measure even the tenor or direction of the stronger will at a certain time. By will Holmes seemed to mean a "conscious" ideal sustained by "unconscious" strength of desire. His science is to determine the intensity of the desire behind various ideals, thus to determine which way society will move. The difficulty is that the direction of the desire measured may differ from the tenor of the idea it sustains: the purports of ideal and of desire may diverge. This is especially important if different people's motives must be compared. People get emotional about the same ideal for the most various motives. Besides, there is a problem in measuring desire thus: the emotional force of desire is "unconscious," however conscious its direction may become. Hence its force is invisible. It is thus hard to measure, especially for a quantitative science which insists, as Holmes occasionally said, that the only reliable verification is according to the sensible, in this case the visible.

Finally, even if the true tendency of the social will might be quantitatively determined by science, the judge's problem would not be thus solved. For the judge still would have to determine which of the wills, or of the various parts of the one social will, are *relevant* to his case and his decision. That implies, however, his own judgment about what kind of case it is: a property case, or a civil rights case, for example. But judgments of *kind* are of *quality*,—as to the appropriateness of a certain claim, for example—not judgments of quantity. One must grasp not the strength behind an opinion or ideal, but the kind of action which it recommends. This process depends, as Holmes himself said in advising judges to forego their own opinions, upon "some attitude of yours not capable of quantitative measurement."[64] The trouble is that his own advice to judges is subject to his criticism: determining the relevancy of the "social will" depends upon just such an attitude.[65] Holmes' counsel for judges is corroded by his own criticism of counsel. The problem is not in the judges' reason but in his criticism: in his pseudo-scientific criterion for reason. More generally, Holmes' own recommendation of science and social science as the only worthy kind of knowledge, is in fact self-vitiating. For if science cannot arrive at qualitative judgments, it cannot sustain Holmes' appraisal of the "worth" of science itself. And thus the "critical acid" of which Holmes was so fond proves so excessive as to destroy itself. This points to the drastic flaw in the very beginning of Holmes' judicial science.

Holmes' science began as a description of law as it "really" is, of the forces which move the law. So beginning, how can it measure or guide those forces and thus instruct the law? For law is inevitably a standard for the use of force, not simply a force. Law is a rule, and therefore looks askance at arbitrary force; it is usually designed to pursue some sort of justice or public good, and thus also looks askance at force utterly without right. If law is not a standard for action (it needn't, of course, be a sufficient standard), it does not exist. Holmes meets this objection by seeing a

[64] "The Path of the Law," *CLP*, p. 181.

[65] In a way Holmes saw these difficulties, but his reaction was to exhort his listeners to greater efforts—"to be as accurate as we can." Appropriately enough, he mistook a difficulty of principle, involving the character or quality of things, for one of degree. Consider the following passage: "Well, in the law we only occasionally can reach an absolutely final and quantitative determination, because the worth of the competing social ends which respectively solicit a judgment of the plaintiff or the defendant cannot be reduced to number and accurately fixed. The worth, that is, the intensity of the competing desires, varies with the varying ideals of the time, and, if the desires were constant, we could not get beyond a relative decision that one was greater and one was less. But it is of the essence of improvement that we should be as accurate as we can. . . ." "Law in Science—Science in Law," *CLP*, p. 231.

standard implicit in the basic forces moving the law: the ideal develops from and by means of the real. Scientific "consciousness" is the culmination of historical development. The difficulty remains. We must have trans-historical knowledge to judge of history's development, to know what is ideal, to know a culmination from a useful tool, a development from a vast concatenation of changes signifying nothing. History doesn't teach; its lessons must be drawn out by judgment. Science can't provide the judgment Holmes needs. It is only a tool for human utility. It doesn't and can't indicate the things men should seek and even the limited range of things that men should regard as useful.

This "descriptive" basis mixing science with historical development gone, all of Holmes' confidences and hopes for the future must be seen as what they are: confidences and hopes. The utopia of human "consciousness," the sanguine faith in history's victor, the expectation that ideas obtain power according to their worth, the recommendation to let the struggle in politics, economics, and ideas go on unimpeded—these have in their Holmesian form little behind them but "faith," that is, belief without rational foundation. It is striking how frequently the "realistic" Holmes chose to rely on what he called "faith." It seems that he was not unaware of some difficulties in his thought. His fundamentally optimistic fatalism was often tinged with a pessimistic skepticism. He saw, in a way, that by making the future his standard of truth he lost the ability to judge now, even as to whether the future will be truthful. Moreover, it becomes dubious whether change is development if its purport appears obscure. The resulting tension leads to characteristically paradoxical statements: "the key to happiness is . . . to be not merely a necessary but a willing instrument in working out the inscrutable end."[66] Need one say that if the end is inscrutable, one cannot distinguish an instrument from an obstacle? Should one then hang one's happiness, and the country's happiness, on the

[66] "Brown University—Commencement," *CLP*, p. 166.

unknown? Holmes' "more cosmopolitan standards" amount to little more than the replacement of the statesman's judgment by condescending calls for change, couched in misleadingly brief and aphoristic rhetoric, resting on no more than blind faith in the future.

To some, however attentive to the argument we have made, this conclusion will sound unnecessarily harsh. Certainly, many of the particular legal decisions and political policies for which Holmes stood, sometimes against the narrow and mean jurisprudence of his contemporaries, can be defended. The point is that Holmes' theoretical defense won't do, and, moreover, that his policies and his defense constantly assume moral and political accomplishments, of both statesmen and philosophers, for which he neither accounts nor provides. Certainly, "theory" has a place in the law. The point is that Holmes' kind of theory preempted the guidance of American law only to show itself incapable of guiding. One may readily acknowledge the importance of legal philosophy, if not of Holmes' elaborately scientific and historical theory. Yet it must be said that such speculations have a very limited place in American law. A few remarks on that place will clarify the role in American legal practice of judicial statesmen like Marshall.

We are still tempted to embrace in the fields of ethics, politics, and the law those methods of natural science which have had such spectacular results elsewhere. The temptation must be resisted. A science exploiting nature for the benefit of man presupposes some judgments as to what is beneficial for man. That knowledge modern science cannot provide. As applied to human affairs social science admits this inability and even prides itself on being "value-free." Judgments of value, however, guide the well-intentioned law-maker and judge. Although we need efficient techniques to assist in what we wish to do, we need first know what to do. Means follow from ends, where not in themselves worthy or unworthy. This orientation by moral and political ends is absent from Holmes' jurisprudence. Holmes turned much of modern jurisprudence to the study of judicial decision-making, but left vacant its essence: a reasonable view of what constitutes justice in America, of the rights and duties of citizens and of the institutions of law, economics, and polity appropriate for the country. A methodological utopia is substituted for sound political counsel.

It is this abstraction from humane ends which is the besetting and deepest flaw of Holmes' thought. It controls his sketch of Marshall, the judge evaluated in terms of the thinker's chill transformation. Marshall's significance for the patriot is described as "union"—with no characterization of the kind of union and its worth for Americans. His significance for lawyers was the raising of law above state—with no estimate of the political advantages and disadvantages of such a momentous achievement. Holmes had no political experience. He hardly read the newspapers, and evidently read very little on the subjects of law, politics, and economics. His visitor Bryce was surprised at his political indifference; his biographer Professor Howe wonders: "If Henry Adams, teaching medieval history, found that the true center of his concern was the American political scene, how could Holmes, teaching American Constitutional Law, remain largely indifferent to the public affairs of his time?"[67] This is distinctly strange in the man who eulogized the place of considerations of social policy in the law. He complained petulantly, as Rogat put it, when Brandeis wanted him to read books in "the domain of fact."[68] Among Holmes' publications and judicial opinions there is nothing focusing on constitutional law in the broad and statesmanlike manner of any one of a dozen Marshallian opinions. Marshall and Holmes each wrote one book. Marshall's comprised the life and especially the military and political accomplishments of Washington, the country's greatest statesman [as Marshall thought], the funda-

[67] Howe, *Holmes*, ii, 31.
[68] Rogat, "The Judge as Spectator," p. 244.

mental founder and savior of its best institutions. Holmes' comprised a series of lectures on private law—in a manner which seems to have bent evidence and presentation to conform to his Darwinian philosophy of history.

Holmes, to repeat what has been said before, assumed as given by history a path cleared by other statesmen. "While there still is doubt," he once wrote, "while opposite convictions still keep a battle front against each other, the time for law has not come. . . ."[69] How strange. That is just the fluid and open time favoring the founder, the law-giver. It is the only time, as political thinkers and statesmen have thought, when, the "cake of custom" broken, extensive improvements in law might be made. It was only this kind of rare circumstance which made possible ratification of the Constitution, Marshall thought. Holmes goes on: "the notion destined to prevail is not yet entitled to the field." Great political deeds need not be attended to, because destiny will watch over us.

As an alternative to Holmes' kind of theory, one must dwell thus on deeds and statesmen rather than on philosophy and philosophers. Philosophy is the pursuit of truth, and nations don't engage in it. Peoples and their leaders talk about and discuss what is the best policy for them. It is, however, policy, their moral, economic, social and political benefit, that is sought, not the truth as such. Such deliberation directed to practical affairs is the concern, of course, of practical judgment, not of philosophy. Justice to the living must be the chief concern of a nation's law, and fair judges and sound statesmen are its bulwark. In the course of his sketch of Marshall, Holmes remarked that "a man is bound to be parochial in his practice," but "his thinking should be cosmopolitan and detached." This is plainly fallacious with respect to any statesman, however true it might be for some philosopher not engaged in governing. Clearly the thoughts of the statesman engaged in his tasks must be fixed on his tasks, and thus circumscribed by the peculiar customs and

[69] "Law and the Court," *CLP*, pp. 294-95.

conditions of his particular nation. Else the man will be a thoughtless practitioner, perhaps a judge who conceives of his task as just playing the game according to the rules (as if rules didn't need politic and fair application), or an impractical doctrinaire. Holmes' jurisprudence encouraged both extremes while discouraging the statesmanlike mean.

Yet there is a place where the laws governing America are touched by moral, political, and legal philosophy. A nation does not philosophize, yet it may be influenced in its purposes, its character, even its institutions, by philosophy. The United States has been often called a "Lockean country," and in my study of Marshall's understanding of the Constitution I have tried to explore the profound truth in this description. The United States is the first "new nation," the first country unequivocally devoted to "modernization," the first particular country devoted to universal or cosmopolitan goals set forth by a modern philosopher. Even the phrasing of the Declaration of Independence comes in part from Locke, as is well known. The country's basis is then peculiarly theoretical, peculiarly concerned with "self-evident truths." The United States' greatest statesman could even say that the country was dedicated to a proposition. The whole civil rights movement for Negroes, the most powerful and massive of modern American political movements, marks that proposition's enduring place in the country's conscience, if not in all its deeds. This does not mean that the country philosophizes; that these notions are fully weighed even by its better statesmen. They are taken for granted, lived by, guiding to some extent the country's deeds. They are embodied in fundamental laws like the Constitution, the great documents of public policy that are revered or respected by almost all. These are in turn interpreted sensibly or foolishly, sometimes magnificently, by the country's leading statesmen as they establish and settle its institutions, then guide it in doing its best according to these revered traditions. Hence the United States has honored the founding generation, Lincoln, and others. Theory has then a place in American law: notably that occupied by constitutional theory or American jurisprudence. It is because the jurisprudence of a judicial statesman like Marshall is so well attuned to the most fundamental concerns of the American order, that his thought is so illuminating about America. He is, *par excellence*, "the expounder of the Constitution."

Our contemporary circumstances make it especially important to distinguish sharply between "theory in the law" and philosophy strictly speaking. Otherwise the law cannot but suffer from the grave problems which have come upon modern moral and political philosophy. To put it mildly, these studies no longer provide the confident guidance from which our country's framers benefited. The signs cannot be missed, ranging from a crude moral skepticism now even fashionable, to philosophic preoccupation not with what is good but with how we know what is good, to fiddling with words, to the mere history of ideas. It may be that this reflects a deep crisis originating with defects in the very origins of modern philosophy. Hence the need for a stricter distinction between the best thought in the sense of philosophy, and the best thought for our country. For it is possible that a country live a self-respecting, honorable, and just life, according to well-founded views of some merit, even as dispute swirls among philosophers about the nature of true merit. The attempt must be made to restore that peculiar soundness for which American institutions were designed. Well interpreted and wisely qualified in accord with our experience, it is probably the best standard of which the country is capable. Without that original view all standards seem lost and a peculiar kind of aimlessness and degradation results. It is as part of such a restoration that my study of Marshall is intended.

A P P E N D I X I I

M A R S H A L L A N D T H E

B U R R T R I A L *

MARSHALL'S conduct of Aaron Burr's treason trial is commonly believed to reflect anti-Jeffersonian bias at the expense of legal principle. Such remains the prevailing opinion among historians, at any rate, despite two recent studies of contrary import. The opinion is in error, and the error deserves to be corrected. Marshall's reputation still suffers from Edward S. Corwin's judgment that the trial exhibits "the one serious blemish on his judicial record." Also, our understanding of the trial itself is clouded by the obscurity attending Marshall's role. And it seems that even modern law has been muddied by the controversy. Congress's official edition of the Constitution, still influenced by Corwin, holds the great Chief Justice's "vacillation . . . between the Bollmann and Burr cases" to be one reason why "the law of treason [is] in a somewhat doubtful condition."[1]

The prevailing belief was most cogently spelled out, if not originated, by Corwin in 1919.[2] He seemed to feel

* This piece appeared in slightly different form in *The Journal of American History*, Volume LIII, September, 1966, pp. 247-58.

[1] *The Constitution of the United States of America: Analysis and Interpretation* (Senate Doc. No. 39, 88 Cong., 1 Sess., 1964), pp. 733-34. See also pp. 728-29.

[2] Edward S. Corwin, *John Marshall and the Constitution: A Chronicle of the Supreme Court*, pp. 86-120. Beveridge, *The Life of John Marshall*, III, 350, 506-09, also implies some vacillation between the Bollmann and Burr opinions, but is nevertheless far more sympathetic to Marshall. Most serious students of the Burr trial have followed

that only political bias, in the crude sense of antipathy toward Thomas Jefferson, could explain what appeared to him as manifest difficulties in Marshall's conduct. Chief among these were inconsistencies between Marshall's decisive opinions at Burr's trial and common law principles, by which the Constitution's treason clause must be interpreted and with which Marshall himself had expressly agreed in *ex parte Bollmann* and *ex parte Swartwout*. Suppose, however, that no such contradictions, manifest or subtle, exist. The allegations of distorted law and of vacillating opinions then collapse. The imputations of political motivation become but speculations unnecessary and even irrelevant to the explanation of Marshall's deeds.

The charge of a sharp divergence between Marshall's views and those implicit in the Constitution could have been questioned long before this, at least since the publication in 1945 of Willard Hurst's fine articles on "Treason in the United States" and on its English background.[3] Yet Corwin's has remained the accepted account of Marshall's behavior at the Burr trial, perhaps because it was not expressly questioned by Hurst. Such an explicit challenge has been made in Bradley Chapin's valuable *The American Law of Treason*.[4] Yet it is not fully satisfactory. Chapin demonstrates that the procedural grounds on which Mar-

Corwin's later interpretation. See Thomas Perkins Abernethy, *The Burr Conspiracy* (New York: Oxford University Press, 1954), pp. 227-49; Richard B. Morris, *Fair Trial: Fourteen Who Stood Accused, from Anne Hutchinson to Alger Hiss* (New York: Alfred A. Knopf, 1953), pp. 119-55, esp. pp. 134-35, 152. See, however, the passing opinion of Leonard W. Levy, *Jefferson & Civil Liberties: The Darker Side* (Cambridge: The Belknap Press, 1963), p. 79, that Marshall only "enforced legal and constitutional standards" in the Burr trial.

[3] Willard Hurst, "Treason in the United States," *Harvard Law Review*, LVIII (Dec. 1944), 226-72; (Feb. 1945), 395-444; (July 1945), 806-57; Hurst, "English Sources of the American Law of Treason," *Wisconsin Law Review*, May 1945, pp. 315-56.

[4] Bradley Chapin, *The American Law of Treason: Revolutionary and Early National Origins* (Seattle: University of Washington Press, 1964), pp. 98-113.

shall in effect halted Burr's trial were perfectly consonant with the common law. He does not, however, expressly confront Corwin's various criticisms of Marshall's substantive notion of treason. Nor does he examine Corwin's crucial allegation of a divergence between the *Burr* and *Bollmann* opinions. In fact he obscures that question by a loose restatement of it. While the recent writers provide the scholarship required for an appraisal of Marshall's conduct, the actual clarification still needs to be done. The purpose of this appendix is to demonstrate that in the light of the findings of Hurst and Chapin, Marshall's opinions amount to an accurate grasp of the Constitution's tenor, that there is no contradiction between Marshall's views at the Burr trial and his opinions previously expressed, and that the imputation of obscure and biased motives is unsupported by any other evidence worthy of the name.

Corwin's argument turns on the contention that Marshall demanded from Burr's prosecutors evidence patently more strict than the Constitution itself required. Article III, Section 3 of the fundamental law prescribes that "No Person shall be convicted of Treason unless on the Testimony of two Witnesses to the same overt Act, or on Confession in open Court." Since Burr did not openly confess, the prosecution had to prove by two witnesses an overt act of treason. Marshall demanded that it thus prove that personal overt act of Burr which constituted the particular act of treason with which he was charged. The indictment charged Burr with a specific act of "levying war" at the island retreat of his associate Harman Blennerhassett. If, as the prosecution maintained, this meant a charge of procuring the assemblage of force on that island, rather than a charge of being present in that assemblage, then that act of procuring, like actual presence, must be shown by two witnesses. "If then the procurement be substituted in place of presence," Marshall intoned, "does it not also constitute an essential part of the overt act? . . . If in one case the presence of the individual make the guilt of the assemblage his guilt, and in the other case the procurement by the individual make the guilt of the assemblage his guilt, then presence and procurement are equally component parts of the overt act, and equally require two witnesses."[5]

Burr's acquittal was then inevitable. The prosecution admitted his absence from Blennerhassett's island and lacked any witnesses to his actual procurement of the assemblage there.

According to Corwin, however, Marshall's interpretation is obviously too stringent. The Constitution does not require two witnesses to the personal overt act of the accused. In accord with the common law doctrine that "in treason all are principals," it requires two witnesses only to an overt act of treason with which the accused may be otherwise linked. "When by further evidence any particular individual is connected with the treasonable combination which brought about the overt act," Corwin writes, "that act, assuming the Common Law doctrine, becomes his act, and he is accordingly responsible for it at the place where it occurred." "Can it be, then," he later asks, "that the Constitution is chargeable with the absurdity of regarding the procurers of treason as traitors and yet of making their conviction impossible?"[6]

The very least that may be concluded from a comparison of Corwin's argument with early national treason law, is that it treats Marshall's problem as unduly "simple." Corwin adopted William Wirt's contention that, since the "entire phraseology" in question comes from an English statute of Edward III's time, it ought to be construed in light of the English common law. This reasoning is not impressive. The Constitution does not follow the famous statute of Edward III precisely. It leaves out the action of "compassing or imagining the death of the king" and includes an express evidential requirement of two witnesses to the same overt

[5] David Robertson, *Reports of the Trials of Colonel Aaron Burr for Treason and for a Misdemeanor . . .* , II, 436, 438.
[6] Corwin, *John Marshall and the Constitution*, pp. 107-08.

act. Thus it is by no means obvious that ancient English constructions ought to control interpretation of the American Constitution on this issue.[7]

In particular, it is not manifest that the Constitution's evidentiary requirements should be interpreted in the light of the common law doctrine that "in treason all are principals." The application of this maxim would make traitors in principal degree of those who are said in common law parlance to have performed only an accessorial role, such as procuring a treasonable assemblage. This could well imply the creation of federal crimes by common law doctrine. Precisely the federal government's authority to punish acts rendered illegal merely by the common law, however, was a hotly disputed issue even in 1807. It was a question actually decided in the negative by the Supreme Court, some five years after Burr's trial. This difficulty is not even mentioned by Corwin, although it was raised by Burr's attorneys and by Marshall as well.[8]

If one presumes the pertinency of the common law, Marshall's failure to conform to its dictates still cannot be demonstrated. The prosecution's indictment was faulty even under the common law. Whatever the comparable culpability of procurer of a treasonable assemblage, and participant in such an assemblage, it seems that under the common law as received from England the accused had to be charged with the particular act of treason, be it procuring or participating, which he had committed. The indictment, however, charged Burr with "levying war"—a head of action long taken to mean actual perpetration—while the prosecution had evidence to prove only that he procured the war levied on Blennerhassett's island. The

[7] *Ibid.*, p. 104; Hurst, "English Sources of the American Law of Treason," p. 316; Hurst, "Treason in the United States," pp. 250-55, 395-417; Chapin, *American Law of Treason*, pp. 3-9, 83-84.

[8] Robertson, *Reports*, I, 547ff.; II, 405; *United States* v. *Hudson and Goodwin*, 7 Cranch (U.S.), 32 (1812). See William Winslow Crosskey, *Politics and the Constitution in the History of the United States*, II, 767-84.

prosecuting attorneys, like Corwin, tried to link Burr with the action on the island by arguing that he was "constructively present." Chapin calls this doctrine "unknown to the common law" in such a context.[9] It was the prosecution and not the defense which here insisted upon the inapplicability of English common law definitions and distinctions. "There is a moral sense," urged Wirt, "much more unerring in questions of this sort, than the frigid deductions of jurists or philosophers. . . ."[10] Chapin has even called the prosecution's "faulty indictment" the "fundamental fact" underlying disposition of the case and in this manner has exonerated Marshall completely from Corwin's charges. It is quite true that Marshall was disposed to interpret the indictment according to its common law meaning, and then to find it faulty. It is also true, however, that he allowed himself to suppose that the indictment's language might be read in the prosecution's lenient manner, as alleging procurement of war with a charge of levying war, and he still would not permit further introduction of evidence unless the prosecution could prove Burr's personal overt act. Even if the charge were taken to be procurement, the Constitution's restrictive intent required that particular charge to be supported by two witnesses—and the prosecution could not provide one.[11]

Thus, even if one grants the adequacy of dubious pleadings as well as the applicability of technical legal doctrines whose bearing was disputed, there remains at issue the sufficiency of the prosecution's evidence in light of the

[9] Chapin, *American Law of Treason*, p. 105; Corwin, *John Marshall and the Constitution*, p. 106. See also Robertson, *Reports*, i, 557ff.; ii, 423-32; Hurst, "English Sources of the American Law of Treason," pp. 327-38, 344-45; Hurst, "Treason in the United States," pp. 252-53, 258-59, 834-35; Blackstone, *Commentaries on the Laws of England in Four Books*, Book iv, iii, xxiii, 34-40, 306-08. See also Alan Wharam, "Treason in Rhodesia," *The Cambridge Law Journal*, November 1967, 192-93.

[10] Robertson, *Reports*, ii, 66, 81, 91-92, 178, 372, 374ff., 388ff.

[11] *Ibid.*, pp. 432, 436, 438.

peculiar intent underlying Article III, Section 3. In a way this is the basic question, for the Constitution's intent might well encompass common law doctrines and enlarge common law meanings.

It is not impossible that the framers of this section presumed that procurers of treason against the United States would be punished as traitors. They could hardly have been ignorant of certain English glosses on "levying war" which authorized this. Yet it must be said that the evidence of their wishes fails to manifest such a purpose. It is not easy to see why Corwin is so certain that Marshall's problem was "simple." In a manner unusual for the constitutional scholar, he discusses neither the words of the fundamental law nor the speeches of its draftsmen.

If words and speeches display any purpose with respect to the crime's definition and punishment, it is one perhaps contrary to that just mentioned. They exhibit the framers' pervasive concern to prevent the use or abuse of treason prosecutions in domestic political conflict by defining the crime strictly and requiring unequivocal evidence. Hurst does not tire of observing that the "outstanding feature" of the treason clause, compared with provisions in colonial and Revolutionary legislation, is that "it is on its face restrictive of the scope of the offence. . . ."[12] It is well known that no offense analogous to "compassing" the king's death was included in treason's definition, that the crime "shall consist only in levying war" and adhering to the country's enemies, and that "giving them aid and comfort" was added probably as a qualification to the last clause.[13] The progressive restriction of the language of Section 3 during its framing, and the language itself, bespeak the framers' concern for a limited definition of treason, perhaps so very limited as to apply most literally only to those who have themselves obviously prosecuted open acts of treason. The requirements of evidence seem to

[12] Hurst, "Treason in the United States," p. 235.
[13] See Max Farrand, ed., *The Records of the Federal Convention of 1787* (New Haven: Yale University Press, 1911), II, 136, 144, 168, 182, 345-50.

reflect this spirit. In fact, as Hurst observes, a motion was introduced in the Convention on August 20 to provide that "Treason against the United States shall consist only in some overt act of levying war against the United States. . . ." The motion was voted down. But it was voted down only after the Convention added to the constitutional requirement of two witnesses the words "to the same overt act." No reference to these happenings occurs in Madison's *Notes*. Nevertheless, Hurst writes, "the inference seems fair that there was a definite intent to require the showing of an overt act as an independent element of the offence, that the first insertion, which made this plain, was stricken probably for artistic reasons. . . ."[14] If Hurst's inference is correct, the superiority of Marshall's argument to Corwin's chief criticism is confirmed by the records of the Constitutional Convention itself. The personal overt act of the accused must be proved. Whether or not Hurst's inference is just, it is at least clear from the words of the document, from the majority of the few speeches in convention on the subject, from *The Federalist* and other pamphlets, from the many citations of Montesquieu, from the ratifying conventions and subsequent law treatises, that the principal purpose of the clause was restrictive. The provision bounds treason prosecutions in order to secure "independent citizens" from the political persecutions which might be part and parcel of the contests of "violent factions," as Madison phrased it in *The Federalist*. Whatever might be their supposition as to the guilt of those who procure the levying of war, then, the framers were dominated by the perhaps contrary wish to surround treason trials with rather stringent limits. Hurst and Chapin suggest that the law of treason, even in England, was becoming more lenient. Corwin's focusing on old English legal precedents overlooks the framers' decisive application to America's popular conditions of an increasingly influential, more or less Lockean, liberalism, a philosophic

[14] Hurst, "Treason in the United States," pp. 403, 402-05, 412ff., 435. See also Farrand, ed., *Records*, II, 337-39.

jurisprudence which regarded the individual's security with the humane solicitude appropriate to a "right" prescribed as fundamental by nature itself.[15]

If the Constitution's pervasive concern for private safety be grasped, then it is easy to see that Marshall's views at the Burr trial, far from contravening that spirit, only articulate it. Indeed, it is the very ambiguity attending the intent of Article III, Section 3, that occasions the complication for which Marshall's crucial opinion from the bench has often been tasked. Marshall believed it "scarcely conceivable" that the term "levying war" was not "employed by the framers of our constitution in the sense . . . affixed to it by those from whom we borrowed it."[16] Thus, his whole disposition throughout the trial was to interpret "levying war" as perpetrating war and hence to look dubiously upon the effort to prosecute Burr for levying war at a place from which he was absent. The Chief Justice granted, however, the possibility of the prosecution's interpretation and did not finally determine the case by an unyielding adherence to common law meanings. In similar fashion, Marshall displayed considerable doubt as to the Constitution's inclusion of the maxim that "in treason all are principals." He indicated repeatedly his reluctance to have an inferior court decide such a "question of vast importance" with such extensive implications, and he never did decide it.[17] Thus the rambling course of Marshall's reasoning amounts to a progressive and flexible, if inconclusive, sifting of arguments to indicate the fundamental alternatives, until a kind of lowest or least doubtful denominator is reached. The theme dominating both the sifting and the choice of a denominator is obvious. The peculiarly restrictive wording of the treason clause reflects the peculiarly restrictive purpose of its mak-

[15] Hurst, "Treason in the United States," pp. 395-417, esp. pp. 395, 410-11, 413-14, 418-19 (n. 124), 430, 811-14; Chapin, *American Law of Treason*, pp. 40, 44-45, 83.
[16] Robertson, *Reports*, II, 402, 409.
[17] *Ibid.*, p. 405.

ers. The Constitution's care in defining treason, while fail-
ing to single out any other crime, bespeaks treason's stature
as "the charge which is most capable of being employed as
the instrument of those malignant and vindictive passions
which may rage in the bosom of contending parties struggling for power."[18] In cases of doubt, then, the law of treason, like penal laws generally but more than any other penal
law, ought to be interpreted strictly. Is this an indefensible
interpretation of a constitutional intent which may be admitted to be not perfectly clear?

Even if Marshall's opinion had contradicted the Constitution's manifest tenor, the prevailing attitude that he
deviated from legal principles in order to spite Jefferson
would not be thereby sustained. For he might simply have
followed his own understanding, however mistaken, of
the Constitution. Corwin's key argument asserts that in the
Burr trials Marshall contradicted his own principles. These
were the maxims which Corwin finds in the common law,
presuming the culpability and even the preeminent culpability of those who procure the levying of war. The constitutional scholar points to only one previous Marshallian
expression of this view. That is a passage from *ex parte
Bollmann* and *ex parte Swartwout* which had been conspicuously debated by counsel and interpreted by Marshall himself during the trial of Burr:

> It is not the intention of the court to say that no individual
> can be guilty of this crime who has not appeared in arms
> against his country. On the contrary, if war be actually
> levied, that is, if a body of men be actually assembled for

18 *Ibid.*, I, 13-14, 81, 100, 105, 148. "As there is no crime which
can more excite and agitate the passions of men than treason, no
charge demands more from the tribunal before which it is made a
deliberate and temperate inquiry." *Ex parte Bollmann* and *ex parte
Swartwout*, 4 Cranch (U.S.), 125 (1807). See generally pp. 125-27.
For Marshall's own description of the misery accompanying indiscriminate executions during domestic strife, see John Marshall, *Life of
George Washington*, I, 395; II, 16ff., 24n.

the purpose of effecting by force a treasonable purpose, all those who perform any part, however minute, or however remote from the scene of action, and who are actually leagued in the general conspiracy, are to be considered as traitors. But there must be an actual assembling of men for the treasonable purpose, to constitute a levying of war.[19]

This is hardly an unequivocal statement that procurers of treasonable assemblies are at least as culpable as perpetrators. The first line quoted indicates that the passage qualifies Marshall's thematic insistence upon an assemblage in force to constitute the crime. Still, it is quite true that there is, at first glance, a certain plausibility in Corwin's presumption that the key phrase, "all those who perform any part, however minute, or however remote from the scene of action," refers to persons who procure the treasonable assembly. This plausibility, however, will not survive a careful examination of the whole passage in question. Corwin's interpretation cannot account for the fact that Marshall requires "playing a part" as a distinct and necessary ingredient of the crime. Corwin supposes Marshall's adherence to a common law definition of treason. This notion implied that all those "leagued in the conspiracy" were traitors if an act of levying war was performed by any one of them. But the passage in question strongly distinguishes performing a part in the levying of war from conspiring to levy war—and requires that a man be engaged in both before he is to be considered a traitor. Corwin's interpretation is thus open to objection on the crucial point.

On the other hand, Corwin's objection to the alternative rendering given by Marshall himself simply comes to naught. The passage can be read as differentiating not between participating in the armed assembly and procuring the armed assembly, but between different kinds of participation in the assembly. During the Burr trials Marshall explained the words as distinguishing between participation

[19] 4 Cranch (U.S.), 75, 126 (1807).

as an armed soldier prepared for combat, and other participation, such as that of an officer supplying the army with provisions or recruiting soldiers.[20] This rendering accounts for Marshall's insistence upon "playing a part" as one ingredient of the crime. Corwin, however, rejects this reading, because it foolishly assumes that a "part" in the action might be played by one "however remote from the scene of action." But is this such a foolish assumption? It is hardly unreasonable to suppose that logistical and recruiting officers are active members of an army mobilized for war, even if they are absent from the place of gathering in force. Corwin's objection, then, cannot be sustained.

It might also be said that Marshall's own reading is in other respects more in accord with this particular passage, and with his general usage, than is Corwin's proposed alternative. The express "intention of the court," as Marshall phrased it, is to show only that persons other than those who have "appeared in arms" might be prosecuted, not that men other than those playing a part in the armed assembly could be. And Corwin's views simply do not correspond with the whole restrictive tone of Marshall's opinion in *ex parte Bollmann* and *ex parte Swartwout*, marked by premises identical to those expressed in the Burr trials, and by a similarly repeated, if vague, disjunction between "levying war" and "conspiracy to levy war." Corwin fails to show a basic inconsistency between the Burr and Bollmann opinions.

With the constitutionality of Marshall's views defended,

[20] "If, for example, an army should be actually raised for the avowed purpose of carrying on open war against the United States and subverting their government, the point must be weighed very deliberately, before a judge would venture to decide that an overt act of levying war had not been committed by a commissary of purchases, who never saw the army, but who, knowing its object and leaguing himself with the rebels, supplied that army with provisions; or by a recruiting officer holding a commission in the rebel service, who, though never in camp, executed the particular duty assigned to him." Robertson, *Reports*, ii, 402; see also pp. 404-05, 427-29, 438-39.

or with merely their consistency vindicated, speculations as to his anti-Jefferson motivation, even if true, lose all relevance in explaining the shape of his opinions during the trials of Burr. In any event, these speculations have never been supported by substantial evidence. It may be granted that many Federalists, and even Burr and his counsel, sought to embarrass Jefferson by showing up his exaggerated apprehensions as to Burr, and his equally exaggerated faith in that villain Wilkinson. It may also be granted that Jefferson himself had reasons to suspect Burr as plotting treason, Marshall as his enemy, the courts generally as Federalist, and the Federalists as determined to make political capital out of Burr's trial. Suppose all this true. It proves nothing as to Marshall's own conduct at Burr's trial. To suppose Marshall a typical Federalist, or governed in his judicial duties by personal enmity and political (in the sense of partisan) opinions, is an entirely gratuitous speculation, especially in the face of the intelligible legal grounds which Marshall set forth. It is a speculation, in fact, manifestly implausible on its face. Admitting Marshall's violent dislike of Jefferson and his principles, one might have expected him to choose better ground for embarrassing the President than that occupied by Burr. Popular fervor ran uproariously against Burr, not for him. It was the Chief Justice, not the President, who after the decision was the object of almost universal vituperation from the press, who was hung in effigy, whose impeachment was covertly threatened in Jefferson's annual message, not to mention the more explicit first draft.[21] Marshall, foreseeing the "bitter cup" of "calumny," "the opprobrium of those who are denominated the world," recognized that "this court" had "many, perhaps peculiar motives" for treating the Presidency with respect.[22] He could do Jefferson no serious damage, and he knew it. A vindictive effort could injure only himself and his Court. And, whatever his

[21] Beveridge, *Life of John Marshall*, III, 530-45.
[22] Robertson, *Reports*, I, 187; II, 444-45.

political opinions, Marshall was undoubtedly possessed of the "political sagacity" with which Corwin credits him. Moreover, neither traitors in general, nor Burr in particular, were any favorites of the Chief Justice.[23]

The fact decisive to the allegations of political motivation, however, is that a close reading of the trial record reveals no substantial political bias of a kind which could help Burr. Apart from the record no evidence worthy of serious consideration seems to exist, and in that source it is really not easy to find any serious bias, personal or political, in Marshall's remarks. Two or three at which the prosecution took umbrage are of a character sufficiently uncertain to occasion as easily wonder about the prosecution's extreme sensitivity, as awareness of Marshall's prejudiced bearing. The remarks might well evidence a certain haste or even insensitivity on Marshall's part. It is hard to see that they manifest a governing political bias against the prosecution. When the existence of such an inference was twice pointed out to Marshall, in fact, he was at great pains to deny that he had meant any "allusion to the conduct of the government in the case before him."[24] In one instance, he actually expunged the remark from his opinion, rather than allow it to continue to give rise, however unintentionally, to such an inference.[25] Insofar as any acerbity steals into Marshall's many statements, it may be most fairly traced to his indignation at the government's clumsy harry-

[23] See Marshall's appraisal of "a traitor, a sordid traitor," Benedict Arnold. Marshall, *Life of George Washington*, i, 381. See also Hay to Jefferson, Aug. 11, 1807, quoted by Beveridge, *Life of John Marshall*, iii, 483; Marshall to Alexander Hamilton, Jan. 1, 1801, John C. Hamilton, ed., *The Works of Alexander Hamilton*, 7 vols. (New York, 1851), vi, 501-03.

[24] Robertson, *Reports*, i, 11n, 189.

[25] *Ibid.*, i, 197. By way of apology Marshall is said to have told the prosecuting attorney "that he had been so pressed for time, that he had never read the opinion after he had written it." Quoted by Beveridge, *Life of John Marshall*, iii, 449.

ing of Burr, an indignation which most scholars, including Corwin, admit to be just.

It is true that Marshall appointed John Randolph, Jefferson's enemy, as foreman of the grand jury. But it is also true that several of Jefferson's closest personal friends were on that jury and that ten of the jurors were administration Republicans and only two, Federalists. More to the point is the fact that Randolph had confessed a strong prepossession, implicitly against Burr.

Finally, Marshall did allow service of the famous *sub poena duces tecum* to the President, but in a spirit far removed from a deliberate challenge to Jefferson's authority. He "would much rather" that counsel arrange among themselves for production of the letters and orders. If the President would only send the papers in question, there would of course be no need for him to attend in person. Should the President be busy, or should the papers be "state papers," that would surely be a reason to be considered should he not obey the *sub poena*. Courts should make certain that the chief executive is not harassed by legal writs. "The president, although subject to the general rules which apply to others, may have sufficient motives for declining to produce a particular paper, and those motives may be such as to restrain the court from enforcing its production."[26] Still, it is a fact that Marshall issued a *sub poena duces tecum* to President Jefferson. The reasons, so far as the trial record reveals them, were connected not with party bias, but with his view of a court's duties, with his particular view, that is, of justice to individuals according to American laws. The "genius and character of our laws and usages" need to be respected; they demand in criminal trials treatment of the defendant "with as much liberality and tenderness as the case will admit." The accused should be permitted all reasonable means, especially in a capital

[26] Robertson, *Reports*, ɪɪ, 535, 535-37; ɪ, 116, 181-82. Compare Abernethy, *Burr Conspiracy*, p. 238.

case, to acquire the papers necessary to his defense,[27] and the President is "subject to the general rules which apply to others."

If any twisting of Marshall's usual notions of Lockean justice can be observed, its tendency is not to spite the wishes of Jefferson and the people, but to conciliate them. The Chief Justice seemed at times to bend over backwards to "pacify the menaces and clamorous yells of the cerberus of Democracy with a sop," as Burr's pathetic accomplice Blennerhassett somewhat elaborately put it.[28] And Burr too thought that the Chief Justice had been disposed to "sacrifice . . . principle to conciliate *Jack Cade*."[29] More weighty than this testimony of the defendants is Marshall's own acknowledgment that he had set Burr's bail higher than "his own ideas of propriety" alone would have recommended.[30] While warning the prosecution from the trial's opening that Burr's overt act was the essential thing to be proved, moreover, he showed himself disposed to allow prosecuting attorney George Hay to pursue his own course.[31] With his sagacious regard for the judiciary's safety, Marshall might well have taken the most scrupulous care in argument and bearing to avoid any imputation of favoritism toward Burr.

Thus, it might be concluded with some irony, Marshall did display a kind of bias during the trial of Burr, but it

[27] Robertson, *Reports*, I, 178, 186; II, 534-35.

[28] Quoted by Beveridge, *Life of John Marshall*, III, 531 (n. 3). Consider an incident which Blennerhassett (not, of course, the most steady witness) recorded. "Did you not do an unprecedented thing," a friend asked Marshall, "in suspending a criminal prosecution and granting two days, in the midst of the argument on a point then under discussion, for counsel to get ready to speak upon it?" "Yes," replied the Chief Justice, "I did and I knew it. But if I had not done so I should have been reproached with not being *disposed* to give the prosecutors an opportunity to answer." Quoted *ibid.*, p. 494.

[29] *Ibid.*, p. 527. Beveridge quotes from several sources expressions of dismay at Marshall's "timidity" in "conciliating" the public.

[30] Robertson, *Reports*, II, 486-87. See also *ibid.*, I, 18-20.

[31] *Ibid.*, I, 85-86, 94, 469-72, 530.

was only a prudent bias toward the popular clamor and toward Jefferson. But even this conciliation of the public was limited by Marshall's devotion to justice as he understood it: protection with "liberality and tenderness" of the rights of the accused. As Marshall put his basic stance: "The interest which the people have in this prosecution, has been stated; but it is firmly believed, that the best and true interest of the people is to be found in a rigid adherence to those rules, which preserve the fairness of criminal prosecution in every stage."[32]

[32] *Ibid.*, I, 100.

INDEX

Abernethy, Thomas Perkins, 270n, 283n

Abolitionism, opposed by Marshall, 50

Abrams v. *US*, 250, 252n

absolutes, rejected by Holmes, 236; difficulties attending his rejection, 246-49

Adams, Charles Francis, 224n

Adams, Henry, 133n, 137n, 265

Adams, Rev. J., 139, 140n

Adams, John, his policy toward France, 122; his overtures to France, 167; chances for his re-election, 172-73; mentioned, vii, 11n, 116, 160, 163n, 231, 232n

Adams, John Quincy, on Jefferson's democracy and the Union, 224n; mentioned, 166, 215

administration, central to liberal government, 64-65, 119

agriculture, and national prosperity, 31; and scientific researches, 31n; cultivators and hunters, 54, 57-58; and citizen virtue according to Marshall, 125, 135; Jefferson's doctrine, 180-82; to Jefferson, 181-82

Alien and Sedition Acts, Marshall's attack on, 15, 17; their constitutionality defended, 17, 87-88; their political imprudence, 171-73; occasion of Federalists' demise, 171-73; mentioned, 167

Ambler, Charles Henry, 123n

amending power, as means of assuring Constitution's permanence, 198

American Insurance Co. v. *Canter*, 21n, 80, 80n

Ames, Fisher, on Federalists' essential democracy, 130, 160n, 165n

ancient political philosophy, *see* political philosophy

André, Major John, admired by Marshall, 126, 126n-27n

The Anna Maria, 132n

The Antelope, 18n, 40n, 49n

argument, Marshall's style, 216-21, *see also* judicial rhetoric and judicial demeanor

aristocracy, few distinguished from the many, 9, 121-22, 124, 126-31, 137; its property arrangements contrasted with Marshall's liberalism, 19; in Virginia, 86n, 161, 163n-64n; Marshall's favor of somewhat aristocratic institutions, 124; few as the upper middle class or natural aristocracy, 130-31; absence of aristocratic republicanism in Marshall's thought, 160-65; aristocratic ingredients in Holmes' thought, 250-51, 251n; mentioned, 117, 170

Aristotle, on healthy democracy, 122; on magnanimity, 127; mentioned, 12, 123n

army, discussion, 94-95, 95n; mentioned, 279-80

Arnold, Benedict, 282n

art, *see* fine arts

Articles of Confederation, discouraged prosperity, 31-32; Marshall's assessment, 46; debility of trade, 83; failure to provide for defense, 88-89; reliance on requisitions and remonstrances, 92; shaken largely by democratic impulses, 148-49; mentioned, 170

Austen, Jane, 129n

Austin, John, 48

Austria, in European balance of power, 91n

Bacon, Francis, on use of fear, 43n; on judicial demeanor, 218; mentioned, 179, 247

balanced government, discussed, 149-54; weakened by democracy, 158-59

balance of power, 90n-91n

Bank of Hamilton v. *Dudley's Lessee*, 67n

Bank of the United States, 168-69. *See also McCulloch* v. *Maryland*

"The Bar as a Profession," 238, 251n

Barron v. *Baltimore*, discussed, 61n; 105n

Bascomb, Henry Bidleman, 31n

Basler, Roy P., 121n, 217n

Bayley v. *Greenleaf*, 30n

Beard, Charles, praises Marshall as historian, xviiin; his constitutional interpretation, 84n

Beasley, Reverend Frederick, 35

Bergh, Albert Ellery, 11n, 184n

Bentham, Jeremy, legal philosophy, x; criticism of Blackstone, x. *See also* utilitarianism

Beveridge, Albert J., his *Life of Marshall*, xi; on Marshall's nationalism, 97; on Marshall and Lincoln, 121n; on Marshall's timidity before Jeffersonian democracy, 214; on Burr Trial, 269n; mentioned, xivn, 13n, 15n, 16n, 24n, 35, 39n, 51n, 56, 84n, 116, 122n, 125n, 150n, 167n, 171n, 213n, 229n, 232n, 235n, 281n, 282n, 284n

bills of attainder, 62

bills of credit, 62n, 74

bill of rights, for people of each state, 61

Bill of Rights, applied to general government only, 61n; merely recommendatory, 79; Jefferson's views, 186

Binney, Horace, 146n

Black and White Taxi case, 255

Blackstone, William, and Bentham, x; influence on Marshall, xiv, 6-7; carrier of sober liberalism to English law, 7; on writ of *habeas corpus*, 14; on property right, 17, 18n-19n; on implied contracts, 29n; his jurisprudence and Smith's economics, 30; on the idle, 37n; definition of law, 47; definition of civil liberty, 58; on judiciary, 68n-69n; on delegation of political power, 120n-21n; and Jefferson, 173; and an enlightened judiciary, 209; mentioned, 70, 182, 255, 274n

Blennerhassett, Harman, 271, 284, 284n

Boorstin, Daniel J., 175n, 179n, 183n, 184n, 185n

Boyd, Julian P., 167n

Brandeis, Louis, 265n

Brashear v. *West and others*, 30

Bridenbaugh, Carl, on liberalism and democracy, 165n

The Brig Wilson v. *the United States*, 76n

Britain, in balance of power, 91n; admired by Marshall, 133; aristocratic, 147; mentioned, 46, 51, 53-54, 55, 83, 90, 90n, 169

Brockenbrough, John W., xvin

Brown v. *Maryland*, discussed, 84, 86; mentioned, 41n, 95n, 107n, 108, 110

"Brown University–Commencement," 263n

Bryce, James, 265

Buck v. *Bell*, 260n

bureaucracy, and liberal government, 64-65; qualifies liberalism's political leveling, 119

Holmes, 254-56; mentioned, 15n

The Common Law, 235, 238, 240n, 241n, 242, 244-45, 259

compassion, in Jefferson's views, 178-79. *See also* humanitarianism

Comte, Auguste, 258

confederation, *see* league, Articles of Confederation

"consciousness," culmination of historical development, according to Holmes, 258-60, 258n, 262-63

consent, title of political legitimacy, 39; required for a nation, 96-101; originated federal government, 117; Constitution ratified only with difficulty, 170; Constitution presumed immortal, 198-99; in a republican manner, 199-200. *See also* social contract

conservation, 179

conservative, 116

Constitution of 1788, purpose, xiv, 150, 150n; ratification, 170, 199-200, 200n; influence on economy, 31-32; an "experiment" in self-government, 149-54; Jefferson's estimate, 185-87; fundamental law, 195-99; written constitution the greatest improvement on political institutions, 196; as political law, 205-06; theory of a written constitution, 206-10; and legislature, 206-10; Constitution's basic postulate according to Gibson, 210; its prospects, 224-25; summary of Marshall's interpretation, contrasted with Holmes', 252-56

Constitutional Convention (of 1787-88), members, 151; 275-76

constitutionalism, origin in Locke and Montesquieu, 58; two

parts, 58-64; Jefferson's view, 186-87; Holmes' view, 248-56

constitutional law, Marshall its founder, viii-ix, 220; its propagation desirable, 143-44

construction of law, according to words and objects, xiii-xiv, 109-110; judiciary's manner of construction, 70-79; according to liberal principles, 73-76; of laws of nations, 76, 79n; of treaties, 76-77, 77n; of political powers, 80-81, 85-86; of Constitution as it bore on the states, 108-12; of treason clause, 277-80; as encouraging respect for law, 218-19. *See also* judiciary

contract, Marshall's doctrine discussed, 26-30, 30n-31n, 47, 62; Blackstone's doctrine of implied contracts, 29n; under control of society, 47; enforcement of strict principles, 71-73; effect of strict doctrine on the states, 109-10, on politics, 221-22. *See also* obligation of contracts, vested rights

Cooley v. *Port Wardens of Philadelphia,* 107-08

Coolidge, Ellen W., 175n

corporation, 21, 97

Corwin, Edward S., his interpretation of Marshall's jurisprudence, xi; on Burr trial, 15, 269-82 *passim*; on basic doctrine of American constitutional law, 26; on judicial review, 202, 208, 209n, 214; mentioned, 90n, 189n, 211, 217n, 224n

cosmopolitan standards, advocated by Holmes, 229-34 *passim*; summarized, 260; evaluated, 263-64

County Court, aristocratic institution, 161, 161n. *See also* Virginia

courts, *see* judiciary

Hardy, Sallie E. Marshall, 50n, 51n, 144n
Harper, Robert, 91n, 158
Hart, H. L. A., revises utilitarian jurisprudence, x
Hay, George, 282n, 284
Head v. *Providence Insurance Co.*, 8n
hearsay evidence, 49-50
hedonism, 175
Henkle, Rev. M. M., 31n
Hepburn and Dundas v. *Ellzey*, 218n
Hillhouse, James, proposal as to Presidency, 189; Marshall's reply, 189-91
historical process, *see* history, philosophy of history
history, Marshall on its writing, 145-46; "natural and right," according to Holmes, 239; displaces nature as basis of Holmes' jurisprudence, 235-39, 243-44
A *history of the colonies*, discussed, xviii-xix
Hobbes, Thomas, and Hart, x; revised by Locke, x; and mores of mass society, 34n; and humanitarianism of Hume and Smith, 34n; on use of fear, 43n; and natural public law, 64n; planned powerful means for modest ends, 81. *See also* liberal individualism
Hogendorp, Charles van, 181n
Holland, provoked Britain to war, 133; commerce and republicanism, 136-37, 137n
Holmes, Oliver Wendell, Jr., on Marshall's preeminence, viii; appraisal of Marshall, xi, discussed, 229-34; his judicial demeanor, 218, 234-35, 235n; his jurisprudence contrasted with Marshall's, 227-68; influence, 227-28, 256; his writings, 265-66; mentioned, 244

honesty, 36-38
honor, admired by Marshall, 131-34, 132n-33n; eroded by "interest," 134-47
Hopkirk v. *Randolph et al.*, 138n
House of Representatives, 152. *See also* balanced government, legislature
Howe, Mark DeWolfe, on Holmes' sketch of Marshall, 229; notes Holmes' attention to history, 244; notes political philosophy in Holmes' thought, 244-45; on Holmes' understanding of science, 258; on Holmes' indifference to politics, 265; mentioned, 235n, 238n
Huidekoper's Lessee v. *Douglas*, 73
human nature, Marshall's views, 8-12, 42, 45, 124-34; Jefferson's views, 173-79. *See also* ethics, interest, virtue
humanitarianism, place in Marshall's views, 30, 34, 34n, 52, 55-58, 243; Jefferson's, contrasted with Marshall's, 173-87 *passim*, especially 173, 175-77
Hume, David, influence on Marshall, 5, 5n, 34n; sums up liberal teaching, 12; on labor, 19; on mores of mass society, 34n; on primacy of courts, 78; on system of checks and balances, 115; his moral doctrine, 130n; on British character, 133; on Locke's republicanism, 164, 165n; and Jefferson, 173; and Lockean natural public law, 208n-09n; and judicial review, 205, 208-09n; mentioned, 35n, 165n, 182
Hunt, Gaillard, 103n
Hunting, Warren B., on contractual obligation, 28, 62
Hurst, Willard, 270-77 *passim*
Hutchinson, Thomas, on witch trials, 10

judicial opinions, designed to enlighten, 216-21; their timing, 214. *See also* rhetoric

judicial review, discussed, 200-12; a variation from the judiciary's civil function, 65; a variation from liberalism in the spirit of liberalism, 195, 208-10; *The Federalist*'s argument, 211-12; Holmes' view, 254; 193-94. *See also* judiciary

judiciary, "civil function," 65-78; power to construe the laws as applied to individuals, 66, 73n, 74-75, 105n, 112-13, 112n-13n; but a tool of law, 66-71, 194; civil function controlled by natural public law, 67-68, 68n-69n; a common law jurisdiction, 60-61, 61n; guided by liberal jurisprudence, 70, 71-78 *passim*, 209; its stature given by liberalism, 77-78; contributes to social peace, 86; contributes to international peace, 89-90; protects general government from states, 112-13; judicial and political power compared, 79-81; the civil function and politics, 65-70, 78-79, 194-95; political consequences of judicial power, 221-23; interpreter of the Constitution, 200, controller of political departments, 200-01, 222-23; construes only civil, not political, law, according to Gibson, 205-10 *passim*; and the executive, 74-76, 205, 206n, 215, 283-84, 269-85 *passim*

—its independence necessary, 69-70, 212-13, 213n; selection and tenure, 212-13; its weakness, 223-24

—its place in Marshall's republicanism, 193-223 (*see* judicial review)

—Jefferson's view, 186

—Holmes' views on the judiciary 254-56. *See also* constitutionalism, natural public law, separation of powers

jurisprudence, defined and discussed, vii, x, 5-7, 266-68; Holmes' definition, 237-38; difficulties in Holmes' definition, 262-65

—relation to political philosophy, vii, x, 266-68, to liberal or Lockean political philosophy, 5-10, 194-95, 243, to liberal economics, 30, 30n, to natural science, 237-38, 259-66

—its propagation desirable, according to Marshall, 143-44

See also law, common law, philosophy, liberal individualism; Blackstone, Locke

jury trial, 78-79

justice, natural, 4-6, 40, 58-62; and force, 52; orientation by justice lacking in Holmes' jurisprudence, 264-66; justice replaced by Holmes with development of law and society, 243-44; implicit in Holmes' view of development, 244-48

See also jurisprudence, natural rights

Kennedy, John Pendleton, 129n

Kent, James, opinion in *Gibbons v. Ogden*, 85

Kercheval, Samuel, 184n, 187n

King, Miles, 184n

King, Rufus, 130, 184n, 188

King v. Delaware Insurance Co., xiiin

Knox, Henry, 165

Koch, Adrienne, 173-86 *passim*

Konefsky, Samuel F., viiin, 111n, 220, 221n

labor (theory of value), and property, 18-20; Jefferson's doctrine, 175-76. *See also* property

sent, democracy, social contract perfectibility of man, 11

Peters, Richard, 119n

philanthropist, 34. *See also* humanitarianism

philosophy, 129, 228-37, 266-68
—ancient, contrasted with modern, 12, 13n, on moral virtue, 127. *See also* Aristotle, Plato, Cicero
—modern, xiv, 4-5, 12, 13n, 245-48, 269, and Jefferson, 179, 182-83. *See also* liberal individualism and entries under particular philosophers
—and jurisprudence, *see* jurisprudence
—and practical judgment, *see* statesman
—and science, *see* science

philosophy of history, Marshall's view, 196; Holmes', 235-39, 243-44, 247-48; underlies Holmes' interpretation of American law, 248-57, flaws in Holmes' view, 257-62; mentioned, 266

Pickering, Timothy, 50n, 80n, 83n, 91n, 117n, 132n, 133n, 153n, 172n

Pierce, H. L., 121n

Pinckney, Charles Cotesworth, 11, 170, 188n

Pitman, John, 105n

Pitt, William, admired by Marshall, 96, 128; on sense of honor, 134

Plato, on democratic freedom, 171; mentioned, vii, 12, 182

Plymouth, 25-26

Pole, J. R., 161n

political religion, Lincoln's, 217; Marshall's, 217-21

politics, defined and discussed, 12-13, 63-68, 76-82, 97, 114-16, 194-95, 222-23; Holmes' 260, 264-66. *See also* government, society

Pollock, Sir Frederick, 235n

popular government, *see* republic

popular sovereignty, 117-22, delegation of power, 120-22, 198-99; Jefferson's democratic version, 154. *See also* the people, consent

population increase, and national strength, 26, 38; and pauperism, 142n-43n; place in Jefferson's thought, 178-80 *passim*

positivism, of Holmes, 236-39

powers, *see* government

precedent, viii, 220

Prentiss, Trustee v. *Barton's Executor,* 106n

press, and party, 158n

Prichard, E. G., 228n

Priestley, Joseph, 183n

primogeniture, and English pauperism, 142n; and Virginia aristocracy, 163n-64n; mentioned, 19

Pritchett, C. Herman, on independence of judges, 213n

private interest, *see* interest

"Privilege, Malice, and Intent," 258

production, Marshall's views, 31-35; encouraged by the Constitution, 32

"The Profession of the Law," 235n

progress, defined and discussed, 38-39; slowed by slavery, 50; Jefferson's doctrine, 175-76, 180; Holmes' doctrine, 235-39, 247

proletarian dictatorship, 250

property, defined and discussed, 18-20; in representative government, 122-23. *See also* right to property

Providence Bank v. *Billings,* and the taxing power, 29; 78

public interest, definition, 22; complementary to private interest, 20-33, 38

public opinion, need for enlightenment, 140-47, 216; as a po-

acy, 102-03; independence of
states, 104-05, 105n; jurisdiction of state governments, 106-
07, 107n, 111-12; according to
Jefferson, 185; states rights and
Justice Johnson, 214, 218n.
See also union

statesman, Marshall as statesman,
viiin; in Indian cases, 52-58;
in reconciling state and general governments, 109-12; in
opposing democracy, 160-61,
170-71 214, 281-85; as party
leader, 166-67; as Chief Justice, 214-21; in establishing a
liberal order, 217; assessed by
Holmes, 232-35
—Marshall's admiration of Napoleon, Pitt, and Frederick the
Great, 95-96; Washington's
statesmanlike qualities, 114,
126-30
—And Marshall's republicanism, 116, 122, 124, 147; and
Jefferson's, 186; contrasted with
partisan politicians, 135; and
Story's *Commentaries*, 143-44;
and the *Life of Washington*,
145; Washington evaluated,
153-54; background of Virginia
statesmen, 161; use of rhetoric,
212
—Holmes' deprecation, 233-35;
subordinated to science, 237,
258-60; and American law,
265-68. *See also* rhetoric, virtue

statistician, man of the future,
according to Holmes, 260

Storing, Herbert J., on Blackstone, 6n; on public interest,
22n

Story, Joseph, on Marshall, xii,
xviii, xviiin; on *US v. Hudson
& Goodwin*, 61n; his *Commentaries*, 70, 143-44, 144n, not
read in Virginia, 224; appraised
by Holmes, 246-47; mentioned,
36n, 45n, 61n, 69n, 73n, 89n-
90n, 132n, 135, 144, 146, 156n,

166, 189n, 215n, 216 218,
225n, 247

Story, W. W., 90n

Strauss, Leo, on difference between ancient and modern
philosophy, 13n; on origin of
capitalism, 20n; on origin of
natural public law, 64n

Sturges v. *Crowninshield*, Justice
Johnson's comment, xvii; 105n,
272n

subpoena duces tecum, 283

suffrage, Marshall's views, 122-
23, 125; Jefferson's views, 185

Supreme Court, Marshall's leadership, 214-21, 224; its political function, 221-24. *See also*
judicial review, judiciary

Sutherland, Arthur E., viiin

Swift v. *Tyson*, 73n, 255

Sydnor, C. S., on suffrage in Virginia, 123; on aristocracy and
democracy in Virginia, 161; on
colonists' society, 162

system, of natural liberty, 25-33,
82-86, 115, 195, 216, 243; of
government, 115-16, 195, 216,
243. *See also* natural public
law, economics

Talleyrand, 233; mentioned, 38,
41, 137, 170

Tawney, R. H., on the "acquisitive society," 23

taxes, 92-93; for support of religion, 140, 140n

Taylor, John, 184n, 186n

Thayer, James Bradley, xii

theology, 35n

theory, *see* philosophy, science

thinker, 228-37 *passim*

Tocqueville, Alexis de, on self-interest, 20; on conformity, 34;
on the middle class, 134; on
"a theory of manufactures,"
135; on democratic despotism,
64-65, 177-78; mentioned,
131n, 142, 194

INDEX